FOOTBALL

– it's more than a kick in the grass

DENNIS STRUDWICK

GSP

Football – it's more than a kick in the grass
Dennis Strudwick

Published by Greyhound Self-Publishing 2025
Malvern, Worcestershire, United Kingdom.

Designed, printed and bound by Aspect Design
89 Newtown Road, Malvern, Worcs. WR14 1PD
United Kingdom
Tel: 01684 561567
E-mail: allan@aspect-design.net
Website: www.aspect-design.net

A copy of this book has been deposited with the British Library Board

ISBN 978-1-915803-22-1

Cover picture:- *Horsham's right full-back for the Club's FA Amateur Cup Replay Tie against local rivals Horsham YMCA. After a 2-2 draw at Horsham's Queen Street Ground, Horsham won the Replay on the YMCA's Ground at Gorings Mead 10-1.*

CONTENTS

Introduction:-		7
Chapter One	How, when & where it all began 1947-1963	11
Chapter Two	Into the Senior game 1963-1966	37
Chapter Three	The Horsham years – 1966-1976 & 1981	43
	Half-time interval – My time at Crawley College of Further Education	85
	Back to football – the second half	88
Chapter Four	Into Administration (But not Insolvency)	137
	Part One – The Sussex Sunday Football League 1976-1981	137
	Part Two – The Southern Football League 1982-2007	157
	The day I met a former player of Stockton Heath.	198
	Part Three – The Football Conference 2007-2015	206
Chapter Five	The Final Whistle – October 2015 to date	227
Chapter Six	'Time Added On' – October 2015 not out	231
A thought for those friends I have lost along the way		235
Acknowledgements		239

Football – it's more than a kick in the grass

or

From 14 Eversfield Road, Horsham to
Buckingham Palace, London.

Thanks to:-

My son Benjamin –
who has stuck by me through thick and thin

&

Janet – my Personal Assistant, Personal Shopper,
House keeper, Chef, Wardrobe Manager, Gardener AND Wife
Thanks both for your support

&

Ursie Emma & Horace Edgar Dean (Mum & Dad);
my siblings:- Gordon Horace, Derek James &
Patricia Ann (sadly, all no longer with us – I miss you),
and Brian Stanley (keep going big Bruv)

&

All my team-mates; all opponents with whom a friendship
developed (my football family); all Directors & Club personnel
with whom I have worked and, of course, all Match Officials!

INTRODUCTION:-

Not even my conceit would have ever allowed me to imagine I could, or would, write a book let alone my memoirs. But I have been encouraged, badgered, even cajoled and not just a little bullied by a colleague and long time friend of over 40 years to follow his superb example. So if you glean any enjoyment from what follows my name is Dennis Strudwick. If I have bored you to the back teeth, blame Keith Allen.

Straightaway I must use some of Keith's words. Keith repeatedly reminds himself and the readers of his own book, his mother frequently said he, Keith, was born lucky. Well, I do not know if I was born with good fortune but it is evident to me someone has been looking after me. I had a wonderful upbringing by right minded loving parents; I enjoyed the warmth of helpful siblings; and guidance from a plethora of outstanding friends. And despite the twists & turns I have taken, and errors, bad decisions and poor choices I have made along life's unpredictable path, I have never been unemployed; I have actively enjoyed participating in multiple sports; I have played in, and have been an administrator of, football, my first love, for about 67 years not out. And along the way I have earned a part-time income and/or my full-time living from the game for 39 of those years. Most importantly, apart from a few football injuries, I have enjoyed good health. So I, too, have been lucky, very lucky indeed. And Keith has always told me, it's better to be lucky than rich.

What follows is not a verbatim account of my journey from 1947 to the present day. It is a simple account of significant moments, and some not so significant passages, along my 'journey' so far. Whilst no offence was intended by anyone at the time, or by me now, please be advised and/or warned, my story does contain profanities and/or humour 'of the day'.

Everything is factually accurate to the best of my ability and recollection but some tales may not be politically correct or woke in today's progressively changing world. Everything I describe is as I remember it. Please be minded, however, of the words of our beloved and late Queen Elizabeth ll about a recent matters within her family, "recollections may vary."

I have endeavoured to mention as many people as I can who have touched my life. Many have made a huge contribution to my development, socially and professionally, while some have played a shorter but no less significant role. I have done my best to remember all of those. But I appreciate picking out particular names is a dangerous game so I hope any I have accidentally missed will forgive me for being omitted. They are all somewhere in my memory bank.

Amongst a chapter of 'Acknowledgements' towards the end of this book I have tried to list those colleagues, friends, opponents and team-mates I

September 2020 – My first visit to Horsham's superb new Ground, the Hop Oast Stadium. For old timers like me the jury may still be out when discussing artificial pitches but this surface provides the perfect arena to hone a player's skills. Wonderful!

have lost along the way. Again, if I have overlooked anyone, I apologise. I mean no disrespect. I also acknowledge the help I have received from many people and other sources of information. As a person who has never consistently maintained a diary I have relied on memory and much external help.

Also, I have endeavoured not to make this story a monotonous trail of "I", "I", "I" or "me", "me", "me" by recalling as many names as I can. But as one colleague impatiently barked at me recently, "It is, effectively, your autobiography. It's bound to be about you. So get on with it! Before it's too late!!" So here goes.

CHAPTER ONE

How, when & where it all began 1947-1963

My mother, Ursie Emma Westbrook was born on the 4th January 1909 at 34 Plymouth Street, Southsea, Portsmouth; a house that no longer exists following a flying visit from the German Luftwaffe on 10th March 1941, which dropped one of many unwelcome loads on Pompey during the Second World War. My father, Horace Edgar Dean Strudwick was born on 2nd January 1910 at 33 East Street, Horsham, West Sussex which during my time gave way to Brewers 'do-it-yourself' store but now houses satellite television equipment. How times change! I have not been able to find any evidence to confirm how my parents met. I can only speculate there must have been a meeting of minds, and bodies, during father's brief spell in Hampshire prior to boarding a ship in Southampton for his first posting abroad after embarking on a career in the Army. But thankfully, for my existence, they met somehow and somewhen.

My life began in the front bedroom of 14 Eversfield Road, Horsham. Home was a three bedroom 1930's council house and I arrived on Tuesday 15th April 1947, about twenty months after the end of the Second World War. Clement Attlee was the UK Prime Minister; Harry S Truman was the Democratic President of the United States; Liverpool won the Football League Championship; Charlton Athletic won the FA Cup; and Jackie Robinson became the first African/American to play Major League baseball when he started at first base for Brooklyn Dodgers. Jackie's selection heralded the end of racial segregation in professional baseball; and my arrival heralded the last of the five children my parents produced together. Given my Dad was not demobbed from National Service until 1st January 1946, having arrived back in England on the 4th October

1945 following the end of World War ll, my parents did not hang around too long before successfully celebrating repatriation.

I was born eighteen years, all but one month, after my eldest sibling. Gordon Horace had arrived into the world on 16th May 1929 at 20 Gifford Road, Bosham, West Sussex, a house that does still exist; and almost eight years had elapsed since the last of my siblings, Patricia Ann, left the womb on 6th August 1939. In the meantime, Brian Stanley became the second born, on 7th February 1935, and then Derek James arrived on 3rd February 1936. So, after having four children in the space of ten years, the latter three in a period of four and a half years, you would imagine my parents might have found out what was causing the reproduction line. So, after eight years had elapsed since Pat's arrival, it is reasonable to assume I was a complete mistake; the result of celebrating the arrival of peacetime. And after six years of conflict, almost all of which I understand was spent apart, who could blame them.

In terms of accommodation I imagine it helped that Gordon had left home by the time I was hatched. He left for the Services whilst still a young man; like father – like son. He joined the Royal Navy on 20th November 1946 as a Leading Airman (LAM) in the Fleet Air Arm five months before I was born. I never lived in the same house as my eldest brother. Prior to that it must have been an incredibly difficult time for people during this period, particularly for Mums & Dads bringing up a family. In my Mother's case, four children in the space of ten years. In my Father's case he had a career as a Signalman to fulfil in the Royal Corps of Signals, no. 2318254, having signed up on 8th January 1927, and to which he had committed the next six years of his life. What is more, the family subsequently discovered he had lied about his age, by adding one year, to enable his enlistment. We thought for years he was two days older than Mum but we now know he was 363 days younger!

Two years later, on 5th January 1929, we understand he embarked at Southampton on the HMT Somersetshire for a passage to India & Pakistan.

Mother must have been about four months pregnant with Gordon at the time and their first born arrived in May, while father was away on duty! Whilst in Rawalpindi, in the Punjab, Dad played a lot of hockey where the local players were exceptionally good. At some point in his army career he tried his luck at boxing. Fancying his chances after three wins he admitted to receiving a *"pasting"* in his fourth bout. I don't think he boxed again. He was also a keen cyclist and had ridden from Horsham to the brand new Wembley Stadium in April 1924 to visit the British Empire Exhibition. He loved athletics, too, and followed it avidly. I have a clear recall of watching televised events from The White City Stadium in London involving British runners, Gordon Pirie, Chris Chataway and Derek Ibbotson, competing against, for example, Vladimir Kuts and Emile Zatopeck. Mother, too, was rooted to the sporting screen whenever horse jumping featured, e.g. The Horse of the Year Show, also from the, now long gone, White City Stadium, before it moved to Wembley Stadium and destroyed the football pitch, following which the event moved to Wembley's indoor arena. Notwithstanding her viewing, Mum never put down her needlework or knitting. She was an outstanding knitter. The constant tittle-tattle of the needles was like a morse code message being dispatched while Jimmie, our white budgerigar, clung like a rodeo rider at the opposite end. I benefitted from Mum's genius skills with several fabulous jumpers. Meanwhile, the whole family was glued to the screen for these fabulous sporting shows. Perhaps this is where my sports gene came from. A love for sport which my parents passed on to their children in increasing measures.

After extending his Terms of Service by two years my father returned to England and married Ursie Emma Westbrook on 15th February 1934; yes, nearly five years after Gordon had been born. This discovery brought about several behind the hand smiles from the rest of us. What's more, they didn't register Gordon's birth until this time! Naughty, or what? Anyway, Dad was discharged 'with the colours' on 7th January 1935 after eight years service. He then signed for 4 further years on the reserve.

The births of Brian, Derek and Patricia followed before he was called up for Army Service on 15th August 1939, only nine days after Pat's arrival. I imagine Dad was not alone in facing such circumstances but, rhetorically speaking, how does a father cope with being called up to go to war within days of seeing the birth of his child, and first daughter. But cope he must have, and he was assigned to the 3rd Div of The Royal Signals, British Expeditionary Forces (BEF). He spoke little about his Army career and/or the second world war except for mentioning his sporting activities and having a wonderful time in northern France, particularly an occasion in Bethune. After he and his colleagues had consumed a great deal of wine they needed to 'borrow' a bus to return to barracks. A competition to determine the best driver was won by the person who could ring the bell the loudest and fastest while still driving the bus. But it was a contest that failed to run its full course. The vehicle, with all its passengers, ended up on its side in a ditch and 'shanks's pony' was the only means to get home. We did, from time to time, try to engage him on his experiences during wartime, particularly in relation to the Dunkirk evacuation in June 1940 but very little was forthcoming. All he would say was, as a Signalman he was amongst the last to leave the beach as he and his colleagues had to destroy all the equipment so it was of no use when it was left behind and was liable to fall into enemy hands. It was clearly a frightening and emotional subject. It was evident Dad was keeping his cards close to his chest so none of us chose to question him further.

Thereafter, upon his return to Blighty, records show he spent 21 days in Ballochmyle Emergency Hospital, for treatment unknown, before completing assignments in North Africa and Italy. Following the end of hostilities on 2nd September 1945 he returned to England on 4th October 1945 and was released from service three months later, on New Year's Day. Meanwhile, his children were growing and he added to the complement within a further 16 months, i.e. me! I was a complete surprise; a mistake, even; the price of a celebration; the cost of six year's lockdown.

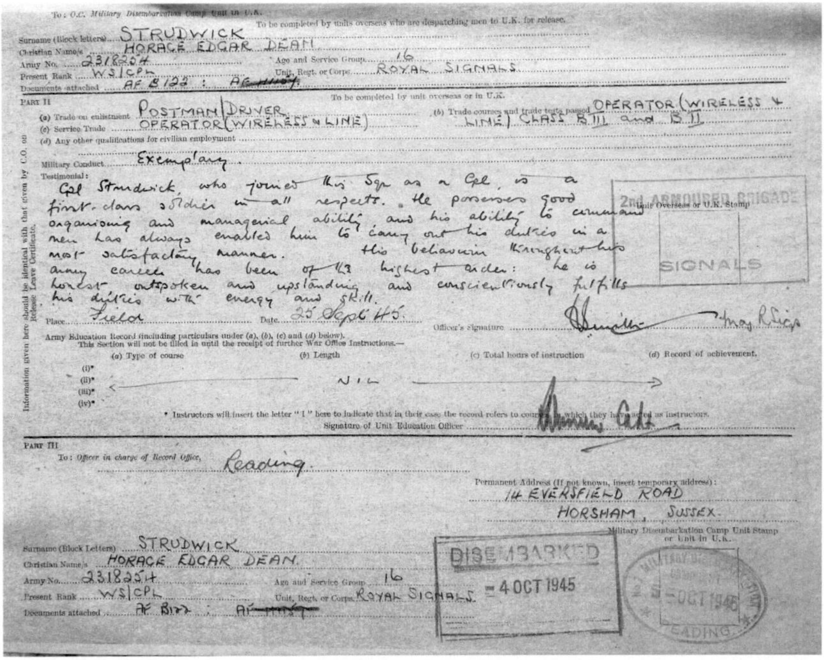

To: O.C. Military Disembarkation Camp Unit in U.K.

To be completed by units overseas who are despatching men to U.K. for release.

Surname (Block letters) STRUDWICK

Christian Name/s HORACE EDGAR DEAN

Army No. 2318254 Age and Service Group 16

Present Rank WS/CPL Unit, Regt. or Corps ROYAL SIGNALS

Documents attached AF B122 : AF ~~…~~

PART II To be completed by unit overseas or in U.K.

(a) Trade on enlistment POSTMAN/DRIVER (b) Trade courses and trade tests passed OPERATOR (WIRELESS & LINE) CLASS B III and B II

(c) Service Trade OPERATOR (WIRELESS & LINE)

(d) Any other qualifications for civilian employment

Military Conduct Exemplary.

Testimonial:

Cpl Strudwick, who joined this Sqn as a Cpl, is a first-class soldier in all respects. He possesses good organising and managerial ability and his ability to command men has always enabled him to carry out his duties in a most satisfactory manner. His behaviour throughout his army career has been of the highest order: he is honest outspoken and upstanding and conscientiously fulfills his duties with energy and skill.

Unit Overseas or U.K. Stamp: 2nd ARMOURED BRIGADE SIGNALS

Place Field Date 25 Sept 45. Officer's Signature [signature] Maj R Sigs

Information given here should be identical with that given by C.O. on Release Leave Certificate.

Army Education Record (including particulars under (a), (b), (c) and (d) below).
This Section will not be filled in until the receipt of further War Office Instructions.—

(a) Type of course (b) Length (c) Total hours of instruction (d) Record of achievement.

(i)*
(ii)* ← NIL →
(iii)*
(iv)*

* Instructors will insert the letter "I" here to indicate that in their case the record refers to courses in which they have acted as instructors.

Signature of Unit Education Officer [signature]

PART III

To: Officer in charge of Record Office, Reading.

Permanent Address (If not known, insert temporary address): 14 EVERSFIELD ROAD HORSHAM, SUSSEX.

Military Disembarkation Camp Unit Stamp or Unit in U.K.

DISEMBARKED 4 OCT 1945

READING

Surname (Block Letters) STRUDWICK

Christian Name/s HORACE EDGAR DEAN.

Army No. 2318254 Age and Service Group 16

Present Rank WS/CPL Unit, Regt. or Corps ROYAL SIGNALS.

Documents attached AF B122 : AF ~~…~~

My Father's 'Military Disembarkation' notice from the Royal Signals passed on 4th October 1945 following the end of the second World War. He was subsequently released from service and arrived home on New Year's Day 1946.

The citation reads:-

Strudwick – Horace Edgar Dean Army no. 2318254
Rank WS/CPL Royal Signals – Military Conduct:- Exemplary

Cpl Strudwick, who joined this Sqn as a Cpl, is a first class soldier in all respects. He possesses good organising and managerial ability and his ability to command men has always enabled him to carry out his duties in a most satisfactory manner. His behaviour throughout his Army career has been of the highest order; he is honest, outspoken and upstanding and consistently fulfils his duties with energy and skill.

Date - 25th September 1945.

Ursie Emma Strudwick (nee Westbrook) &
Lance Corporal Horace Strudwick no. 2318254

Obviously, it was a long time before I began to understand and appreciate the existence of my siblings. I was much younger than them and they didn't want a baby brother cramping their style. And I still didn't see anything of the eldest, Gordon, as he was based at the Fleet Air Arm centre, first at Ford, West Sussex, then Lossiemouth and finally at Yeovilton. He had begun to work for De Havilland and then Westlands, both aircraft manufacturers; work that eventually took him to Toronto, Canada in the early 1950s. That was quite an adventure in those days. But as much as he wanted to extend his stay in the 'new world' he could not persuade the young lady he had met in Somerset, Margaret Cox, to join him. Margaret enjoyed a tranquil life in the hamlet of Pitney with her parents, Bill and Rhoda. I can't remember how Bill earned his living but he kept chickens in the grounds of their charming stone built thatched cottage. Rhoda ran the local Post Office from a room attached to their house. She cleaned the village school and played the organ in the beautiful local church. They were celebrities within their community. And for Margaret to swap this peaceful, tranquil existence for a city life 3,500 miles away was a call too much to make. So after about a year in Canada Gordon returned home on the Queen Mary, departing from New York, bringing with him a reversible jacket for his baby brother. It was plain brown one side and 'lumberjack' style on the other, creating a perfect camouflage when playing in St. Leonards Forest, which I did a lot with my mates. I wore that jacket endlessly. It didn't last long enough for me to outgrow it, it literally fell off me! Whilst in the Big Apple Gordon made a homecoming record for his "Mom" at the top of the Empire State Building, the tallest building in the world at the time. It was a venue that was to become important in my memory and eventually played a significant role in my life.

So, by mid-1947 our family was complete, barring any more accidents. Gordon subsequently settled in Somerset and married Margaret. Times, I imagine, remained pretty tough for Mum & Dad bringing up three boys & a girl in a three bedroom council house during the years following world conflict. And I think I remember witnessing the demolition of air-shelters in the street. But that is very vague. Indoors, Brian & Derek shared one bedroom; Pat & I the other, while I was very small. In subsequent years our 12 year age range worked in the family's favour as the eldest boys started lives on their own two feet, leaving Pat & I with our own rooms, at last. Meanwhile I had eventually grown old enough to become of some significance to the siblings with whom I lived at 14 Eversfield Road, albeit mainly as a gofer. But I looked forward to annual holidays in Somerset, falling in love with Cheddar Gorge and the beach at Weston-super-Mare which seemed endless when the tide went out. Neither I nor my siblings recall Gordon showing any inclination towards sport, apart from an appreciation at arms length. He was an aircraft enthusiast, by now working on fighter jets, the Sea King, the Phantom, the Harrier Jump jet, the Lynx helicopter and, I remember him telling me about a revolutionary aircraft ejector seat that operated under water. All very exciting, I am sure, and interesting stuff but it didn't butter my toast.

Brian and Derek, on the other hand, showed great enthusiasm for most things sporting. Brian was very statistically minded and analytical. He maintained records of most things along with a huge scrapbook with cuttings on any sport related competitive contest. I still have it. I tried to maintain it for a while but I wasn't as diligent as my elders. Besides, the book had become extremely fat with its additions and had no covers. It was all I could do to keep it together. But it contains some historic pictures and newspaper cuttings.

Brian played football, in goal, for several local teams in Horsham including East End United who he described as a bunch of rogues who were quite successful on their day. He also played for Roffey, a suburb of Horsham, and the neighbouring village of Southwater, having met and courted one of the villagers, Betty Rowland. Brian & Betty subsequently married and chose FA Cup Final day in 1960 for their wedding ceremony. Dad and I couldn't believe it, even though neither of us had any allegiance to Blackburn Rovers or Wolverhampton Wanderers. We made it plain, though, it would take quite a while to forgive them, albeit our protests were disingenuous and we didn't allow the clash to take the gloss and the pleasure away from a beautiful day. By now Brian had turned his attention to different sports. He had taken passionately to darts and bar billiards which I suspect accompanied, and may have even interrupted, the odd glass of ale. He also served as Southwater's cricket umpire for many years. During the more active era of his sporting prowess he also enjoyed cycling, particularly with brother Derek. Along with a few companions Derek cycled from Horsham to London to watch the Queen's Coronation on 2nd June 1953. I imagine it was far easier and safer to cycle on roads in those days but the bicycles were not so well equipped and the return journey would have been in the region of 75 miles, at least. Wow! I would think this would have evidenced the acronym of his BSA bike really did stand for 'Bloody Sore Arse'. Sadly the day coincided with the loss of the only true blood grandparent I knew – Mum's mother.

Derek's main sporting interests, however, were football and cricket. Having followed in father's post war footsteps with employment in the Post Office Derek joined as a Telegraph Boy and played regularly for Horsham PO cricket and football teams. I accompanied him on several cricketing day's out and sometimes, when in my early teens, I made up the numbers when players could not get off duty. Derek's main interest, though, was football. And by all accounts he was a good attacking inside forward. I think he fancied himself as a bit of a Johnny Haynes, but probably only a small bit of that wonderful player. But like his sporting colleagues, working for the Post Office limited his availability and he never reached his full potential. He, and his best friend Robin Stepney 'tried out' for Horsham and Redhill. Derek's work prevented his progress whereas Robin went on to make 213 appearances for Aldershot in the Football League. Thereafter, Robin, a family friend as his father was also a Postman, coached football in several European countries and subsequently became Assistant Manager to Keith Burkinshaw at Tottenham Hotspur. Later, during my own career, I got to have frequent contact with Tottenham so I asked after Robin. He was known for constantly whistling wherever he went and was an immensely popular figure amongst all the players and staff. Meanwhile, back at home, Derek pursued his football locally while turning out occasionally for Horsham Reserves before meeting his wife to be, Maureen Gatland. Now Horsham wasn't a particularly small town, quite a bustling market town actually, but Maureen had been born in and raised at 64 East Street, Horsham, smack bang opposite the home where Derek had begun his life before moving to Eversfield Road.

As I write this a very, very early memory springs to mind. In their teenage years Brian and Derek were curiously known as 'Snaz' amongst all their friends and subsequently many work colleagues. I haven't the foggiest idea why or where this name came from. Perhaps because of the years that separated us it wasn't a name that was often affixed to me except for the few who knew us all. The few who carried it over to me were probably those with older brothers and/or Collyer's Grammar School in their veins. In those early days, however, the two Snaz's used to take me to a Gym Club run in a 'Nissan' like hut in Horsham Park by a superb athlete called Eddie Boxall. I remember little more than that, other than being allowed to climb on, and balance on, all the equipment and then being used as the topping on the human pyramid. These gatherings in Eddie's Gym were probably the early days of the modern 'work out', seriously therapeutic for the older lads, just good fun for me. I have no doubt in this day and age there might be 'safe guarding' concerns but I can assure everyone, I came to no harm and it was a darn sight better option for my development than spending my evenings in front of a computer screen playing games.

Patricia followed Derek into the Strudwick family and she stretched the influence of the sporting gene even further. Being brought up in the company of three robust boys, and eventually a fourth male sibling, gave Pat a resilient personality. The post war years were tough for everyone, let alone for a young girl living in the company of three brothers, only for a fourth to turn up. It was quite natural for her to develop a mental strength and I trust she would not mind if I called her a 'tom boy'. Pat was magic, and made of stern stuff. She was a good all-round sports woman. She played all the school/social sports e.g. rounders, hockey and netball. But in her age group she was an outstanding athlete, in particular sprinting, hurdles and long jump. She was very successful at school in these events and one year she qualified for some national school championship finals to be held in Northumberland. Northumberland is a long way from Sussex in any era but in the mid-50s it was an exceptional journey for a young school girl to make; so too was the competition. She returned home winless but with the comfort she had done her best. The winner of the events in which Pat took part, hurdles and long jump, was a young lady from Wells, Somerset, called Mary Bignall. A few years later Miss Bignall was to become Mrs Mary Rand, Olympic Champion and world record holder. After these heady school days Pat subsequently met and married Brian Pavey, a local footballer for Billingshurst. Brian was a gem of a guy; good enough for our household of

Pompey fans to overlook his allegiance to Arsenal. Like Pat, Brian came from a big family. He survived Pat although he did not enjoy good health towards the end of his life which came in a road accident. We lost Pat, a smoker, with a bronchial complaint, aged 49. After Pat, there was me.

Of course, I knew little of the struggles in the recovery from the war. But as I became cognisant with events I appreciated Dad was in a secure job with the Post Office, albeit it was a job that left Mum with one major sadness. In those days there was a postal delivery on Christmas Day so Dad had to work. Mother always regretted that Father never saw his children open their Christmas presents. Her feelings were hurt even more when her best friend, Mrs Johnson who lived in an adjacent street, happened to innocently say she posted all her cards on Christmas Eve so they would arrive on Christmas Day! I'm not sure Mum ever got over that disappointment. But it didn't prevent her keeping an impeccable home and she also 'cleaned' for a lovely family in the smart end of town, to help make ends meet. As well as the infant memory of appreciating the indescribable comfort and security gleaned from having my hands washed by a parent, one of the earliest of my memories is being looked after by my Grandmother one day a week and being taken to a coffee shop in Middle Street, Horsham. Needless to say the shop is no longer there but the memory of dark brown oak seating with high back seats, higher than church pews, is still firmly etched in the back pocket of my mind. My sister frequently told me I was too young to remember that, but I do. I remember, too, ration books and being limited to two ounces of sweets, but even then, only when they were available. Two ounces!! No jumbo sized bags in those days. And no risk of obesity in those austere times. As time moved on I began my school days starting at Clarence Road Infants. Apart from playing and running in the massive playground at every opportunity, I have only one indelible memory. The image of the rotund Headmaster, Mr Woodrow, is permanently stuck in my memory. He painstakingly taught us how to form and shape the letters we wrote. Thank you Mr Woodrow. I have taken pride in my hand writing ever since.

First school photograph – Clarence Road School circa 1953.

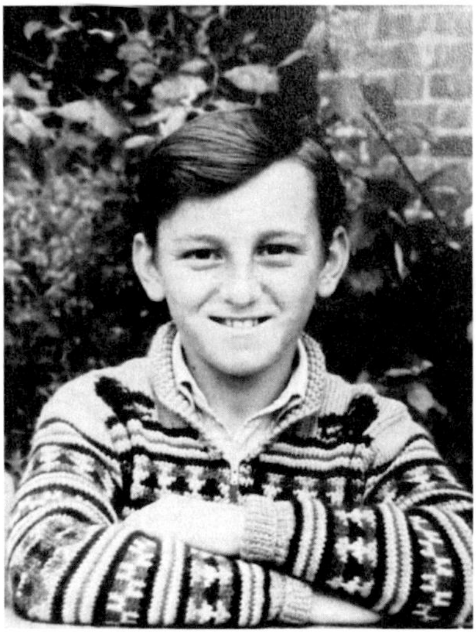

Another school photograph – Chesworth School circa 1957 and an example of Mother's knitting skills.

Despite the difficult years following WW2 I was lucky to have enjoyed regular holidays. My parents didn't own a car in those early days so initially our holidays were day trips by train to London, Littlehampton, Worthing, Brighton and, of course, Portsmouth. The Naval city had been heavily targeted by the enemy during the war. 67 official air-raids had taken out 20% of the city's housing stock between July 1940 and May 1944 and had killed 930 inhabitants. A decade on, bomb sites still heavily scarred the streets. Wherever we went in the city, or whatever we did, Mum had to visit the market in Charlotte Street, Portsmouth's answer to London's Petticoat Lane, and The Landport Drapery Bazaar. On one particular visit to the Department Store, during my immediate post Santa Claus believing days, and while the country was still recovering from wartime, I was invited to choose my Christmas present. Wow! I chose a football related board game that used magnets to move the players. I chose well. I was very happy. But I could not believe my parents' response. *"Is there anything else you would like?"* It was not until years later did I understand and appreciate the significance of this further invitation. The doom & gloom of wartime was clearly lifting. And I have never forgotten my parents generosity. That gesture, alone, was the best Christmas present I have ever had. The memory, along with many others, remains vivid, cherished and has lasted over seventy years so far; longer than any material gift. My eyes still water at the thought of that moment. Thereafter the days out in mother's home town were to stand me in good stead in the years to come. Indeed, it was on these early trips to Pompey that Dad introduced me to Fratton Park where the youngsters like me were carefully ushered to the front row of the terracing, passed overhead in the smallest of cases, ensuring an uninterrupted view of the gloriously lush green grass. It is against this backdrop another early memory has stayed with me to this day, i.e. Blackpool FC's bright tangerine shirts and dazzling white shorts. Despite my allegiance to Pompey's blue shirts, white shorts & red socks, Blackpool's tangerine remains, for me, the most attractive kit I have ever seen. But shame on me, I cannot remember if Stanley Matthews was playing that day. Never mind, I would catch up with him later in my career.

It was around this time, when aged about six I think, the football bug showed it had really bitten me. Gordon and his then fiancé, Margaret, bought me a football kit for Christmas. I would, and should, have been grateful. But I threw a shameful selfish tantrum. The kit was green & white in the Arsenal style. Who on earth played in those colours? Not even Plymouth Argyle played in this kit. Not that that would have helped, even if they did. I should have realised. As mentioned earlier, Gordon had never shown any interest in sport, particularly not football. He didn't have a clue who played in what colours. I am sure to have got a slap or two for being ungrateful. But I ask you, who played in green shirts with white sleeves – nobody!! And nobody any good, that's for sure.

After the statutory time, two or three years, I moved from Clarence Road to Denne Road Junior School, subsequently to be renamed Chesworth. I can't think why. The school was in Denne Road! My first brush with local politics, perhaps. It was, however, at Chesworth where another teacher left a lasting impression on me, Mr Forester.

Mr Forester was sports minded. Desk bound lessons apart we were outside, weather permitting, as much as time and the curriculum allowed – in the playground, on the sports field or simply studying nature on the nearby River Arun. The school had properly organised sports day events and I quickly learnt I could run; fast by comparison with my fellow pupils. I didn't lose a race at Chesworth but I was well beaten into third place in a county final. That hurt. I was devastated. Defeat left a bad taste. But it was a great lesson. Although I didn't appreciate it at the time, it taught me to deal with disappointment, even at this young age. Learning to deal with disappointment is important but it is something children seem to be protected from these days. For me, I recall that first feeling of defeat but it helped to learn how to deal with it.

I believe it was in my penultimate year at Chesworth when organised football was arranged for us. I was selected to play for a team representing Horsham Primary Schools against Crawley Primary Schools to be played at the All Saints School, Roffey. I was made Captain. On being told the news I remember racing around the play ground at Chesworth, as fast as I could, bouncing a football. I was so chuffed. Some would now say I was being big headed but aged 10 or 11 I would not have known what that was. I realised I had been noticed, and we all like to be noticed. I was very happy, and proud too. We won the game 3-1. I scored two and a good friend, John Grant, scored one. The 'blue touch paper' in terms of football had been lit. And when next in the playground, in a game of skittles where two teams played against one another and endeavoured to knock over the opponent's skittle in a circle, guarded by a 'goalkeeper', I recall the ball being thrown towards me. Instead of catching and throwing the ball at the skittle, as was customary, I chose to head it at the target. To my surprise, and the annoyance of the opposing 'goalkeeper', I scored by knocking over the skittle. Such an insignificant event so why has this minutiae stayed in my memory? I can even remember the name of the beaten skittle minder, a lad who was, and for many years remained, a good friend, Michael Stringer. So why such recall after 68 years? Maybe because it was a first sign I had a love, and possibly a reasonable eye for a ball.

THE VICTORIOUS HORSHAM TEAM

Second Half Rally Beat Crawley

HORSHAM PRIMARY SCHOOLS 3, CRAWLEY PRIMARY SCHOOLS 1

CRAWLEY settled down quickly in this match, played on the All Saints' School, Roffey, pitch on Saturday morning.

The visiting team launched a series of powerful attacks on the Horsham goal, and it was not until some minutes from the start that the home team began to warm up.

A good goal by Crawley towards the end of the first half might well have proved decisive.

However, Horsham were inspired by an early second-half goal, and the ensuing ding-dong struggle ended in a 3—1 win for them. Home team scorers were Strudwick, of Chesworth (two) Grant, of Greenway.

Pictured above is the Horsham team, drawn from five local schools. It was: I. Walker; Saunders, Cottington; Dunn, Daubney, Riley; Sumner, Strudwick, Garton, Grant, Fiest.

The first team picture I appeared in. Horsham Primary Schools XI about to take on Crawley Primary Schools 1956/57 season. Age and mice have taken out two players in the back row, one of which was Bob Reilly (extreme right). The remainder are Back Row (left to right):- Ian Walker, ? Saunders, Dave Cottington, John Grant, (plus two) Front Row:- Geoff Sumner, Den Strudwick, Colin Garton, Robin Daubney & Harold Fiest.

In my final year at Chesworth School I made the 'select' team again. I recall we played Crawley Schools, again, this time away from home. I cannot remember exactly where we played, nor the score. I think it was a draw but somehow this photograph has survived the intervening years.

Horsham team in the back row:- Ian Coomber, John Grant, ??, Tony Stones, Roger (Gunner) Jackson, Eric Greening, ??, ??, DJS, ??, John Hewitt (methinks).

The Eleven plus exam success won me a place at Collyer's Grammar School, Horsham in September 1958. Brian and Derek had both attended Collyer's so I was pleased to have matched their achievement. I even applied for, and was successful in being given, a place in the same School House, Mercers. History had repeated itself. But unlike my brothers I was no academic. I failed miserably at Latin and French; kept my head above water in English, Maths, Geography & History; and loved the sport, although the football pitches were neither in good condition nor were they all level. Inspired by another good sporting teacher, Mr G E (Ted) Palmer, I broke into the U/14 football team during my second year, at the age of 12. I won the athletics 'Victor Ludorum' (Triple jump [hop, step & jump in those days], 100 yards sprint, 110 yards hurdles and sprint relays); the Gymnastics competition; swimming races & diving contests in each of my first two years. I told you I was lucky. I could not, though, master cricket. I think the ball was too hard. And neither could I get the hang of 'fives', a game like squash but the racket was substituted in favour of a gloved hand. The school had a fives court but I was not the pupil with an eye for the ball in this sport. Great game, good to watch, but I did not grasp it. Fellow Eversfield Road'ite, Tommy Smallwood was a fine exponent. Football was my game.

Collyer's School U/14 team 1960/61

Back row (left to right) – Alan Lancaster, David Hill, ? Saunders, Martin Burgess, Stuart Morden, Richard Ogle, ? Middlemiss, ? Sawyer

Front row (left to right) – David Cottington, DJS, Gordon Johnson, Michael Stringer, Mark Daniels

At the end of my first year at Collyer's the school inherited a great deal of money from a distant historic benefactor. This enabled the playing fields to be levelled, new classrooms & science block to be built, together with a new gymnasium and new modern equipment installed. While construction was underway the school found ways to meet its physical education responsibilities, but understandably these activities were truncated, with the exception of a new pursuit that quietly crept into the school's curriculum. Following the recruitment of a new teacher, in History & Sport, if I remember correctly, a rugby pitch was marked out and furnished with posts on a plot untouched by the renovations. The new teacher was Mr Peter Sibley, a player for the famous London Rugby Union club, Blackheath. His influence was evident: his preferred sport was imposed on us all. I, for one, made a clumsy attempt at moving the action forward whilst only being allowed to pass the ball backwards to a team mate. I found it exceedingly difficult. Happily, for me though, the coup eventually failed; the 'H' posts disappeared and Collyer's returned to being a football school. As for Mr Sibley, good teacher; great bloke; wrong sport. During the transition, and the return to normality, I looked elsewhere to get my sporting fixes.

My super supportive sister Pat, and her footballing boyfriend Brian helped. They took me to a few FA Amateur Cup Finals; my first visits to Wembley, the National Stadium. Pat was clearly feeding my football gene. The games I recall seeing were:- Woking v Ilford (1957/58), in which my PE Teacher "Ted" Palmer was a linesman; Hendon v Kingstonian (1959/60); and Crook Town v Hounslow (1961/62). Little did I know then it was a Competition in which I would eventually play in early Rounds of this national tournament and I would play regularly against some of the aforementioned clubs.

The local Athletics Club, the Blue Star Harriers, through their superb long distance runner John Luxford, who lived in the same street as me, tried its hardest to persuade me to pursue an athletic career. But I remained focused on football. I became a member of the Horsham Boys' Club. This gave me most of the football I needed, small sided indoor games as well as

11v11 outdoor matches. I also extended my participation in sport by joining the Horsham Swimming Club. I had frequented Horsham Swimming Pool from a very young age. Thanks to my pocket money I had owned a season ticket from the age of 8, when the minimum age was 10! I visited morning, afternoon & evening during the summer months and had taught myself to swim. Subsequently I became the Club's first choice breast stroke swimmer and had won the boys & men's diving competitions, static board & spring board, from the age of eleven. When too old for the boy's competition I continued to win the men's for two further years. And then, incredulously to me, because I was not a strong front crawl swimmer, I was picked for the water-polo team! I was under no illusion, I was only selected to make up the numbers, but I wasn't going to say no. With the sporting gene in full bloom I felt I was a boy of many parts, with some of them occasionally working. And when the school's construction work was completed the new gymnasium provided the opportunity for yet another new sport. We had a trampoline! I jumped for joy.

I took to the elastic 'bed' like an excited kangaroo. Practising twists, turns and somersaults complemented my diving. I couldn't get off it, apart from the times I disrespected it and it threw me off and I crashed painfully to the floor. I mastered it to a modest degree, sufficiently well to win a place in the South of England 'Open' Trampoline Championship. I was severely outclassed by the top performers. When the eventual winner threw a double front somersault in his first warm-up exercise I knew I was out of my depth. But I ended up in a satisfactory 8th out of 16 entrants after two disciplines, i.e. a compulsory programme and a freestyle routine. It was an earnest and modest attempt but it would never overtake my love of football which by now, as I was later told by the best goalkeeper I ever played against, Crawley Town's John Maggs, had infected me like a disease. How right he was. I had been infected at birth. What John didn't say was, the disease was incurable.

I began to make the school's first XI by the time I had reached the 4th year. The Spring edition of the School's magazine described me as *"Occasional*

Appearances – Strudwick – His ball control is good but his physique has made it difficult for him to be successful in the First XI. He may well develop into a really good player." I maintained my place more frequently through year 5. Through years 3 & 4, though, home games were in short supply while the playing fields were upgraded. On many vacant Saturdays, therefore, I took to spending the money I earned from my paper rounds on travel to, and watching the world's best team, Portsmouth FC. Between the ages of 12 & 16, or thereabouts, I would take the train from Horsham to Portsmouth (3s 6d – half priced fare); eat my packed lunch in the gardens of the City's Guildhall, looking up my grandfather's name on the War Memorial, on every trip. From there, using the knowledge my parents gave me of Pompey's streets, I would walk the 2½ miles to Fratton Park; enter the stadium in Frogmore Road (1s 6d); buy a programme (6d); and purchase a ticket for the North Stand (1s 6d). At the end of the match I would take the shorter walk back to Fratton train station hoping the train home would not turn up before

Collyer's School First XI – 1962/63

the Pompey Mail arrived on the streets. This was my gift to Mum, enabling her to read familiar names and see all the news from her hometown. Printed on blue paper, of course, the Mail always carried the caricature of a sailor on the front page. The sailor giving a two handed thumbs up indicating a win; if the thumbs were horizontal, a draw; if the thumbs were down, it was a defeat. My parents were never negligent during my upbringing, quite the opposite, but with today's level of awareness and safeguarding, I am not sure there will be many young teens able to enjoy the freedom I was lucky enough to experience and enjoy. A great day out watching the mighty Pompey, all for less than 10s, i.e. 50p in today's money! Unbelievable. My sister Pat accompanied me once. While waiting at the station for the train home we were joined on the platform by the whole Leeds United team, including the stupendous John Charles. They all autographed a programme for us. A magic moment for a football nut like me.

Meanwhile, whilst playing at every opportunity for Horsham Boys' Club Youth team I qualified for selection for the Sussex Boys' Clubs Representative team which subsequently led to my first trip abroad. In 1963 The Boys' Club's Association took a team to Duren in Germany, an industrial town between Aachen and Cologne. Before our departure we collectively agreed not to become involved in any discussion about the war. Although this might have been an odd thing for such young boys to have considered it proved to be a wise decision. Each of us subsequently agreed, there appeared to be a lot of TV programmes about the conflict; not that any of us understood what was being said. We were hosted by the families of the German players. Paul Kaufmann and his family were very kind and generous to me but the teams we played were less charitable. They won all three matches we played, comfortably!! Nevertheless, it was a super trip. We were treated wonderfully well and the Kaufmann family gave me my first introduction to the duvet. It was like sleeping under a three foot high mushroom! A weird experience, to begin with but comfortable and warm. The whole team and accompanying officials were taken to some exciting places and attractions, including Cologne. What a beautiful city; it is well worth a visit. The sight of the Cathedral, when walking out of the railway station, was mind blowing.

The pre-tour bonding of the Sussex side involved two training sessions at Woodside Road, Worthing, the home of the town's Athenian League team. It was my first experience of playing on/at the Ground of a senior adult football pitch with a stadium like environment. The surface was excellent, well covered with grass and, unknown to us starry eyed kids the sessions were being observed by Worthing's Manager, Dick Tarrant. Dick was a well respected former player of considerable repute and when his playing days were over he became a coach with identical standing. It was music to my ears, therefore, and considerably flattering when at the end of these brief sessions he asked me to come training at Worthing and join his club when I had finished my schooling, and when I had the time and means to travel. For the time being I wound down my final school year by making my first move into adult football with Broadbridge Heath FC, a local village side that played in the Horsham & District League.

It was a difficult transition in terms of physicality but with a best friend from my street, Barry Goacher, we coped well, mainly by youthful effervescence and naive arrogance. The villagers' pitch was horrendous, even on a good day. It was sited in a seriously sloping field, better suited for cows or goats, behind The Shelley Arms. The playing surface became a bog on just the threat of rain. I remember one particular cup tie we played against a team two Divisions higher than us, Billingshurst, that was played in a quagmire. By today's standards there isn't a Referee in the world who would have let us play. The pitch would have been deemed too dangerous. I hadn't found, nor did I find, anyone who considered mud dangerous in those days of the early '60s. Remember Derby County's Baseball Ground? We just played. The match ended all square, 6-6, and was headlined in the local paper as *"The match of the century."* I scored three, including two penalties, one with left foot and one with right foot, in that match and

Broadbridge Heath FC (circa 1962/63 season)

Back row:- Barry Goacher, Colin Fielder, Arthur Edwards, Mick Lilley, Ted Timms, Phil ?

Front row:- ? Dennis Istead, Bob Fisher, Dennis Strudwick, Don ?

notched again in the replay which we won on our equally muddy opponent's ground 6-4. I concluded this part of my football education by playing the following season for Horsham YMCA, a team emerging from the lower Divisions of the Sussex County League. It was very helpful to play with the likes of Billy 'Dinger' Bell, a former Horsham wing-half, and Danny Cherriman, a stereo-typical bustling centre-forward. Good fellows, not without ability, and with a shedload of experience when it came to football.

On 23rd October 1963, armed with sister Pat's knowledge on how to get to Wembley, I took myself off to the National Stadium for an International match. I say *"took myself off"* because I have no recollection of who else I went with. I just knew I was going to see some of the best artists in the game that had, by now, become an obsession in me. The fact that the match was a celebratory fixture marking the 100th Anniversary of The Football Association was completely wasted upon me. I just knew I was going to see some of the best players in the world as, for the first time in the history of the game, a single National team was going to take on a team representing the Rest of the World, a FIFA XI. So there I was, a goggled-eyed 16½ year old amongst 87,000 people.

Managed by Alf Ramsey, a player I saw playing for Tottenham Hotspur in one of my first visits to Fratton Park, and a person I very fleetingly met later in my life, England fielded a perfectly balanced team:- Gordon Banks, Jimmy Armfield, Ray Wilson, Gordon Milne, Maurice Norman, Bobby Moore, Terry Paine, Jimmy Greaves, Bobby Smith, George Eastham & Bobby Charlton. The substitutes were:- Tony Waiters, Ken Shelitoe, Ron Flowers, Tony Kay & Joe Baker. The Rest of the World team was managed by Fernando Riera and comprised:- Lev Yashin, Djalma Santos, Karl-Heinz Schnellinger, Svatopluk Pluskal, Jan Popluhar, Josef Masopust, Raymond Kopa, Denis Law, Alfredo di Stefano, Eusebio & Francisco Gento. The subs:- Milutin Soskic, Luis Eyzaguirre, Jim Baxter, Uwe Seeler & Ferenc Puskas.

The England team, then, contained four players who would win the World Cup three years later. The FIFA XI was full of great players, some not household names in the UK, but Yashin, Santos, Schnellinger, Kopa, Law, di Stefano, Eusebio, Gento, Baxter, Seeler & Puskas were names I was familiar with but previously could only dream of seeing. And FIFA fulfilled its promise to ensure all substitutes would be used in the second half. The governing body was, though, let down by Santos FC who refused to release Pele, and AC Milan who refused to release Cesare Maldini. Also, Soviet-Georgian, Mikheil Meskhi, who was replaced in the squad by Slovan Bratislavia's Jan Popluhar, was falsely reported by the USSR Football Federation as injured and unable to play. The player's subsequent biography confirmed his Federation did not inform him of the invitation to play. It seems avoidance of the truth is endemic in this nation's history. Notwithstanding this absence, I saw the two greatest goalkeepers the planet has ever produced play in a match against one another; I saw my favourite player, The Lawman, score for The Rest of the World (82 mins); and England's most prolific goalscorer, Jimmy Greaves, win the match in the final minute, after Terry Paine had opened the scoring in the 66th minute. I told you I was lucky!

Circa July 1963 – Collyer's School Horsham

The last P.E. period for Class 5C. Left to right:- DJS, Patrick Parker, Terry Yates, David Newnham, ??, Ian Rattray, ??, Harry Loomes & 'Basil' Austin.

CHAPTER TWO

Into the Senior game 1963-1966

During my final year at Collyer's I was awarded my school 'Colours' for sporting achievements. The gift of a uniquely designed cap, a scroll to wear beneath my blazer badge and a new tie would not remotely interest anyone outside Collyer's. But they meant much to me and are still somewhere in my archives. Then with GCE examinations completed, not wholly successfully on my part with passes in Mathematics and English Language only, the school term ended in July 1963 with the customary dunking in the town's open air swimming pool, fully clothed in uniform, including school cap & tie. A moment of huge relief which manifested itself into immense fun and laughter. So, to much delight, the school days were over. The discomfort of walking home dripping wet that day was barely noticeable and quickly forgotten. And thoughts of what might lay ahead were not on the agenda.

For my part I had left school uncertain about the direction I wanted to take, other than be a footballer. I had not, though, been sought after by any club, let alone any major club, so a full-time future playing the game remained just a dream. I was not good enough. Worse still, I was not even good enough to get noticed, well, not that I am aware of! While seeking inspiration and/or opportunities, I continued to work for a furnishers, Hoads of Horsham, who had given me employment during school holidays. Having started doing all the 'boy's' jobs I was trained to measure, quote and fit all types of floor coverings. A useful skill that I turned to in several subsequent years in my own home(s) and for friends. But the magnetic pull of football remained irrepressible. I took up Dick Tarrant's invitation to join the training at Worthing FC. The contacts I made pointed me in the right direction for a career at the level for which, as chosen by others, I was best suited. What followed was a 60 year role of playing in and administering the world's most popular game, and it is not completely over just yet.

I was lucky to be able to pair up with two other Horsham lads on the adventure with Worthing FC. Ted Streeter, aka Sticky, and brother Michael, also imaginatively know as Sticky, lived in an adjacent street to me and, being a little older, provided a vehicle and did all the driving. Barry Goacher accompanied us for a while but he clearly had not been infected by the football disease as I had been and his interest soon faded. I was still contaminated. The journeys up & down the A24 every Tuesday & Thursday for training were hilarious and not, on reflection, without a little danger. The A24 in those days was single carriageway for the whole journey and I remember, during a period of upgrading the road to dual carriageway status, the passengers distracted the driver, Micky I believe, to the extent we ended up in a field. And, of course, how can I ever forget the smell of Worthing's seaweed, an infamous tourist distraction, as we reached the town boundaries and/or the twice weekly fish & chip suppers at C&S Fisheries on Findon Valley Road.

The elevation I had made by joining Worthing was immediately evident. All the players changed and trained together. There was no noticeable segregation of the three teams within the Club. The principle of 'if you don't train you don't play' was indelibly imposed in my mind. It focussed everyone's attention. On match days all aspects of a player's kit were provided, except for boots and, of course, undergarments. The players were looked after well off the pitch, too. When playing at home, at Woodside Road, home and visiting players all sat down for dinner after the match. And even while I was in the 'A' team, where I began my time at Worthing, due to the journey I had to make home I was always invited to enjoy the hospitality. All the players had access to the Club's internal and external professional physiotherapists. All they had to do was follow instructions and turn up wherever required, on time. Nothing was left to chance. Under the management of Dick Tarrant and the Chairmanship of

Harry Bloom everything was very professional. We were taught to follow good disciplines and were looked after very well. And to help the process the Club had a unique character in Sam Chetwynd.

Although my time at Worthing was brief, just over two seasons, it provided an excellent learning curve. The Club had some good players who had earned promotion from the Athenian League First Division the season before I arrived; so Woodside Road was a good and happy place to be. Following pre-season training my introduction was to be invited to attend the first First XI game of the new (1964-65) season; a home match against Barnet, the Premier Division Champions from the previous season. Typically for the opening game of the season, it was a scorchingly hot day. I could not help but be impressed by the strength & fitness of the players and their ability to cope with the hot weather. In front of a crowd I would estimate to be in excess of 2,000 people Barnet won, 2-0. It was clearly going to be a tough campaign for the likes of Richard Tarrant (the Manager's son), yachtsman Brian Cudmore, Roger Allport, the effervescent (and local Police Officer) Ray Knight, the uncompromising Gerry Offen, David Bloom (the Chairman's son) and my travel buddy Micky Streeter. They need not have been too concerned about this first reverse, the Rebels, as Worthing was known, were to lose only six more League games during the season and they finished fourth in the table. A highly credible performance.

Like most young players I wanted to score goals, so I played in the forward line. Competition for front players within the Club was stiff and opposition defences were even stronger. But after a few games in the 'A' (third) team I regularly made the Reserve side. Both teams were managed, administratively, by Sam Chetwynd. Sam took care of just about everything, e.g. making sure the players knew where to meet for the next fixture; travel arrangements and laying out the kit & medical equipment. Sam also provided the entertainment. He loved to talk about his career in football, i.e. how he coached & befriended world class players. The tales would often begin with a subtle name drop like, "when I met this raw young player called

Di", pronounced Dee, "I could tell he had potential." He rattled on about how he coached Di and what he did to perfect the player called Alfredo Di Stefano with whom he was still good pals. With Sam's guidance Di became a Real Madrid hero and played for three international countries, Argentina, Columbia and Spain. Ferenc was another of his prodigies, and Sam tried in vain to coach Ferenc to kick with his right foot but decided he was quite good, or at least good enough, with his left. Ferenc, in this tale, was Ferenc Puskas who played for Hungary and Real Madrid! These were all, of course, complete 'cock & ball' stories created by Sam's vivid and most amusing and elastic imagination. We were kept spellbound by his parables; tales of Jeffrey Archer proportions, composed as he went along. Sam was a colourful, fascinating character and popular with everyone.

I mentioned above Harry Bloom and Dick Tarrant. Harry had a well respected car sales business in Worthing and ran the football club with the same meticulous care. Commitment was also his forte. To my knowledge he rarely missed a match and was frequently seen at the ground on training nights. Without losing his love for Worthing FC he subsequently became a Director at Brighton & Hove Albion FC and within three years he was made Vice-Chairman. I understand he was the 'calming gel' between Chairman Mike Bamber, of frequently unpredictable mood, and Club Manager Alan Mullery. Harry literally 'died with his boots on' so to speak, on the club's coach making its way to an away fixture at Stoke City. The Club is now 'chaired' by his grandson Tony, son of Harry's brother Ronnie. The Albion remembers Harry fondly and has honoured his involvement by naming a restaurant after him (HB's) in the Club's new Stadium, the Amex, at Falmer. A nice way to remember a good man; a football man. And to show just how the 'football disease' is indiscriminate in infecting families, another of Harry's sons, Ray, who was heavily involved at Worthing FC is now a Director at the Brighton club, on the Board with his cousin Tony, the Chairman.

I made a lot of friends at Worthing and many happy times remain in the memory bank. A person who made an early impression upon me was Ray

Knight, the Club's 6'3" centre-half. Ray was a happy-go-lucky type of person who had a good sense of humour and a sharp wit. As a Police Constable he resembled and applied the image of a typical 'village bobby' to his law enforcement duties within the comparatively large seaside town. He was also self effacing. Using his height and stature he admitted adopting a lofty approach to a drunk whilst 'on the beat' one night as he, the drunk, struggled to keep his feet when making his way home after a good night out. Noticing the man had long winkle picker shoes on Ray asked, *"Do your toes go to the end of those shoes?" "No,"* the man said through an alcoholic haze, *"does your head go to the top of that helmet?"* As a footballer, despite appearing to be a little uncoordinated, Ray was effective. He was downright awkward and difficult to play against. He was the same in training. He didn't mind who he nudged, barged or elbowed. Whoever was in his way, they were there to be tackled. And they knew it and/or very quickly found out about it.

Another first team player who helped me along the way, within and outside football, became a friend for life. Wilf Hugill was an established and an accomplished defender, mainly at full-back when I met him at Worthing. During his National Service Wilf played for Glentoran in the Northern Ireland League where he briefly came across a very young George Best. I cannot remember in what capacity he met Bestie, but I imagine George was still only a boy. A little later Glentoran rejected George for being *"too small and light"*. After that setback local football scout, Bob Bishop, advised Manchester United, *"I think I have found you a genius."* Bob was clearly a good judge of a player.

Wilf had joined Worthing FC in 1958. By the time I arrived he had become Club Captain and regularly represented Sussex at senior level. Like Bobby Moore, Wilf was steady and reliable; not the fastest player on two legs but what he lacked in speed he made up for in good positioning and guile. And he never lost his cool. At 'our' level, Wilf was a 'great'. He was followed each week by his fiancee, who subsequently became his wife, Sonia. Sonia, by the way, was always accompanied by her sister, Corrine, who married another player, Phil Tidy. They were all very kind to me during my early 'discovery' years at a senior club. Very sadly Phil took his own life in the years following the end of his football career. But, back to Wilf, he was professional in every aspect of his business and social life. He was a master craftsman in carpentry and the best way I can sum up my admiration for this friend is to metaphorically stand back and truthfully say, Wilf built his & Sonia's marital home; a magnificent family house in Tarring. Not many of us can say that. It was a very very sad day when our friendship ended with his passing on 10 March 2015. I was extremely proud when, at Sonia's request, my condolence letter to the family, and eulogy to my great friend, was read at Wilf's funeral. We then lost Sonia on 12 February 2021. I am pleased to say, though, I have happier times with Wilf & Sonia to report a little later. In the meantime, although my friendship has been taken away, my love for these people will never diminish.

Wilf & Sonia Hugill – Wilf played for Steyning, Worthing, Horsham, Eastbourne United & Sussex. He also managed and undertook 29 'aid' trips in 8 years to Romania, driving a hired lorry loaded with equipment for a school in Ghidigeni and gifts for the pupils, following the downfall of the country's Communist President Nicolae Ceasescu in December 1989. He was supported throughout by Sonia who was a renowned and an immensely popular Teacher in Worthing.

CHAPTER THREE

The Horsham years – 1966-1976 & 1981

As the 1966/67 season approached Ted & Micky Streeter both left Worthing to join Horsham FC which was undergoing something of a revolution under a new Manager, Pat Tobin. Ted became Pat's Assistant and managed the Reserve team. Wilf Hugill also left the Seasiders at this time to join Horsham's new regime. I continued at Worthing under the Reserve team management of Tony Murrant, an ex-Horsham & ex-Worthing player, who also doubled as my chauffeur. Thanks Tony. I recall the train journey between Horsham and Worthing, which I had to take on quite a few occasions, was laborious after suffering at the hands of Dr. Beeching. But at 19 years of age it wasn't insurmountable. Besides, I was playing football for Worthing and that was something to feel good about. And there were likeable team-mates to meet, Alan Poland (a very good goalkeeper); Gerry Rawlings (a competitive, no, rugged half back); Colin Woffinden (a skilful midfielder) and Dave Smith (a tall commanding centre half who liked the bath water hotter than anyone else could withstand). The journeys had to be done. It was always a delight to play at Worthing's Woodside Road Ground; the pitch was kept in immaculate condition. Travel to away fixtures was always well organised, car or coach travel to most but as many games were against London based sides I recall everyone travelled to Victoria by train where we were picked up by a coach to complete the journey to the likes of Hayes, Hounslow, Finchley, Uxbridge and Edmonton.

Employment wise I was now working with Ted Streeter at Woodside (no connection to Worthing's football ground) Civil Engineering in Three Bridges. I was the Company's bookkeeper, payroll clerk and general Office dogsbody. Indeed, most of the time I was the only one in the Office! Ted was a surveyor, and so was Peter Mackie, a Scot who liked a wee dram and a bet, often together. The Company operated as a Ground Worker in the house building industry, constructing the roads, footpaths and foundations up to the damp course. The owner was Jim Keaveney whose personality and sense of humour matched the size of his waist – big! I learnt a lot about the Irish and their way of life; met a lot of lovely people; and picked up my first lessons in 'street wisdom'. Business was fast, furious and a bit 'cut throat' at times. It was often difficult to get building materials and/or machinery at the right place, at the right time, and above all at a good price. And worst of all, large contractors were often slow to pay up. This gave us frequent cash flow issues, which appears to be an endemic problem in the construction industry. But it was an enlightening time of life during which I was generously given all the time off I needed to play football. They were good days.

Leaving work aside for a moment I continued making the 40 odd mile round trip to Worthing, three times each week (Tuesday, Thursday & Saturday) to play football. But I began to keep a vague eye on the revolution taking place at Queen Street, Horsham. It was, after all, my home town club who I had watched from a very young boy having initially been taken by my father. In those early days Horsham played in the Metropolitan League against many Football League 'A' teams. I recall little of those occasions other than swinging like a budding gymnast on the pitch perimeter barrier and/or passing the half-time interval by carrying a board around the pitch announcing the winning tote numbers or playing my own game of football with a group of other young supporters using the side netting at the 'bottom/YMCA end' goal as our target. These days predated the current thirst for statistics so I have no idea what crowds Horsham FC attracted but I clearly remember exiting 'The Hut' Ground along the narrow lane leading to Queen Street, the A281. Supporters could only shuffle their way to the road where, on a Saturday (there were no floodlights in those days so I do not recall any midweek games) Dad would divert on our journey home to buy a bag of winkles! As the seasons moved on, and I was able to attend without parental care, my mates and I would attend matches using the benefit of a 'hedge ticket'. Shamefully I admit, we entered Horsham's Ground illicitly via the adjacent Horsham YMCA Ground on Gorings Mead, and through a gap in the hedge behind one of the spectator Stands.

Horsham FC moved on too, to the Corinthian League and subsequently the Athenian League. I was becoming a more serious follower and had started to notice particular players, e.g. Ernie Manouch, (a magnificent goalkeeper), Glynn Jones (a majestic centre-half), Owen Parker (a skilful wing-half), and John Elphick (an outstanding bustling centre-forward), all from the Horsham locality. By now, I was watching from the terraces of the new spectator stand on the Gorings Mead side of the Ground, with Dad and several of his Post Office work mates. And as time took its toll on the earliest of the faces I cheered new personnel slowly began to break into the side. Unlike today, when players come and go in quick succession, teams sixty odd years ago were more stable and the teams evolved. Players like Tony Winkworth, John Browning, Billy Bell, Roy 'Cogger' Mobsby, Tony Lee, Roy Scutt, Keith Brister, Geoff Crowther, John Chalaye, Denis Stillwell, Gordon New, Jimmy Carter, Dave Stripp, Dave Collyer and Don Cocozza (aka Donkey Ozza) became local heroes. I leave until last, the mention of the club's most prolific and successful centre-forward, Micky Browning. Micky was capped by the Football Association when he won an England place in its Amateur International XI; the only player I know of 'capped' whilst playing for Horsham. Mickey was an outstanding player and a good man.

So, armed with all these childhood through to early adolescence memories, which clearly played a significant role in the development of my 'football gene', it was not a difficult decision for me to make. In or around October 1966, I decided to swap my allegiance from Worthing to Horsham. Whilst harbouring an ambition to eventually play at the highest level I could, having not progressed beyond Worthing's Reserve Team, I felt in the short term at least, I could play Reserve Team football at Horsham – my home town team – without travelling 40 miles three times each week. I made the move purely for my own convenience and, hopefully, my development. I was aware Horsham had undergone great change since the appointment of Manager Pat Tobin. Like all/any club engaged in such a transition plenty of new players had arrived, Some were from far afield, directly recruited by Pat since he knew their capabilities, e.g. George Wakeling, John Gregory, Keith Welham & Terry (Tex) Wiltshire. Others were more local, from senior clubs within the county e.g. Wilf Hugill, Brian Riggs & Mick Streeter. The affect of the changes brought about by Pat was having an immediate impact. At the time I signed Horsham had reached the final Qualifying Round of the FA Cup; not that I, at the age of 19, knew of the structure of this Competition and/or what happened next should Horsham win their forthcoming tie. I did not expect First Team affairs would concern me any time soon. I did not, therefore, consider I was jumping on a 'band wagon' that was rapidly gaining pace. Quite the opposite, I was joining a club that had been relegated at the end of the previous season from Athenian League Division 1 to Division 2 having won only five of its thirty League fixtures in the 1965-66 season. It was the first time in the Club's history it had suffered relegation. So it's little wonder the Club Committee ordered a change of management. Taking all that into account there was one other major reason to join Horsham; the Club had just invested £5,000 in floodlights. This was a major factor in attracting new and better players. For me it also meant being able to play midweek fixtures throughout the winter, enabling more matches, and to train midweek evenings at a sensible time. I was able to leave behind running around Broadwater Green, Worthing, with only street lighting showing the way. All that remained is the memory of Roger Johnson (I think it was) crashing into a newly planted tree, breaking it and its supporting stake, in two. It was so dark.

After a couple of training sessions I was given an opportunity in the Reserve team. One of my early appearances, and probably the very first, was a Sussex Intermediate Cup fixture at Slindon, a village near Arundel. It was a game we felt we should win, indeed, we were expected to win. Despite the relatively short journey we travelled by coach. Upon arrival we couldn't find the Dressing Rooms. I cannot remember who, if anyone, was in charge of our arrangements but there was no sign of a reception for a visiting football team. The coach driver made what appeared to be a fair and obvious conclusion by taking us to the village hall. It was quickly evident nobody was expecting us, and there were no changing rooms, so we prepared for the match on the coach. What was quickly evident to me was, Horsham Reserves played in 'hand me down' kit from a previous season's first team strip. And, my word, some of those guys must have had extraordinarily long arms! (see picture).

Horsham Reserves at Slindon – Sussex Intermediate Cup – circa November 1966

Back Row (left to right):- Alan Lancaster, Phil Skingsley, Dave Barton, John Steele, Micky Byrne & John West.

Front Row (left to right):- DJS, Jeff Cox, Roy (Cogger) Mobsby, Nigel Moore & Keith Etheridge.

The atmosphere brightened when a photographer made his presence known and informed us his camera work would appear in the next edition of the West Sussex County Times. Not a bad start to my Horsham career, I thought, my 'fizzog' in the paper already. Anyway, Slindon gave us a fright. We scraped through to the next round by a margin of 2-1. We changed back on the bus and departed quickly, complaining the lack of any appropriate welcome, and dressing rooms, had undermined our preparations. We were brusquely told we had gone to the wrong hall. At the correct venue there were proper dressing rooms with showers and hospitality had been laid on. We left, a little red faced but more importantly, we left as winners.

Under its new management the First XI had commenced the season well, steadily building what it hoped would be a promotion campaign. Pat Tobin and Ted Streeter were younger than the management team I had experienced at Worthing and were applying new styles of play. England had not long won the World Cup with new patterns of play, i.e. with overlapping full-backs and without conventional wingers. Pat & Ted were excellent coaches and were following the new trends. Their methods were proving successful.

As well as a good start in the League Horsham had progressed through four qualifying rounds of the FA Cup. Victories over Dorking, 3-0; Fleet Town, 3-0; and Woking, 2-1 had led to a final qualifying match against local rivals Hastings United, of the Southern League. Unlike the Corinthian, Athenian and Isthmian Leagues whose membership claimed amateur status the Southern League had always been acknowledged as a professional competition. Since its formation in 1894 the Southern League had frequently provided clubs to the Football League. It had a history of close ties to the full-time game and frequently Football League players ended their careers at Southern League clubs. Rather uncharitably, therefore, the Southern League had gained a reputation of being a 'Football League graveyard', metaphorically speaking. As if to underline the unflattering nickname, the leader of Hastings United's attack against Horsham was ex-Tottenham Hotspur & England centre-forward Bobby Smith. My father was amongst the 3,297 people at Queen Street on the 15th October 1966 that saw goals from Mick Mears and John Gregory, a penalty, defeat their professional opponents 2-1. Despite carrying a little more weight than in his full-time professional days, a still classy centre-forward, Bobby Smith, scored for Hastings.

So, Horsham had reached the First Round Proper of the FA Challenge Cup for only the second time in its history. The last occasion was in the 1947/48 season when, as a Sussex County League side, they faced another former England centre-forward on Saturday 29th November 1947; this time with disastrous consequences. Horsham opened the scoring against Notts County before going down 9-1. Ron Smallwood put Horsham ahead in the second minute but County replied though the great Tommy Lawton (3); Jackie Sewell (3); Jack Marsh (2) & Tony Freeman (1). The attendance at the County Ground was 24,815.

Nineteen years later, for their victory over Hastings United, Horsham was rewarded with a home tie against Swindon Town in the First Round. Having been granted permission for the Club to postpone its Reserve team fixture I joined the rest of the second string players, and my father, in the record Queen Street crowd of 7,134.

Horsham was able to field its strongest available side:- Ian Page, Geoff Crowther, Wilf Hugill, Ron Philpott, Brian Riggs, Don Hollands, John Gregory, John Tomlinson, Mick Streeter, Brian Griffin, Keith Wellham & Brian Hardcastle as substitute. They approached the game in-form and were full of confidence. But their task was formidable. The Robins included one-club man John Trollope, who eventually completed over 700 Football League appearances, Mel Nurse, Dennis 'Bullets' Brown, Willie Penman and England U/23 International, Don Rogers.

Pat Tobin liked his teams to start at a tremendous pace. Horsham obliged. The Robins were immediately put under the cosh by Griffin, Streeter, Hugill and Gregory. Swindon weathered the storm and struck back at lightening speed through Penman, Rogers and Roger Smart. Pat would also have instructed his side to follow another golden rule, when playing against a team that was perceived to be superior, e.g. a full-time professional team, keep them out for as long as you can, do not concede early, stay in the game. The purpose being, it would be far harder to get back into the game against a pro side. Horsham succeeded for 26 minutes; not really long enough. Goalkeeper Page attempted a short goal kick to Hugill. I was sitting in the temporary accommodation at the far end of the ground so I did not have a clear view but there appeared to be some hesitancy. Rogers reacted in a flash. He whipped the ball in the net. Horsham argued the ball had not left the penalty area but Referee Reg Paine* was having none of it. Swindon were ahead and did not look back. That is not to suggest they had it easy for the remainder of the game, on the contrary, Tomlinson, Streeter, Griffin & Wellham rattled Swindon's cage at every opportunity. The Horsham team left all they had on the pitch. Swindon had to wait until the 70th minute to score their second, through Nurse. It was not until the 86th minute that Swindon put the game beyond all reasonable doubt when 'Bullets' Brown fired home. Excitement had captured the town in the weeks since the draw had been made and it all concluded with a wonderful game. I had no part to play whatsoever but my appetite for the future had been indelibly whetted.

I knuckled down endeavouring to secure a regular place in the Reserve team. There was some stiff competition from some good players. Obviously, I cannot remember them all but I recall Keith Cook, Denny Ringrose, Dick Hounsome, Richard Collier and the absolutely outstanding Dave Owens. On his day Owens was a truly magnificent player, worthy of a far higher standard of football. I recall a game in which his good friend and

---

* Reg Paine subsequently became Head of the Refereeing Department at the Football Association. We were to become working colleagues in the football industry and good friends. But I never asked him about the disputed goal at Horsham v Swindon!

travel buddy, Cook, scored a fine goal. Owens decided he had to produce something better, and he did just that. He scored directly from a corner kick. I believe to this day he did it deliberately. He played for it, and achieved it. Dave Owens went on to play a few games for the First XI but only Dave Owens can tell you why he did not progress far, far further in the game. One of the most skilful players I played with.

I do not recall missing many, if any, games for the Reserves but I knew I was finding it difficult to adapt to Horsham's style of play. I was moved back into midfield but Ted Streeter decided the defence needed more cover and speed so moved me into the back four. I became accustomed to the 'overlapping' full-back role, left & right as I could kick with both feet, and not infrequently as a 'man marker' in the centre of the defence. I quickly began to enjoy life in my new position(s). Providing I chose, tactically, the right time to go forward I was able to support the attack on the side I was playing. But I was expected to provide defensive cover whenever we were attacked on the opposite side. I also enjoyed the occasions I was asked to play a specific role, in front of the traditional centre-half for example, marking a deep laying centre-forward like Lewes' Micky Morgan. My pace also enabled me to play as a sweeper behind the centre-half. I particularly enjoyed games when selected to play this role as I felt, and assumed, I was being given greater responsibility to provide cover to both sides of the defence. The simple truth is, I just enjoyed playing. I don't think I could cope with so many circumstances of the modern game where players are not given full playing time. I wanted to play every week, and midweek as well if we had a fixture. I was finding the defensive role much easier, too. Unlike a forward/striker who spends much of his time facing his own defence to receive the ball before turning to attack, a defender is, or should, always be facing the ball. The role should be much easier to play. If the ball and/or an attacker gets behind a defender, the defender could be in trouble. So I always endeavoured to stay goal side; a golden rule.

The fundamental roles of a Reserve team are to support the First team.

It should provide a vehicle for front players not currently being selected, to return to the 1st XI; it must develop Reserve players to challenge for 1st XI places, to create competition; and provide a common Club strategy for all players whilst maintaining an equal level of fitness for everyone in the Club. The bond amongst the players was, therefore, strong. There was no room for egos; any such traits were soon brought down to earth, and the humour was occasionally coarse. It was character building stuff. Tex once recalled a story from a previous club of his where, after training, two team mates were heard chatting in the showers. He didn't say who but I suspect one was Tex. In summary, with the shower hammering down one colleague said to another, *"Am I annoying you?" "No, why?"*, came the reply. *"I just thought I would be"* said the first person. *"Why would you think that?"* said his mate. *"Because I am peeing down your leg!"* Argh!! I don't know what happened next.

My 'aquiline' nose attracted multiple comments, mainly from Tex. He was positive I was the only person he knew who could smoke cigars in the rain! Apparently, if I attended a wedding I could cut the cake simply by nodding my head! And if Keith Cook and I ever attended a fancy dress party together we could go 'back-to-back', as a pick axe!! The 'Dressing Room' humour of the day would probably be considered politically incorrect in the present day. But I am not aware of anyone being offended, they always answered back with their own wisecrack. And if you wanted to give banter you had to be strong enough to take it. Besides it was also incredibly funny. Tex Wiltshire had an encyclopaedia of jokes. It was a challenge for anyone to tell him a story he had not already heard. Almost everyone failed, as Tex delivered the punchline almost a soon as the story had begun. I didn't know it at the time but, give or take the ups & downs of not knowing if you were in the team, and of course some poor results, I was embarking on the eleven most happy years I spent in football. And as much as I disliked Tuesday & Thursday evenings, training sessions were not to be missed.

I do, though, recall missing one Thursday evening. But my excuse, which in my view was unique, did not dissuade the 'judges' from imposing a fine upon me – the proceeds of which went into the end of season tour fund. It was early afternoon when I received a telephone call from my work colleague, Peter Mackie. Peter was in Scotland with his mother following the passing of his father. He asked me to accompany his wife and three young children on a flight that afternoon from Gatwick to Glasgow so the family could all be together at the time of the funeral. Peter's wife Mamie used to be a hostess for Caledonian Airways. But she had lost her confidence after

Apologies for the slightly damaged photograph. In addition to over 300 appearances for the First team, I served my time in the Reserves. I am not sure in which Suburban or Athenian League season this picture was taken but I believe we won the League Cup.

Pictured, left to right:-

Back row – Frank Knott, ??, Malcolm Bailey, Jess Lee, Paul (Doughy) Baker, ??, Mark Tidy, Ted Streeter

Middle row – Keith Cook, DJS, Denny Ringrose, John Grant, Micky Byrne, Dick Hounsome

Front row – ??, Jimmy Wond, Roy (Cogger) Mobsby, Dave Foreman, Dave Owens.

she dropped out of a flight she was due to work on, because of illness, and the flight crashed. So we all boarded a flight around 5pm; disembarked at Glasgow and said our goodbyes; and after the formalities I immediately boarded the same airplane for the flight back. I was still eating a dinner when we landed back in Sussex and a moustachioed gentleman emerged from the flight deck excitedly referring to the duration of the flight back by saying, *"It's a record chaps, 47 minutes, it's a record"*. Having arrived home late my mother disbelieved my story, told me off for being too late to go training and clipped my ear. My team mates were equally unimpressed and duly enforced a financial penalty. I thought it was all a great experience. I was pleased to have helped my friends and I had been to Scotland and back in less than three hours.

Back at Queen Street I had settled in to my new environment comfortably. I enjoyed playing in my new position and do not recall missing many, if any, matches. Most of all I felt a sense of pride wearing the Amber & Lincoln green of my home town Club, even for the Reserve team. The focus of the Club, however, revolves around the First team so I have no records on how we, in the 'Stiffs', concluded our season. But I can confidently say we won more of our Suburban League games than we lost. We all got on well, I was enjoying myself, so I had no thoughts or ambitions of a First team place yet. With the First team playing so well, making such a challenge was beyond my reach, for the time being at least. Besides that, the Reserve team was not without success of its own.

As time moved on, so did my work. Woodside Civil Engineering collapsed and I joined a 'sister' company called O'Brien & Joyce based in Smallfields, Surrey. Thankfully they were football friendly. Indeed, during my employment one of the Partners' sons started a Company football team, ingeniously called OBJ. The team played in the Sussex Sunday League. After initially being banned, Sunday football had become a growth industry. I had put 'a toe in the water' during these early days with a team called Mundane Casuals, formed by a group of old Collyerians. Inevitably, I was eventually coerced into turning out for OBJ. At the time, I just played whenever I had the opportunity. I considered it broadened my experience. Looking back, with my eyes set on progress at Horsham, turning out on a Sunday for the work's team was an imposition. I felt coerced. But, as much as I tried, I couldn't resist the opportunity of a game. OBJ was a happy place. I still have the occasional lunch with two of my ex-colleagues, Jackie Watson and Bridget Flanagan.

So my first season (1966/67) at Horsham concluded and I had been converted from striker into a defender, predominately at full-back. I think we finished in a respectable position in the League. The First team had been revitalised after the previous season's relegation and finished third. Sussex rivals Eastbourne United, managed by ex-Charlton Athletic defender

In the Stiffs, methinks circa December 1966.

Back row:- ??, Phil Skingsley, Keith Etheridge, John Grant, Dick Hounsome, DJS.

Front row:- Graham Langford, Roy 'Cogger' Mobsby, Peter Dove, Dave Foreman, Dave Owens.

Gordon Jago, won the League by four points from Ware and were seven ahead of Horsham. In a Christmas fixture United had convincingly beaten Horsham 3-0 at The Oval, Eastbourne. So in the return fixture in midweek towards the end of April, when honours were still up for grabs, Horsham sought revenge. And while leading 2-1 that looked a possibility. But, for the second time in the season the new floodlights failed. The lighting reduced to half power. After a lengthy interruption Horsham wanted to continue but Eastbourne, understandably in the circumstances, refused. There was much angst amongst the crowd. Honours had eluded Horsham by the time the match was re-arranged as the season's final fixture. The medals had been decided but Horsham took some consolation in a 1-0 victory by an 80th minute goal from Brian Griffin. Between the abandoned and re-arranged game, though, Eastbourne defeated Horsham in the Sussex Senior Cup Final to retain the trophy. So, a 'double' for our Sussex rivals and we were left empty handed and pre-season training was just six weeks away!

In the evening warmth of mid-July, beginning with a run from Queen Street to Horsham Cricket Club and then 'increasing demand' sprint exercises up the side of Denne Hill, training was tough. And there was little or no sight of a ball during the early weeks of pre-season. Competition was fierce and the number of ambitious participants was high. This always led to a fair amount of anxiety, i.e. would I make it this season. During the years that followed I learnt not to panic. There always seemed twice the number needed and/or expected for the commencement of a season during the early weeks of training. As the season approached and the training got fierce the numbers dwindled. But the reduced numbers just increased the intensity as the selections for the first pre-season friendlies were awaited. Everyone was keen to win a place in the team. I confined my anticipation to hope rather than expectancy. But, bingo, I was in the first line-up; a friendly against APV Athletic, known locally as a very successful works team from Manor Royal, Crawley.

We fielded a young side, with several players from the Reserve team and a few newcomers. One debut maker, Barry Steer, joined Horsham from APV in the summer. He opened the scoring for his new Club. Horsham'ites Russell Penticost and Graham Langford scored our other goals in a 3-2 victory. I don't remember how I played but it wasn't good enough to win a place in any of the remaining pre-season friendlies and subsequently the opening game of the League season. So it was back to the Stiffs!

I carried on as I left off the last season; defending like stink and attacking whenever possible. I had by now been voted the fastest player in the Club and was awarded a cloth badge portraying the Road Runner, Beep Beep! Mother sewed it on the backside of my training shorts because that was the only place anyone was going to see it. All the players in the two squads mixed well, trained together, swapping experiences, learning, all the while bonding. The dressing room humour/culture was off the Richter scale, hilarious. A 'bad mistake' culture developed. Anyone admitting making a mistake, like the player, Micky Harrington, who wasted an hour of his working day waiting to admonish a fellow motorist that had blocked in his vehicle, only to realise his car was parked further along the road, was ridiculed unmercifully. Numerous times players turned up for training missing a vital item in their kit bag, because someone else had packed their bag. Bad mistake! In all these cases the biggest error was owning up to making a mistake in the first place.

So Horsham was a good place to be. But the First team commenced the 1967/68 campaign indifferently. After a 6-0 crushing at the hands of Crawley Town in its last pre-season friendly Horsham won only three of its first seven competitive matches. The next seven comprised three draws and four defeats. Three wins from fourteen outings was less than what Pat Tobin expected. I don't know what he was thinking but after a 2-0 defeat at Edmonton I was pleased to receive a message, *"No training on Tuesday, you are to report to Crawley 6pm on 24th October for a Midweek Floodlight League match."* My first competitive start, against Horsham's nearest and fiercest rivals. For a local lad like me this could not have been a bigger/better start to first team life.

Crawley's Town Mead pitch sloped and was compact. The crowd was very close to the pitch and the dressing rooms were not 5 star. The 'New Towners' boasted several former full-time professionals e.g. Roy Jennings at centre-half *(22 goals in 297 appearances for Brighton & Hove Albion)* and Roy McCrohan *(a wing half for Norwich City, Colchester United & Bristol Rovers).* Jennings opened the scoring for the Newtowners, from the penalty spot. Keith Cook volleyed home from a Keith Welham cross for our equaliser. It was a goal that gave him particular joy as his father, Fred, was Crawley's Manager. Debut maker Peter Dove, all 5'5' of him, was a star in midfield. And I, according to the local paper, *"settled down after a shaky start to play competently."* The attendance was 861, not bad for a 'subordinate' League encounter. We drew 1-1.

Four days later I was selected for my first Athenian League fixture, a home game against Harrow Borough. We won 3-1. Dave Legrice scored first, Keith Cook added a second and then Peter Dove scored his first Horsham goal. Within the next three weeks I was selected for four more games; Woking in the Mithras Cup, which we lost 2-1 but I set up Don Hollands for our goal; Tooting & Mitcham United in the Floodlight League, a 2-1 win with goals by Streeter and Legrice; a 3-2 victory over Lancing in the Sussex Senior Cup, where Streeter, Steer & an own goal were our scorers; and a 1-0 win at a boggy Windsor & Eton. Steer was on target again in a match we were, reportedly, very lucky.

So, after participating in four wins in six matches, and only one defeat, I do not know why, or cannot remember why, my run in the first team ended at this point. I must have been disappointed. I was not called upon again until I was used as a substitute for a Midweek Floodlight League game on 20th February against – Crawley Town! Again, we drew 1-1. George Wakeling was our goalscorer with an 84th minute equaliser. Four days later I was included in the team that took on and defeated Ruislip 1-0, thanks to a Keith Welham thunderbolt. *(Keith Welham had lucky legs; lucky they didn't break, they were so skinny. But he had a shot more powerful than I had ever seen and/or subsequently saw.)* I was not then selected until 12th March for a floodlight game at Southall. We won 2-1 with both our goals coming from John Wayling. I did not make the First team again that season. The campaign drew to a close with Horsham in bronze medal position, again. Great rivals Lewes were crowned champions ahead of Aylesbury United.

As I approached my third season with Horsham I realised just how unfit you can get in the few weeks between the end of one season and the beginning of preparations for the next. The pain and stiffness after the first couple of sessions was indescribable and begs the question, is it all worth it? Of course it is!

Having made nine appearances in competitive matches in 1967/68 I probably harboured hopes of pressing for a few more games in 1968/69. And it started well. I was selected for the first pre-season friendly, against Merton Rushmere, and we won 2-1 with goals from wonderful Wellham and Keith Cook. But disappointment was to come. I was not chosen again until an Athenian League fixture on 26 October. I am sure to have been frustrated and, no doubt, disappointed by this omission but I know I would not have been confident enough to have questioned the Manager's decision. I am sure I would have got on with business as best I could to be sure I didn't let anyone down. I wanted my place back. But competition was stiff.

In the closed season, and the weeks that followed, Ray Smith, John Warman, John West, John Eales, Gordon Guile, Ray Major, Frankie Childs, Ricky Maddox and Dai Mason had all signed. And Micky Browning re-signed. Wilf Hugill, Barry Steer and Brian Griffin were amongst the leavers who joined Eastbourne United. I hung on and the order came after training on Thursday 24th October, *"you're in on Saturday. Report to Queen Street at 1.30pm."* Sadly, we lost. Even more sadly Don Hollands, one of the toughest players I ever shared a pitch with, block tackled an opponent so strongly his momentum took him over the opponents shoulder and Don broke his arm when landing on the pitch. He walked off unaided cradling his broken limb with his good arm.

I had to wait nearly four weeks for my next appearance; a Premier Midweek Floodlight encounter at Southall. Western Road, Southall was quite a big ground but when it is as empty as it was on 19th November, it was not inspiring. I replaced Ron Philpott, now there's an inspirational player!, and we drew 2-2. My enduring memory of my visit to Southall, on this occasion, was spending another 90 minutes after the game looking for Ray Major's contact lens. Having swept the dressing room floor, and carrying out a finger tip search through all the mud, Ray found it stuck to the leg of his trousers!

My next match was only four days away; a 3-0 Athenian League home win against Uxbridge in which John Warman grabbed his first goals (2) and the irrepressible John Gregory notched one. Gregory was a superb midfield player, tenacious and creative, in the John McGovern mould. An Uxbridge player was cautioned for fouling me when neither of us was in possession of the ball. If I remember the incident correctly, he decided to express his frustration at something by grabbing me around the throat. Well, it is a physical contact game!

Despite the good result I had to wait a month for my next outing. As Christmas approached we played Wingate at home and won 3-0. Langford, Warman & Smith scored; my best effort hit the crossbar; and the victory took us to the top of the League. A victory over county rivals Eastbourne Town on Boxing Day enhanced our position but two days later disaster struck. Horsham to Herne Bay over the Christmas holiday period was not a kind gesture by the fixtures Secretary, but that is what we were dealt. It was something I was to become mindful of later in my career. A trip to Herne Bay always had a disincentive affect, but on 28th December, Mmmm! We experienced one late withdrawal, Frankie Childs, which George Wakeling filled. We sent a strong side but after Phil Skingsley conceded a third minute penalty we crashed 4-0. I can't remember if I paid for the poor result but I didn't make the team again until 25th January, as a substitute in a Sussex Senior Cup tie against Three Bridges. Another new player, Paul Delea, made his debut; John Eales and Ray Major scored our goals in a 2-1 win. I cannot confirm if I got on the pitch in this match but I was just about ever-present for the remainder of the season, making a further 23 appearances before the season's end.

Amongst those games I managed to score my second goal, although it was during a very disappointing 2-1 defeat at home to Rainham. The local newspaper led with the words, *"When a full-back is your best forward you know you are in trouble...speedy Strudwick was up to score, but it was too late."* On another occasion, in the 15th April defeat of Maidenhead United, the media report stated, *"It was another great hearted display by left-back Dennis Strudwick and a grafting performance by John Gregory. If Gregory commanded the midfield, Strudwick was a real terror both in defence and attack. He rarely lost his grip on tricky right winger Woolley yet found time to boost the attack numerous times. It was Strudwick's amazing ability to be up with the attack and back with the defence, almost at the same time, that led to Horsham's second half clincher. He started the move with Gregory near his own goal and almost finished it off with a flashing shot blocked by the goalkeeper. Frankie Childs finished it off."* Well, it was my birthday!

As the season wound down we took on Eastbourne United in the Sussex Senior Cup Final at The Goldstone Ground, Brighton. It was the most important game, in terms of profile, I had played in so far. Eastbourne were on the cusp of finishing second in the Division above us and were about to be promoted to the Athenian Premier Division. I remember being extremely nervous. My legs were like lead. Our task, against a team inspired by Roy Osborne, proved to be as tough as it sounded. We lost 3-0 in front of a 3,570 crowd. I was rubbish.

Our penultimate League game was at home to Boreham Wood. Our Hertfordshire opponents won 3-0 to clinch the Championship, and promotion. We concluded our programme in fifth position with the return fixture against Herne Bay, a much more convenient date to make the longest journey; lucky Herne Bay. We drew 1-1; Denny Ringrose and Dave Stewart made their debuts.

Two 3rd place finishes and a 5th place was clearly not good enough for Horsham's Board. Change was afoot, and Pat Tobin left. I was sorry to see Pat go. He was the first Manager to give me individual and specific coaching. I knew my pace gave me the ability to provide cover for other members of the defence but any positional sense and tackling skills, particularly tackling skills, that I developed was entirely due to Pat, with Ted Streeter's help. The players anticipated radical changes; and we didn't have to wait long. A new Manager was unveiled at the Club's Annual Dinner in June. Roy Osborne, who masterminded our defeat in the Sussex Senior Cup just two months ago was appointed Player/Manager. Roy was an accomplished player. He had played for Redhill and Sutton United, for whom he appeared at Wembley in the FA Amateur Cup Final in 1963. Unfortunately for Roy, Sutton met an emerging Wimbledon side, who won 4-2. Roy had a bubbly personality which was evident in a photograph that quickly came to light. Walking out of the tunnel at Wembley in the company of the other 21 players, all of whom had gloomy faces focussing hard of the task ahead, Roy was last out and was seen waving like a windmill to family, friends and fans. He was happily lapping up the great occasion.

'Ozzie' brought with him from Eastbourne former Horsham players Wilf Hugill & Barry Steer as well as Rodney Ralfe, who became known in the Dressing Room as Arthur Askey. Tex Wiltshire also returned after a spell at Cray Wanderers. Dave Black, a FA Amateur Cup Finalist with Chesham United, also joined. Dave was an interesting fellow. We noticed he twisted & turned and bent over backwards, seemingly to avoid heading the ball. He wore a well fixed hair piece! With an attractive programme of pre-season friendlies the Club was in buoyant mood. Crystal Palace was the first to visit Queen Street in the 1969/70 season. And, to my delight, I was to make a start.

After the game the reports read, Mason, Skingsley, Hugill, West and Strudwick *"did a sound job against the class of opposition they faced"* and went on *"Skingsley and Strudwick worked hard and gave little away."* Nice words but we lost 5-1! We had been well beaten. The Selhurst Park outfit was quicker and stronger. Barry Steer scored our lone goal. And it got worse. We were thoroughly beaten in our next match, 3-0 against a Dagenham team containing at least a couple of England Amateur Internationals, as well as John Still who went on to became a successful Manager. We won only one of our five pre-season games, 4-3 at Haywards Heath, and I didn't play in that one! Fortunately the competitive season started considerably better, for me and more importantly, the team.

We lost only two of our first 13 fixtures between 16th August and 4th October. And I played in all the games. It was my best start to a campaign so far. A home win over Harrow Borough was followed by a draw at Epsom & Ewell, then another home win against Edmonton, in which we met our old friend John Gregory. Then came our first defeat, a loss to Eastbourne Town 3-2 at Queen Street. Osborne & Steer were our scorers. The same pair scored in a 3-3 draw at Uxbridge; Steer bagged 2. We then played a goalless draw at home to Windsor & Eton before losing 1-0 to our friends at Dagenham. As usual the Daggers were able to field an exceptionally strong side, even in this secondary competition, the Mithras Cup Semi-Final First Leg Tie. They pummelled us, but we kept them out for 80 minutes when a rasping shot beat our outstanding goalkeeper, Keith Etheridge. As Dagenham tried to increase their lead Tony Bass got the better of me as he cut in from the bye-line and with tremendous power smashed a shot towards the goal. It was of such speed and power it caught Keith completely unaware. The ball passed between his gloved hands and crashed into his forehead and over the bar. He rucked me for letting Bass get his shot in: I rucked him for not catching it. Then we laughed at our good fortune.

The second leg was no laughing matter. For some reason our team was shuffled. I was moved 'up front' for example, John Grant came in for Phil Skingsley who was named as substitute. Phil came on when Tex Wiltshire sustained an injury. We worked very hard but lost 3-1 to a Daggers team that was less convincing than four days previously. Jimmy Bean scored our goal.

Between the two games against Dagenham we defeated Lancing 3-0 in the FA Cup Preliminary Round. We followed on with a 4-0 win at Whyteleafe in the FA Amateur Cup; a 2-1 win at Haywards Heath in the FA Cup; and a 2-0 victory at Farnham in the Amateur Cup. We then faced Southwick in the FA Cup.

Southwick were a good County League club, and had been for many years. Their team for this match included Dave Virgo (an excellent goalkeeper), Micky Cull (a solid reliable central defender), Gary Cross (hard tackling defender – soon to become a team mate), Brian Doherty (a tricky left winger – I was right back!) and Gerry Offen (putting it politely, an uncompromising defender. What Gerry lacked in artistry he made up with aggression.) It was a hard game, and physically very tough. Luckily for me Docherty was not at his most slippery and was substituted. This enabled me to get forward more, where I frequently came into contact with Offen – once too often! No love was lost in our tussle to get the better of one another, we were both winners. Eventually Gerry caught me across the thighs as I aimed to go past him. He was having none of it. I crashed to the turf. I managed to complete my role in our 2-0 win but it was the end of my best run in the First Team so far, and the beginning of the end to my season. For a short while, at least, I became a regular visitor to Mr Rixon, the Club's private physiotherapist. Mr Rixon was one to allow you to play if possible, provided no further damage would be done. So after a fortnight's intensive treatment I was nominated as a substitute for the Third Qualifying Round of the FA Cup against Littlehampton Town. I am not sure if I took to the field but the experiment clearly had no prospect of succeeding and I remained a patient for a further six weeks while Mr Rixon prised muscle tissue off the damaged, but not broken, femur.

On the first Tuesday of my period of inactivity I watched training from the comfort of the grandstand. The usual activities had all taken place and the session was concluding with a 'warm-down' game in which role plays of match situations would be practiced. Despite being team mates, players are naturally competitive, some more so than others. Phil Skingsley and John Warman were two of the latter kind. They were red blooded, for sure. And red haired as it happened. So when they clashed, in what to many would have been a mundane challenge, the blue touch paper was instantly lit. A fight broke out. Roy had the unenviable task of asking them both to leave the Club. With the greatest of dignity, and respect for the Manager and the Club, they both left instantly without a further word being spoken. It was a sad incident which touched us all. And the Club lost two good players. The following day, 8th October, Horsham played Leatherhead at Queens Street in a Premier Midweek Floodlight League match. I watched from the sideline. In an otherwise quiet match, having already been cautioned for delaying the taking of a free-kick, Tex Wiltshire accidentally kicked the Tanners goalkeeper, Cuthbert. Tanners' captain Bobby Adam became involved and exchanged punches with Tex. Both were sent off by Referee Alan Turvey. There were further fireworks on 5th November when Tex was sent off again. Once more, having already been cautioned, Tex was sent off following an 'off the ball' incident spotted by a Linesman. New Manager Osborne was suddenly having a tough time.

My recovery continued but after playing a couple of games in the Reserves a setback awaited. I received notice to attend hospital to have my tonsils out. Not a major operation but not an insignificant procedure as an adult. Facing a further period of incapacity, having courted for three years, Myra & I arranged our marriage at short notice. The quick scheduling had family & friends counting the following months but they were wasting their time. My mind was on a return to the team before the end of the season. Records confirm I returned on 25th March for a Premier Midweek Floodlight League game against Finchley. The game ended even 1-1 and so did my season. It was a disappointing closure for me, after such a good start, but for the Club it was mission accomplished. The First Team went on to win the Athenian League Second Division Championship.

24 West Sussex County Times, Friday, April 17, 1970

The reserves take a deserved bow

Let opponents back into game with easy one

Horsham Res. 2, Worthing Res. 2

Despite the heavy conditions Horsham Reserves played some attractive football against a weakened Worthing side in Saturday's Athenian League game at Queen Street.

Plenty of openings were created, but they were unable to convert them into goals. It was Malcolm Bailey, with one of his characteristic bursts through the defence, who opened the scoring midway through the first half.

In the second half, playing down the slope, Horsham continued to have all the play but still the many chances that were made were all missed.

They finally scored a second goal through Rick Conley midway through the period when he shot through a crowd of players and the ball trickled over the line.

Then, as has happened so frequently, they allowed their opponents to get back into the game with an easy goal. This gave Worthing the incentive to go all out and they scored a second soft goal five minutes from the end when the defence stood and watched the Worthing player come from blind side and place the ball past Etheridge for the equaliser.

Horsham made a frantic effort to try to snatch the winner, but Worthing held out to earn a point.

In the limelight for once are members of the Horsham FC reserve side without whose backing the Hornets' promotion prospects would have been dimmed. They are (l. to r., back) Dave Fitzgerald, Mark Tidey, Peter McBride, Will Puk, Den Strudwick, Den Ringrose, Keith Etheridge and "spongeman" Ray Childs. Front: Ron Blair, Rick Conley, Keith Cook, Malcolm Bailey and Les Setters.

It was not a great feeling to lose your place in the First team but it was no imposition playing in this Reserve team. At least ten had gained first team experience.

Back row:- Dave Fitzgerald, Mark Tidy, Peter McBride, Willie Puk, DJS, Denny Ringrose, Keith Etheridge, Ray Childs.

Front row:- Ronnie Blair, Ricky Connelly, Keith Cook, Malcolm Bailey, Les Setters.

The excitement during the approach of a new season is always high. But adrenalin levels in the advance of the 1970/71 campaign were fuelled by the challenges of a promotion and a plethora of new faces arriving for pre-season training. The passing of time does not allow me to remember them all but they included Ross Gumpright, John Ford, Peter Kenchington, Jimmy Wond and the return of John Gregory. Others did not complete the intense sessions, organised by Roy Oz and Ronnie Barber, that took place in the large open spaces of the newly acquired headquarters of the Horsham Rugby Club. Without doubt, competition for places was going to be stiffer than usual. Promotion attracted better players, and more of them. And looking at the fixture schedule, or at least the games for which I was subsequently selected to play, the programme was frightening. I was selected for, and played in, 11 games in 31 days.

Newcomers Ford & Gumpright, plus two recruits from last season, Bean and Black, all scored in the opening friendly. We beat our neighbours, Horsham YMCA, 4-0. We won only one more of our warm-up fixtures, a 4-3 victory over Redhill in the Abbeyfield Cup, played on behalf of a local charity. Our final friendly was against our fiercest rivals Crawley Town. Despite a 4-2 defeat in which I endured mixed fortunes, having assisted in one of our goals but then gave away a penalty for Crawley's fourth, I made the line-up for the opening League match of the season, a home game against Letchworth.

We started well. A 4-0 win over Letchworth was followed by victories over Dorking and Hornchurch without conceding a goal. I claimed an 'assist' in Barry Steer's goal against Dorking. Our defence was then breached at Eastbourne United but goals by Steer 2, West and Ford secured a 4-2 win. We then earned a clean sheet away against Leyton, 4-0, in which I had a goal disallowed, before losing to Dorking 1-0 and getting thumped at Chichester City 5-2 in the Sussex Senior Cup, despite leading twice through Steer and Ford.

We needed to recover quickly and thank goodness Barry Steer was on fire. Our next opponents were Eastbourne United, newly relegated and struggling a bit following the loss of several players, some to Horsham! After the nightmare at Chichester I was left out, doh!, but made the bench so I was able to enjoy the celebrations for a 6-0 win, albeit through reflected glory. All the goals came in the second half and Barry Steer scored five!!

I missed one further game before starting on a run in which I believe I played in almost every game for the remainder of the season. The run commenced with an appearance in the centre of defence, alongside the reliable John West, at Three Bridges. We won this Amateur Cup tie 3-0 on a boggy inconsistent surface. Three weeks later we were knocked out 4-1 by Redhill, one of Roy Osborne's former clubs, in a game I started as a substitute but took to the field when John Gregory was injured.

The following week we went to Chesham for an Athenian League Cup Tie. We were without Ross Gumpright, on honeymoon, and John West, injured. Jimmy Wond replaced Gumps, for only his third First team appearance, and scored a hat-trick in a 3-1 win! I stood in for West in the centre of the defence, again, a position I enjoyed despite my lack of height. It was a super win. We were all delighted for Wondy. And, according to the West Sussex County Times, my performance at the back, with Wilf Hugill, was as valuable as Jimmy's.

Three days later we returned to earth with a 4-1 defeat at Carshalton Athletic. And four days hence we lost at home to Edmonton. These setbacks were followed by six straight wins – four in the League, including a 6-0 triumph over Chesham; a midweek League match at Wokingham where I had another goal disallowed; a 4-1 over East Grinstead in the County Cup; and a 1-0 victory in the reverse fixture against Chesham, where I had yet another goal disallowed. I began to believe there was a conspiracy against me.

The New Year, 1971, commenced with five wins. The first, a 2-0 home win against Hounslow, saw another of my efforts ruled out by the Match Officials. We were in the top three in the League and progressing in the

County Cup. The season was going well. By the time we reached the Quarter Final of the Sussex Senior Cup I'd had six 'goals' disallowed. So when I notched at APV Crawley, only to hear Tex scream *"he's disallowed it"*, clear thinking deserted me. But my loud protests were drowned out by laughter. It was a wind-up the whole team was in on. My response was to score again in a 5-0 win. Like a London bus, nothing for months, then two come along.

As February drew to a close we came off the rails big time. News reached us prior to a trip to Aylesbury that Keith Welham who, with Jimmy Wond had returned to Cray Wanderers, had passed away during a Tuesday evening training session. Keith was always at the front of any runs during training, but not on his final session. Training at Cray had started with a road run and Keith had been geed up for not leading the race, as he usually did. When the group returned to the dressing room to put on their boots Keith keeled over and fell on Jimmy. Not suspecting anything but a prank Jimmy nudged Keith to say, 'stop mucking about'. He wasn't. And nothing could be done to help. Keith was, I think 26, and he left behind a wife and three children. We were all devastated at losing a friend and such a popular player at such a young age. For many it was a first experience of bereavement. Our minds were elsewhere. We lost 5-1.

We won only 4 of our final 14 games of the 70/71 season, 10 of which had been League games. One of the defeats was our exit from the Sussex Senior Cup at the semi-final stage. Lewes took an early lead through Graham Sweet and as much as we battled, in a game described as *"not for the faint hearted"*, we rarely got the better of our opponents. Former colleagues Ray Smith and Malcolm Bailey were a constant threat. Six minutes from time Lewes stretched their lead. We gave away a free kick about ten yards outside our penalty area. We organised ourselves while a Lewes player received treatment. Play restarted with a Ray Smith free-kick which Sweet got his head to and the ball inexplicably slipped through Dai Mason's hands. Inexplicably, that is, until some of our eagle eyed players reported Colin

Newstead had dunked the ball in the Trainer's bucket before Smith lobbed the ball into the danger area for Sweet to head home. A cunning trick by Newst, a player who was to join Horsham a few seasons later. Adversity really does breed strange bedfellows. John Ford pulled a goal back in the closing minutes but it was too late.

Another match amongst this inglorious run of results was a midweek draw at Hounslow. Hounslow were bottom of the League so this was a match we should have expected to win if we were to maintain any hope of promotion. It should have been 'a piece of cake'. Perhaps that kind of thinking got under our skin and undermined our preparation. Add to that the ambiance of Hounslow's ground, in those days. There are many reasons why their stadium was not twinned with the Santiago Bernabeu, Madrid. It was one of the most uninspiring grounds I had the good fortune to play on. And on a Monday night, well that just added to an apathetic performance by us. We struggled to draw 1-1. Having also drawn our previous three games we saw promotion slipping away. The mood of disappointment in the dressing room was tangible. Roy Oz kept his comments to a minimum, he knew it was not the time to issue rollockings. The room was silent when the door burst open and a Club Committeeman, Ted Horrox, rushed in and hung his raincoat on a peg. He proceeded to tell us exactly what he thought of our performance and how we had let down the Club. He concluded his dressing down with the words, *"That's the last you see of me!"* He left as quickly as he had arrived. We were all shell shocked. I am not sure how much time elapsed, but we were still silent when there was a timid knock at the door and Mr Horrox reappeared. Without a word he recovered his raincoat from the peg and, for the second time, made for the exit. Tex leapt to his feet and shouted, *"I thought we'd f**king seen the last of you!"*. Mr Horrox walked out under the door. And, as far as I can remember, he kept his word.

At least the season ended on a higher note. We won our last two League fixtures 3-0. The penultimate game was at Harlow where goals by Tex

Wiltshire, Micky Howard and Barry Steer put us in with a chance of a fourth place finish. But we had to avoid defeat against the only club that could take that place from us, Carshalton Athletic. The game was billed as Roy Osborne's last, as a Player; he had been appointed Manager for the following season. Oz had been a wizard. He had transformed the Club's fortunes and he concluded his regular playing career with two goals whilst leading us to a 3-0 victory which secured a respectable fourth spot in our first season back in Division 1 of the Athenian League. And we had reached the Semi-Final of the Sussex Senior Cup.

It had been a decent season for me, too. After the previous year's 18 appearances I had made 53 outings, including pre-season friendlies. It had proved to be a consolidating campaign for the Club, too. Micky Howard, a power house of a centre-forward had joined from Eastbourne United and Richard Summerfield, aka Snitch, and Terry Molloy represented the

All ready for the 'off'

This is the squad that Horsham FC team-manager Roy Osborne (right) helped—not too often—by "spongeman" Ray Childs (left) hopes will retain the Sussex Senior Cup, take the Division 1, Athenian League, title, and help justify selection to the new division of the Isthmian League.

They are (l. to r., back): Rick Collier, Den Strudwick, Andy Tasker, Gary Cross, Colin Newstead, Dai Mason, Dave Hutchins and Rick Summerfield. Front: Terry Molloy, Peter Medhurst, Keith Mills, Tex Wiltshire, skipper Bob Adam and Barry Steer.

young generation who had broken into the First team ranks. The prospects for further progress looked bright. And the rumours of anticipated new signings supported that optimism. I hoped I would still have a role to play. Competition for places was going to be harder than ever; and so it proved to be, as we became known as 'The Hornets" following a competition organised by the Club in conjunction with West Sussex County Times. (Personally, I have never been able to reconcile the 'Hornets' with a team playing in Lincoln green & Amber – black & yellow, perhaps, but not green & amber.)

The customary multitudes turned up for the early sessions for the 1971/72 pre-season training but the quality of the serious contenders for places has gone up by a few notches. Colin Newstead, Andy Tasker, aka Whisker, Gary Cross (Cranky) and Peter Medhurst (Primrose, because he always seemed to wear a yellow shirt) all joined from Lewes. Bobby Adams (Tanner) and Keith Mills (who became known as Jimmy Sticky boots, because only a bailiff could get the ball off him legitimately) signed from Leatherhead, known as the Tanners; 6'3" centre-forward, Dave Hutchins moved from Tooting & Mitcham United and John Lock arrived from Worthing. John was a member of Wilf Hugill's highly successful Sunday youth team, Durrington, and fifty years on he remains a dear friend with whom I am still in regular contact.

The results of pre-season friendlies endorsed all the optimism that greets a new campaign. A brace each from Newstead & Wiltshire, plus one from Steer brought a 5-0 win over Horsham YMCA. Wiltshire and Summerfield then scored in a 2-0 victory over Eastbourne Town before new signing Dave Hutchins bagged four in an 8-0 thrashing of Haywards Heath. We then conceded two goals in the last four minutes against Crawley Town to go down in a closely fought match before trouncing a Brighton & Hove Albion side 5-0, in which Steer notched a hat-trick. Reports suggest I played in at least three of the above games, more likely four, so I was hopeful for a place in the starting line-up of another competitive season. But my hopes were dashed.

The League season, however, did not start as well as expected for the Club; four defeats and four wins in the first eight games. And I didn't even make the bench. It was the perception of local players the Manager was always more likely to pick players he had brought to the Club from afar, otherwise, why bring them. It seemed it was always easier to leave out a local player, who may have already been at the Club, rather than disappoint a player who was persuaded to join, and was prepared to travel. It was obviously not a theory that could be proven. I am certain to have let my feeling known by moaning a lot, perhaps even sulking a bit, but my allegiance to the team/Club never wavered and my efforts, particularly in training, never fell short. On the contrary, on training nights in Horsham Park Ozzie nearly always concluded our drills on the opposite side of the Park to our exit. The session, therefore, ended with a sprint of perhaps 300 yards, or more, to the car park. I remember Dave Hutchins, whose long legs had not been used to coming second in a dash, bemoaning his new status as a 'runner-up' as a little guy with a big nose and a Road Runner badge on the arse of his shorts went passed him. Anyway, just over a month into the season, I made the team as a midfielder for game number nine, away to Harlow Town.

In the build up to the game I must have visibly been wearing my heart on my sleeve. The local written media reported my appearance as my final match for the Club. When describing the game it said, *"Harlow ripped through a frail (Horsham) defence despite a memorable swansong by Dennis Strudwick who was seeking pastures new after failing to gain a regular first team place. Strudwick showed what Horsham would be missing when he intercepted a ball and found Peter Medhurst who shot narrowly wide."* It must be difficult for anyone disinterested in football to appreciate the heartbreak of a player not selected for the team he loves, or just the team for which he feels good enough to play. I do not remember how close I came to leaving at that point or what options, if any, I had to choose from. I recall a few seasons before this incident, in the late 60s I think, when I considered an inquiry from Crawley Town. Fortunately for me, as it happens, the Town Mead Manager, Stan Markham, contacted me to say he was unable to progress his approach as he had spent all his budget acquiring the services of Nobby Upton, a midfielder from Brighton & Hove Albion. So, just as in that case, business moved on after our 3-3 draw at Harlow. But despite the favourable note in the local rag I failed to impress Roy Oz. I was left out of the side for the match against Carshalton Athletic the following Tuesday which ended in a 1-0 defeat. The next day, Cross and Medhurst made a surprise move back to Lewes, just three days before Horsham were due to meet the East Sussex club in the FA Cup. As a consequence Ozzie persuaded me to stay at Queen Street. It was a decision I did not regret. Indeed, it was one I never sought to make. I managed to fulfil a further 46 appearances, in all competitions and friendlies, for my hometown Club during that season – re-starting with that game against the Rooks, i.e. Lewes.

Harrington and Hutchins scored Horsham's goals in a tense First Qualifying Round battle in which Lewes hit the woodwork before we got on the scoresheet. I missed the following midweek match, the opening game of the Premier Midweek Floodlight League, against Guildford & Godalming, because of a work commitment. It's true it was not a fixture of huge importance but it was the competition in which I made my Horsham debut, so I had a soft spot for it. In this particular fixture Terry Dyson, the former Tottenham Hotspur winger, played for Guildford and created problems for Horsham's defence throughout the 90 minutes. I would have enjoyed the test of playing against such a top player. G&G won comfortably, 4-1, but the result was expunged when Guildford withdrew from the Competition. A city the size of Guildford, without a football club, was unthinkable.

A few days later we entertained Ringmer, the Sussex County League Champions in a FA Amateur Cup Tie. The County Leaguers gave a great account of themselves and led 2-1 for a long period of the game. But having got back into the contest in the 63rd minute we snatched the winner with three minutes remaining. Hutch scored all three of our goals. He was proving to be a considerable asset despite getting a lot of stick for not using his height advantage to greater effect. We used to joke that he wasn't as tall when he jumped. Dave's reply was always the same, *"How many goals have you got?"* His point was well made. Few, if any, could better his challenging question. Hutch's contribution to the team was a guarantee of at least twenty goals per season.

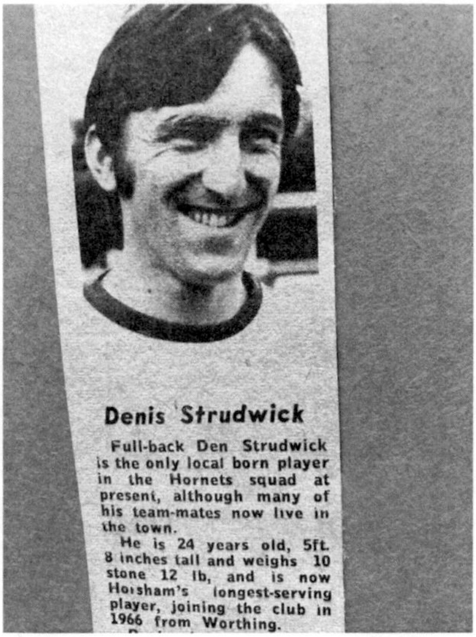

Being without a midweek fixture, after the Ringer match, the following week I made myself available to play in a Charity friendly, twenty-four hours later. I had to; it was against a Portsmouth ex-Pro team. I cannot remember, and I cannot find any notes on who played for the visitors. I don't recall any really famous names. But they turned out in blue, white & red and they had all, at some stage, played for the mighty Pompey. That was good enough for me. For what it's worth we won 9-4.

Back at the business end we were approaching the end of October and, in the games in which I had been involved, we had not been defeated since that 'friendly' loss to Crawley on 9 August. We had made further progress in the FA Cup by winning at Woodside Road, Worthing 3-1.

As we were playing against a few former team mates, e.g. Micky Streeter, Roger Weekes, Keith Cook and Russell Penticost it was a satisfying win. But I didn't help. After moving 2-0 ahead, under pressure from Streeter and Weeks, I sliced a clearance past Dai Mason. The ball flew like a rocket into our own net. The game then turned feisty. The Rebels' Dave Treagus clashed with Colin Newstead and then Newst was on the receiving end of a body check from Gil Harding that launched him over the concrete pitch perimeter barrier and into the crowd. Newst had the last laugh when he put the game beyond doubt by scoring our third goal.

We then progressed in the Amateur Cup, again playing against several former colleagues now with Lewes, i.e. Gary Cross, Peter Medhurst, Malcolm Bailey, Ray Smith and Ross Gumpright. We won a scrappy game 1-0. Scrappy it may have been but it was good to have knocked the Rooks out of the country's two major tournaments in under a month.

We then won an astonishing match at Leatherhead in the Premier Midweek League. The Tanners were flying at the time, having experienced tremendous League and FA Cup success and fame. When we took an early lead, and quickly doubled it, there was a tangible mood amongst us all of, "Oh dear. What have we done now? What will the consequences of that be?' Neil Brister, whose father had played for Horsham, came on and scored a sensational goal. Like his Dad, Neil's left leg, and foot, was like a wand. With Neil's inspiration we went on to win 5-1. It was a great night, too, for our own former Leatherhead Tanner, Bobby Adam.

Three days later we were knocked out of the FA Cup by those dastardly rivals at Crawley, 3-1. That was not considered good preparation for our Amateur Cup Tie the following Saturday, against our neighbours, Horsham YMCA. The town buzzed during the week preceding this game between Horsham's two senior sides. And it was worth the wait.

To add spice to the occasion the YM's team was heavily populated with former Hornets, Keith Etheridge; Billy Bell; Ian Booth; Alan Lancaster; Ron Moulding; Ken Awcock and, the still formidable, Micky Browning.

Indeed, Micky was a pain in the backside of our defence all afternoon. Despite leading twice, through goals by Keith Mills, Browning scored YM's first and set up Hoath for their equalising second. With minutes remaining, and I remember this vividly, Billy Bell caught us out with a direct free-kick on goal. Oh no, I thought as the ball cleared our heads. We all turned simultaneously and watched helplessly as Dai Mason pulled off a fantastic finger tip save, to rescue our skins and reputation. Looking back, it was a fantastic game; not one for the purist maybe but great for the spectators, who now had a replay to look forward to.

We had little time to consider exactly how we planned to restore the perceived gap between the levels at which we and the YM played as we had a Premier Midweek League fixture on Tuesday. As it turned out, the game against Tooting & Mitcham United was what the doctor ordered, i.e. a chance for us to test ourselves against a team at least two Divisions above us, Horsham v YM in reverse. The game could not have gone better. We won 6-1! Dave Hutchins scored a hat-trick against his former club. And we enhanced our position at the top of this midweek competition.

So, when Saturday arrived we were brimming with confidence but not without a little nervousness on my part. As a Horsham born person, this match meant a lot. And like so many matches in which I played, I was the only player in the team, that came from Horsham. By saying that I do not mean my team mates were any less mindful of the importance of the game, it just added to the significance for me. But something we all heard outside the dressing room, as we were preparing for the match, stirred us and has remained a clear memory ever since. A 'reserve' YMCA goalkeeper, Paul (Doughy) Baker, once a Horsham Reserve player, was doing his best to fire up his colleagues and supporters along the touchline. As some memories fade with the passing of time, it's funny what does stay with you. As if it was only yesterday I clearly recall Doughy shouting, *"Horsham, they couldn't score in a f**king kick-about!"* We won 10-1. Micky Harrington scored 3; Dave Hutchins, Tex Wiltshire and Colin Newstead all scored a brace, and

Alan Lancaster, an old school pal and Horsham team mate, completed the rout with an own goal. Doughy's war cry had an affect opposite to that which he intended.

Our undefeated run continued for a further five matches which included two games against Boreham Wood in the final Qualifying Round of the Amateur Cup. We drew at home, 1-1, when fellow full-back Andy Tasker scored. We then won the Replay 3-1 at Meadow Park, Boreham. I recall it being a tetchy affair during which we won few friends among the Hertfordshire club's fan base; they were ferociously partisan despite

The Horsham team on 6th November 1971
FA Amateur Cup Third Qualifying Round Replay
HORSHAM YMCA 1 versus HORSHAM 10

Standing:- Andy Tasker, John West, Tex Wiltshire, Dai Mason, Dave Hutchins, Keith Mills, Barry Steer

Seated:- Colin Newstead, DJS, Bobby Adams, Micky Harrington, Terry Molloy

Mascot – Peter Osborne

being fairly small in number. But they had little reason to complain. This was one of our best performances. We also won a Second Round Tie in the Sussex Cup, 1-0 at Bognor Regis, thanks to a Barry Steer goal. In the Bognor side that day was Jack Pearce. Jack has since been Manager and Chairman of his club, and remains a Board member at the Nyewood Lane outfit to this day. He has given Bognor Regis Town FC great service, in anyone's language. I subsequently became a good friend and a colleague of Jack's. For now, though, we had a visit to Hounslow on the agenda. As you will have gathered, the Denbigh Road venue was neither inspirational nor a happy hunting ground. As well as the woes I experienced with Horsham I was once on the losing side for Worthing Reserves, 9-1! I was again on the wrong side of the result. We lost 3-1.

We lost our next game, too. But, at least it was a League Cup tie and did not affect our promotion push. At another uninspiring venue, Cheshunt won 2-0. The only positive words I have for the Theobalds Road ground are, it was level. There was little or no spectator accommodation, there were large grass areas surrounding the pitch, i.e. no terracing and little or no seating. But I guess when clubs like Chestnut and Hounslow do not command a crowd there is little incentive to provide facilities that will not be used. I felt for Ron Fuller who made the journey to Cheshunt as our substitute, his first appearance for the First XI I believe, and I hoped he would have more opportunities in the future. Ron was a popular fellow who never let the side down, whoever he played for. His bushy beard made him resemble Trevor Hockey, a rugged Birmingham City player. Ron became known in the dressing room as a 'poor man's version' of Hockey. Ron Fuller was also called "Gerd", as a play on words with that great German centre forward, Gerd Muller.

After a win at Wokingham, where Newst got the only goal of the game, our promotion challenge took a hit with a 2-1 defeat at Eastbourne United in the final game of the calendar year. The Eastbourne side contained a famously familiar name, Wilf Hugill. Ron Fuller took my place in the back four that day but I returned three days later for the New Year's day fixture at, of all places, Herne Bay. The Athenian League's Fixtures Secretary clearly had a wicked sense of humour, and had applied his witticism on us again. Indeed one season when, I think it was Worthing, was scheduled to play at Herne Bay on a Bank Holiday the visitors queried having to make such a journey on a Bank Holiday Monday. I was told they received the answer, *"Well, you're both coastal clubs!"* Mmmm!! Anyway, when it was our turn to bear the brunt of this person's drollness, on 1st January 1972, we drew 2-2. Not a bad result against a consistently difficult team to beat.

The following Saturday we travelled to Hendon for the First Round Proper of the FA Amateur Cup, the first time in 33 years the Hornets had reached this stage of the Competition. Hendon were consistently one of the best non-Football League teams in the country. With Peter Swannell in goal; Tony Jennings in defence; Peter Deadman in midfield; and Rod Haider & John Connell up front, all Amateur Internationals, our task was a formidable one. Bobby Adam* was at his outstanding best, tackling strongly and marshalling the whole of the defence. He was ably assisted by Rick Summerfield, aka 'Snitch'. Although 'Snitch' was incredibly quiet, frustratingly so at times, he was developing into a fine player. We were

---

* *At about 5'8" tall Bobby Adam was not the tallest centre-half/sweeper I ever played with. But he was, by a country mile, the best organiser of the defence. In one match, I recall injuries forced Roy Oz to ask Tex Wiltshire to play at left back. Tex shuddered at the prospect, and so did the rest of us. Tex was a 'touch' player, with flair and improvisation, not one with rigid discipline. But Roy's emergency plan worked, thanks to Bobby. After the match Tex articulated his thoughts on Bobby in his colourful East End language, "He (Bobby) had me on a piece of string! Go here; go there; moved ten yards forward; drop five yards back; clear it; head it, tackle; don't tackle; stay goal side..." Bobby played Tex's game for him, just as he controlled the back four every week. Bobby was a conductor. Follow Bobby's advice and you will not go wrong. Bob's only weak point was to not see eye to eye with Referee Alan Turvey. Mr Turvey dismissed Bobby six times during the '70s.*

more than making a game of it. But late in the second half I found myself exposed. I challenged for the ball and, allegedly, tripped Rod Haider in the box. Frankly, I thought I did well to get near a player of Haider's class! The Referee shrewdly awaited the outcome rather than make a hasty decision, which might have been a penalty. Haider regained his footing and cleverly stabbed the ball past Dai Mason. But we nearly forced a draw. In almost the final minute, Barry Steer's powerful header flew past the post a foot wide of the goal, and suddenly our Cup run was over. It was back to the League.

We welcomed Finchley to Queen Street seven days later. It was our first home League fixture for three months. We won 3-0; Mills & Hutchins 2 were our scorers. Three days later we needed an own goal to overcome Wokingham. I was a substitute, having been replaced by the returning Gary Cross. I am sure I would not have been happy to have been 'dropped' after playing a part in a 3-0 victory. It would have fuelled my theory about home based players being easier to leave out than 'imported ' players. But the team is bigger than any one player, so move on. And move on I did. I had to. Our next fixture was a Sussex Senior Cup Third Round tie against Burgess Hill from the County League, and I was in. According to the local paper I was *"prominent throughout the game"* and after dispossessing a dangerous opponent I *"hit a shot cum cross that scraped along the crossbar."* I sought to secure my place and, by and large, succeeded. I was selected for 15 further matches in the final three months of the season. Three of these matches were in successive weeks against Worthing in a Quarter Final Tie of the Sussex Senior Cup. We drew the first match, at home, 1-1. Newstead scored our goal and after a spat with my former colleague, Phil Skingsley, in which I ended up laying face down on the pitch, Skingsley was cautioned for walking on my back, bottom to shoulders. It wasn't easy to get a caution in those days. In today's game it would have merited a dismissal.

The Replay seven days later at Woodside Road was also drawn, after extra-time. Steer was our goalscorer in a match in which the Rebels took no prisoners. Although we had a few escapes of our own the 'Man of the Match' was Worthing's Goalkeeper, Malcolm Arnold. He saved the Seasiders on several occasions. 120 minutes of passionate football and the goals came within a minute of each other during the additional time.

Queen Street hosted the second Replay and after two close encounters the third match was no anti-climax. Being in Division 1 of the Athenian League we were playing in a Division above Worthing but the Rebels were doing particularly well in Division 2. It is fair to say they put us 'to the sword'. But two goals from Steer, either side of Worthing's goal by Trevor Still prevailed for us. 'Chunky' Still, 5'4", even in boots with long studs, was a thorough nuisance whenever I played against him and a person with whom I was pleased to conduct some business a little later on during our professional lives.

At this point of the season I still wasn't making the side consistently. But after missing an away draw at Finchley, which was not a bad ground to miss, actually, I was re-instated for a home game against Marlow. We won 1-0. And according to the West Sussex County Times I was *"one of the few players showing any real drive and dash"* adding, *"after a downfield burst my low drive evaded four teammates in front of goal."* Steer was again our match winner.

Despite missing a 1-0 win over Eastbourne United I was back in the team for the tricky encounter at nearby rivals Dorking. The Meadowbank Ground was always a tough place to visit. Dave Hutchins and Graham Sweet, who had recently joined us from Lewes along with returning Peter Medhurst*, scored our goals in a 2-2 draw. By now I felt Roy Oz was playing

---

* It was a pleasure to welcome Peter Medhurst back into the team. He was a fun guy and a prankster. He always played with a smile on his face. A tough tackling midfielder who contributed with a goal or two at important times. He persistently 'got a flyer' at sprint exercises in training just to wind up everyone else. His favourite trick, however, was to be the first to leave training, return to the dressing room, and gather everyone's socks and shoes and leave them in a pile. You would not believe the amount of guys

Gary Cross and I in alternate matches. So after missing the midweek trip to Chesham, and a good 1-0 win, I was back for a game against Aylesbury United. Graham (Boo Boo) Sweet was the icing on the cake. He bagged three in a 7-0 win; Mills and Medhurst each grabbed a brace. How could I not keep my place after winning 7-0? But I didn't!

---

who could not remember what socks they had put on that day. Peter was always laughing. I recall a Newick Rangers match in which our goalkeeper, Russell Cummings, thwarted the opponents attack by safely gathering the ball. As he put all his energy into throwing the ball back into play his momentum spun him round and the ball flew out of his hand and into his own goal behind him. Whilst the rest of us was gutted by this crazy error the stunned silence was broken by Peter's chuckling, followed by his constructive comment, *"That's the worst goal I have ever seen."* It wasn't long before his contagious laughter infected us all.

There was, of course, multiple pranks played amongst the squad throughout every season. So perhaps it is time to admit to my own stunt. I once poured a packet of soap powder into the bath after training. With the water running so fast no effort was required to stir up the foam & suds for them to reach the ceiling. The whole room was a mass of bubbles. I had not taken into account how slippery the foam would make the fully tiled room. The suds made it dangerous, but they gave the walls and ceiling a super clean.

In another stunt, which I believe occurred after the end of a season, I am pleased to say I was neither a participant, nor a victim of the circumstances. A group of players agreed to represent the Club at a village festival by taking part at a five-a-side tournament. It's the sort of event that can last much of the day if you win a few games along the way. Consequently, wives & girlfriends joined the group of eight or nine players taking part. They were accompanied by a mutual non-playing friend who generously invited them all to some hospitality at his (very nice) home at the end of the day. A stop at an Off-licence ensured the liquid refreshments were taken care of by the 'guests' while the host rustled up copious amounts of a shepherd's pie style dish complemented by a variety of beans. All was ravenously consumed. Cries for a second helping were satisfied with one player, frequently mentioned in this diary, particularly demanding "more of that mince, please." When all was consumed, and appetites were satisfied the host announced, "You have just consumed twelve tins of Lassie meaty chunks!" Arrgh! They had forgotten and/or overlooked, their host was a representative for a pet food Company. I'm glad I missed that one.

I was then absent for a 3-0 defeat at Hertford Town which was a setback to our promotion ambitions. But after playing in a 1-1 draw against Tooting & Mitcham, in which Hutch scored against his former club, yet again, I was included for the Senior Cup Semi-Final against Chichester City. We owed Chichester something for an embarrassing defeat a season or two ago. But we were staring defeat in the face by the fourth minute of the second half. Having fallen behind in the first half through City's speedy forward, Wing, he stretched their lead further in the 49th minute. Ouch, 2-0 down! Keith Mills then changed the game, but not in a manner to which we were accustomed from our own skill-master. Chichester's skipper and schemer-in-chief, Paul Flood (not the former B&HA one with who I played with many times for Newick Rangers), was caught by a heavy tackle from 'Jimmy Sticky Boots'. Flood was left limping badly; the crowd went crackers and Flood eventually left the field. The balance of the game turned. Newst scored; I cleared one off the line with goalkeeper Dai Mason beaten; Mills equalised; and suddenly Newst got the winner. Three goals in fifteen minutes. We were in the Final.

After victory over Chichester, my season wound down with five more appearances. Two were in the Athenian League, which we won; 3-1 at home to Harlow Town, on my birthday, so a good present; and home to Letchworth 4-0. I played two in the Midweek League in which we lost to Leatherhead, avenging their 5-1 home defeat earlier in the season, and a goalless draw with Walton & Hersham. Then came the Sussex Senior Final against Whitehawk at the Goldstone Ground, Hove. And the occasion did not start well.

As the disappointing crowd of 1,413 gathered we prepared in the dressing room. Bobby Adam, our Captain, had broken a bone in his wrist in the match against Walton nine days earlier. The lower part of his arm was in plaster and despite a heavy covering of sponge Referee Gerry Collyer refused permission for Bobby to play. The plaster of Paris presented a danger to other players. Snitch Summerfield was immediately drafted in and played magnificently, as if his life depended on the result, ignoring the stitches over his eye also collected in the Walton match. To make matters worse we fell behind when Hawks' winger Colin Banks latched on to a back pass from Tex Wiltshire to Dai Mason, and netted. Reportedly I showed our attack how it should be done when I *"beat the left winger, tore up the wing and crossed the perfect ball to the far post which Colin Newstead could not reach."* But all else went right on the night. Summerfield and Hutchins scored. Although we were red hot favourites to beat the County Leaguers, Whitehawk gave us one hell of a fright.

The Final at the Goldstone Ground, Hove was my final appearance of the season. Two days later the Club played and won its last game of the campaign, against Hounslow (3-0), to land fourth place in the League. Of my 46 appearances, in all competitions, I had been on the losing side only 6 times. I featured 14 times in League games, losing only one. Apart from being in & out of the side on a few occasions, it had not been a bad season for me personally. I was ready for the next campaign. Before that, though, I had a new challenge ahead of me, commencing in September 1972 – just as my mind would be fixed on challenging for a more permanent place in the team.

Half-time interval – My time at Crawley College of Further Education

After the failure of my employer, O'Brien & Joyce, I had begun work as the Cost Accountant for T&E Homes, a Developer based in Reigate. Following a period establishing myself I was allowed to enrol on a day release course to study for an ONC & HNC in Business Studies. I successfully passed my exams at the end of each of the following three years. And whilst I will return to the football aspect of my life, my 'story' would not be complete without mentioning the most influential and inspiring teacher it has ever been my good fortune to meet, John Kendall. There were, of course, other teachers and subjects on this course but John, as a lecturer in Business Communication, was the most outstanding. He used his own methods, it is true, but he had charisma and delivered the most compelling tutorials. He also made the point, this was further education; none of us needed to be there. We were all adults so he would treat us as adults.

John focussed his teachings on a few basic principles. In no particular order:-

- write your message as you would say it
- try to use no more than twenty words in a sentence, otherwise the reader will have forgotten how the sentence began by the time they reach the end
- brevity emphasises stress – length dissipates it
- write in a manner and tone that will get you what you are hoping to achieve.

He would set us tricky situations to which we had to respond in a way that would achieve our aims. So, for example, when Mrs Kendall had been wrongly accused of allowing the horses at her riding school to churn up the village green in Scaynes Hill, I believe, we were asked to compose a response to the accusing Local Authority, on her behalf. It was a tricky task that required tact and diplomacy as well as a degree of assertion. We were given a week to submit our responses.

When we handed our letters in an old school time 'dread' feeling immediately came over me. It would be mine that gets read out. Lecturer John placed his chair on top of his desk. He climbed on top of the desk and onto the chair. He pushed his spectacles to the end of his nose. From his lofty position he looked down upon the whole class. Oh no, he looked at me now several feet below him in the front row. My letter replicated the work and style of letters produced by me and many, more senior members, at my office. And, peering over the top of his spectacles, John launched into his critique by reading aloud in a 'toffee nosed' accent, *"I am in receipt of your letter and note the content"*. *"I hope you f**king did"* he said, *"that's why I wrote to you!"* Severely embarrassed, it was my turn to walk out under the door. But I wasn't alone. While I shrank beneath the desk John read another. *"I* *am writing..."* the next student's letter began. *"I know your are"* said JK *"I've got a f**king letter from you"*. Turning back to me John asked, *"What are you trying to say?"* I mumbled something inaudible. John replied *"Would, thank you for you letter do?" "Yes"* I whispered meekly. *"Well say that"*.The lessons had been learnt. I have never made the same mistake again. And I learnt from all the other examples he picked upon. John was brilliant; unforgettable.

It wasn't all doom & gloom, though. When given the task of describing/illustrating the British educational system to a foreign visitor I chose to demonstrate the structure by using a flow chart. JK awarded my work with a 100% mark, a mark that I remember lost me a fiver in a side bet with a classmate. And JK's tutelage helped me earn an 84% mark from the Examination Board for a thesis I wrote on the British Pharmaceutical Industry. I will never forget John Kendall and his lectures; an outstanding teacher whose lessons on how to communicate would play a major role in my future.

John's ear bashings apart, I inevitably squeezed in a bit of football. Despite our small class of twelve, including eight males, we entered the College six-a-side football tournament. We won!!

Back to football – the second half

The 1972/73 season approached. Training was hard, as usual. Having spent much of the summer swatting for exams the running up Denne Hill seemed harder than ever. But pre-season started well enough for me to feel optimistic about what lay ahead. I played in five warm-up friendlies, losing only one, to Kingstonian, and winning four, against Ringmer, Burgess Hill, Haywards Heath and Brighton & Hove Albion, 4-0! Nevertheless, that last Thursday night's training session always ended with an anxious wait, to see if you had made the team for the opening game. So I was very pleased to make the starting line-up for the first League game of the season at home to the re-named Edmonton-Haringey. It was good, too, to meet up and face two former team mates in George Wakeling and John Gregory. I remember them both with great affection. George was a deep thinker of the game and inevitably developed into a successful Manager. When playing he was meticulous in his preparation. I noticed he always bandaged one ankle, for medical reasons I assumed, until one particular match during his time with Horsham. When pulling on his socks George shouted, *"S—t, I've bandaged up the wrong ankle!"* It was a superstition issue he had got himself into. We laughed and never let him forget it. It was good to see our former team mates but it was even better to win the game 2-1. Wiltshire and Steer were our scorers. My own curious habit was to put on my left boot first and then be last out of the dressing room, and onto the pitch. Don't ask why, I cannot explain. I was last out of the changing room after the game too! But that was just tardiness.

Next up was a delightful 3-1 win at Dorking and then even more gratifying 3-1 win over Hounslow; a match in which me and my opposite number for the visitors were described in the Press as *"both having a liking for adventurous play."* A visit to Redhill in the League Cup brought us down to earth. We lost 2-1. But a fine and somewhat unexpected victory, at least the margin was not expected, in a Premier Midweek League match at Kingstonian by 5 goals to 2 lifted our confidence. People like our scorers that night, Tex Wiltshire, Terry Molloy, Keith Mills and Colin Newstead (2) were always confident in their own ability, they were that good; Keith Mills especially. As 'Sticky Boots' Mills put us 3-0 ahead by half-time by back heeling the ball into the net I remember him shouting towards the bench, *"Roy, you'd better take me off now, I've caused enough damage."* The three goal winning margin set us up well for the journey four days later to Herne Bay.

It was never easy to play at Herne Bay. We often seemed to suffer a

Horsham FC circa 1971

Standing (left to right) – Ron Barber, Roy Scutt, Roy Osborne, Peter Medhurst, Gary Cross, Barry Steer, Tex Wiltshire, Andy Tasker, Dai Mason, Richard Collier, Graham Sweet, DJS, Geoff Holtham, Tony Lee, Ted Horrox.

Sitting – John West, Dave Hutchins, Bobby Adams, Colin Newstead, Mickey Harrington

Crouching – Keith Valentine, Dave Fitzgerald, Peter Osborne, Keith Mills, Terry Molloy, Ray Childs.

few injuries as the long journey to an extremity of Kent appeared on the horizon. These were flippantly christened 'Erne Bay ankle'. This particular fixture was no exception. Andy Tasker, Gary Cross and Barry Steer had all suffered injuries in recent games. And on the morning of the match Steve Ibbitson, a former Scunthorpe United apprentice with Kevin Keegan, newly signed by Roy from Eastbourne United, became a victim of flu. Roy Oz was a troubled Manager upon arrival at Winch's Field, Herne Bay. When pestered by the host's tannoy announcer for the Horsham line-up Roy asked for a bit more time. It wasn't long before there was another knock on the dressing room door and a request for the team. Roy frustrated the announcer again. A little later the third knock on the door was much harder than the previous two and was followed by a pleading voice, *"Can I please have the team to announce to the crowd before it's too late?"* An equally frustrated Roy rattled off at top speed, *"Freeman, Hardy, Willis, Lofthouse, Shorthouse, Sh*thouse!"* The announcer's voice sounded more relieved when he replied, *"Hang on a minute. Who was right back?"* The dressing room collapsed into laughter. Unhindered by our troubled build up, we won 2-1.

I was then a 75th minute substitute in a 1-0 FA Cup defeat at Lewes and then another substitute appearance in the 33rd minute of a goalless draw at Eastbourne United in an Athenian League fixture. I wasn't restored to the side for another 3½ weeks, for the trip to Tooting & Mitcham United. In the non-Football League Boardrooms of power League chiefs were plotting a re-structure of the clubs. Horsham FC was hoping to be part of the reshuffle by gaining a place in the Isthmian League. It was important, therefore, for us to get a good result against the established Isthmian club. Our 6-0 win suggests we achieved that aim and I got on the score sheet. Big Hutch scored a hat-trick and 'Sticky Boots' notched two as he again *"cheekily back heeled the ball into the path of Den Strudwick who slammed in number five."*

This match was the first of four in eight days, in different competitions, before a return to League action at home to Letchworth on 4th November. Hutch and Newst each scored a brace in a 4-0 win. We scored four in our next match, too, at Wokingham Town. But our hosts also scored four, one when my *"last ditch tackle failed."* It was only the second point we had dropped, out of twenty, in our first ten League fixtures. There was only two points for a win in those days.

Games were now coming thick and fast, and no complaints about a congested fixture list. A 2-0 win over Addlestone, in which I assisted Terry Molloy to score, preserved our place at the top of the Midweek League. A 3-1 win at Bexhill Town put us in the Third Round of the Senior Cup but the game was marred by a serious injury to Andy Tasker. The game was held up while we awaited for an ambulance to take 'Whisker' to hospital with a suspected broken leg. Ron Fuller took over for his first game of the season. Then came a run of seven League matches, in which I played in five, from which we took maximum points to make our Championship hopes a real possibility.

The run began with a very important win over our closest rivals, Carshalton Athletic. Matches against Carshalton were always tight and competitive. They always fielded a good team, playing a passing game, ensuring the man on the ball was always well supported and had options. We won 2-1, which completed the 'double' over them this season. Next came Aylesbury United, in the pouring rain. There were puddles in several areas of the pitch when the match began, but there was no Dave Hutchins. The weather prevented Hutch arriving on time. We began the match with ten men and we were a goal down by the time he took the field. But it was a good job he made it; he scored a hat-trick in a 4-2 win. Then came Grays Athletic 2-1; Letchworth Town 3-1, to which, unusually, we travelled by train and taxi; and finally the return match against Edmonton-Haringey. Tex Wiltshire and 'Yours Truly' got the goals in a 2-1 victory.

We had a break from the League challenge seven days later when we took on, and defeated, Shoreham 3-0 in a Senior Cup Third Round Tie.

Thereafter, my season fell apart. I managed five games in subordinate competitions before my final League match on 31 March. In one of these less significant games Horsham recruited yet another outstanding player, Steve Cosham. After joining from Crawley, 'Coshy' scored a brace against Redhill in the Midweek League, a game that we won 4-1. Keith Mills and I completed the scoring. We lost the final game I played, a League game at Gray's, 1-0. Of my 33 appearances in the Lincoln green & amber that season 13 had been in the League and the loss against Grays was the only time I finished on the losing side. My teammates, though, went on to win the League without further help from me. The Athenian League then lost sixteen clubs, Horsham amongst them, to the Isthmian League, in a major restructure of the Leagues. I was to become used to League restructuring projects later in my career.

My summer of 1973 was consumed with revision and the examinations at the end of my third College year so, once again, I was probably a week or two behind the rest of the squad when pre-season training and friendlies started. The first of the three warm-up matches in which I featured was not until 4th August. It was clear that day competition for places was going to be tougher than ever. The abundance of players enabled us to field two 'first' teams on the same day. We sent a strong side to Arundel to play the County Leaguers, now managed by Wilf Hugill and I was selected for what looked like a tougher test against Bishops Stortford, FA Amateur Cup Semi-Finalists. In the heart of Stortford's defence was a fellow I have already mentioned, John Still, with whom I was to become very well acquainted in later years. John went on to be a Titan in the non-League game, and became the only person to steer three clubs (Maidstone United, Dagenham & Redbridge and Luton Town) from The Football Conference into the Football League, and keeping them there. A magnificent football man. We drew 2-2 with Stortford and then drew again in a match with Woking. The final pre-season game was a 3-0 win at Southwick. New signing Ray Radford, who had previously given us a hard time in his days with Erith & Belvedere, opened his account with Cosham and Mills completing the scoring. We then had a week to wait before the start of the new League season – in a new League, too. This is the worst week of the year, waiting to see if you were in the team for the opener. I do not expect any non-football enthusiast or non-participant to understand just how strong the feeling of anticipation can be. I can only liken it to the hopes and excitement of a five year old when sent to bed on Christmas Eve. I was particularly pleased, therefore, to have made the starting line-up for the Club's first game in the Isthmian League, a home match against Harlow Town.

We started well and deserved our 1-0 half-time lead, thanks to a Barry Steer goal. The second half was more even and we looked like capitalising on the change to 3 points for a win until seven minutes from the end. I suffered an *"indiscretion"*, according to the newspaper, and handled the ball in the penalty area. The penalty was converted. In a moment of madness, I was responsible for losing two points! But I kept my place for the next fixture, away at Staines Town.

Steer was again on target, this time with a 25 yard blockbuster after only six minutes. New signing from Redhill, Glyn Garfield, affectionately known as 'Sobers', was resolute in defence having replaced Bobby Adam who was injured in the match against Harlow. We then lost Steer to injury in the second half, and he was missed. We succumbed in the 77th minute but hung on for another 1-1 draw.

After just two League games we started on our run to Wembley Stadium with a FA Cup Tie at Deri Park, the home of Rainham Town. This was another London suburb ground that did not get the adrenalin going; quite the opposite, in fact. It must have been difficult for the Rainham players to raise positive thoughts and enthusiasm to play at their home stadium. Visitors had to make a genuine physical and mental effort to raise any exuberance for the prospect of playing a game of football on its unreliable surface. Despite being more or less level the pitch was bumpy and sparse in grass, even at this time of the season. And as we were about to leave the dressing room someone, I can't remember who, washed the oils from their hands under the tap in the communal bath. The tap and the pipe connected to it, came away from the wall and water spurted out of the gaping hole. Plumbing services were immediately called to avoid the room from being flooded. But all's well that ends well. We won 2-1 thanks to two goals by Steve Cosham. The winning goal came so late in the game, i.e. the 90th minute, the home club Chairman had been on the telephone to book a coach for a replay at Horsham on Tuesday! Bad mistake!! He had to call back to undo his booking.

So our scheduled midweek League fixture at home to Wokingham Town was able to go ahead, but the game proceeded without Steve Cosham who dropped out at the last minute with a sore throat. Keith Mills was elevated from the substitutes bench and promptly scored a hat-trick. Newst had opened the scoring and was subsequently the architect of our 4-0 win but 'Jimmy Sticky Boots' took all the applause when he was replaced by Graham Sweet 15 minutes from the end. The Club won its first £25 prize for the margin of its victory.

Our next match, four days later, took place on one of the hottest days of the year. And we got roasted. Chesham United visited Queen Street and their wingers, Ken Beavan and Stewart Atkins were our achilles heal, so much so the local media reported "*Tasker and Strudwick were kept so busy they didn't get time to aid the attack.*" Goals by Mills (2) and Sweet enabled us to hang on for quite a while but we were eventually beaten 5-3. It seems I lost my place as a result of this match, on the 8th September: I played only two further games until 2nd March. My case wasn't helped when on 30 October, against Tooting & Mitcham I broke my nose in a clash of heads. With a nose my size, once described as 'aquiline' by a school teacher, this was no small problem. I was taken to Crawley hospital, kept under treatment until 3.00am the following morning, and told to return later that day to the 'day ward' for an operation. As the name of the ward suggests, surgery was complete within a few hours and I was sent home with both nostrils fully plugged with cotton wool and sticky plaster from ear to ear. I was taken violently ill that evening with headache & sickness which resulted in a 'home' visit from my GP, who complained bitterly to the hospital about the dangers of releasing patients too quickly after a head injury and treatment. As a result, I was confined to the 'injury list' for two weeks before I could consider recommencing training.

It wasn't long after that before I started playing again, in the Reserves. And like most other players at the Club, I continued to play Sunday football, to regain and maintain fitness. By now many of us played for the same Brighton based Sunday team, Newick Rangers. I don't know where the team's name 'Newick' came from, our home pitch was at East Brighton Park. Newst, Medhurst, Cross, Hutchins, Sweet and Ibbitson were among those who regularly turned out for our legendary friend and Manager, Ron Eastwood, in the Sussex Sunday League. The Competition had grown from absolutely nothing. Sunday football had been banned until about the '60s when Ron Pavey and Tom Foster decided to start the Competition. In the League's earliest days players played under assumed names to avoid detection and a subsequent suspension from authorised competitions. But it wasn't long before Sunday football became a growth industry in Sussex. And it was something for which I was grateful at times like this, needing fitness. And the chance to play with good senior players, not knowing it was soon to play a major part in a career change for me. In the meantime, on 20 December 1973, my son Benjamin was born. I was present for his arrival. It was frightening and exciting, all at the same time. Benjamin was in great shape, thank God, but I still haven't fathomed out how or why you girls manage to endure that experience. Notwithstanding having to adapt to the new environment, football was never far from my mind and I carried on hoping for a return to First team action. The opportunity came on 2nd March, at Finchley.

We had played Finchley in the reverse League fixture seven days earlier.

It was never considered ideal that two clubs should be scheduled to play one another so soon but with cup ties disrupting the programme it may sometimes have been unavoidable. It was more important to ensure every club had a fixture, especially on a Saturday. So we headed off to Summers Lane, Finchley a week after being held to a 1-1 draw at Queen Street. It had been a disappointing result so Ozzie made four changes to the line-up. Cosham returned at centre-forward after a bout of flu, replacing Mills; Cross moved from central-defence to right-back to replace Garfield; I filled in for the injured Tasker at left-back: and a new signing from Crawley Town, Roy Priestley, joined Bobby Adam in the centre of defence.

As usual we travelled to north London in cars driven by Committee members. Players tended to stick with a driver of their choice. Some, for example liked a quiet ride, enabling them to sleep, and some preferred a more lively white knuckle ride which might include music and/or the thrills & spills of being driven by Frank King. Frank had a regular group of punters prepared to put their lives in Frank's hands, and his vehicle, a large Zephyr Zodiac I think it was, the type with bench seating. We terrorised Frank. A separate book would be required to articulate all that went on, on our travels. In summary, the windscreen washers & wipers were constantly being switched on. So, too, were the headlights encouraging multiple drivers travelling in the opposite direction to give Frank an advisory flash of their own headlights. On one occasion, when driving through one of London's suburbs, the otherwise very quiet 'Snitch' Summerfield said to Frank, *"A lot of people up here seem to know you, Frank."* Passengers often gave Frank incorrect directions to a ground leading him into a cul-de-sac on more than one occasion; and I was in the car once when we commenced a journey to Essex with the bonnet on the safety catch. I cannot remember who was responsible for that stunt but I have my suspicions. Thankfully a conscience was soon pricked and Frank was informed. Until then it looked like the bonnet of his car was about to fly up into the air. Frank, of course, had not noticed it vibrating. Like he didn't notice the car beside him when he decided to make a late change of lane on another trip. The car swerved to avoid Frank's unexpected manoeuvre and collided with a bus. Frank carried on, oblivious to the incident. Luckily, for all concerned, this happened in the middle of a busy London suburb where traffic was moving comparatively slowly. It was unlikely, therefore, any injuries occurred and the three pairs of eyes starring out of Frank's rear window saw only a couple of bruised vehicles.

The practical jokes became too much for Chairman Geoff Holtham. He banned a number of us from travelling with Frank. When Frank informed us he could not drive us to a particular match we told him we would go on strike. We hid behind the cycle shop at the top of the drive leading to our ground. Frank went into a panic mode and advised the Chairman of our absence, and that he couldn't find us. A truce was quickly declared on condition we behaved ourselves. So we piled into the Zephyr and set off once again. After a short amnesty it wasn't too long before the pranks recommenced unabated. We all absolutely loved Frank. And Frank loved being part of the team. He worked wonders for the Club and he, and his magnificent contribution, will never be forgotten by any of us.

Anyway, back to the Finchley fixture. The journey must have been uneventful; I have no memories of this particular trip. But I remember clearly what happened as we gathered in the dressing room. Members of the party randomly trickled in, in good time for the match. Travelling from different starting points, and in different modes of transport, we did not all arrive together. The 'London boys', for example, travelled independently and under their own steam. Others travelled in cars from Horsham. I had already arrived when the 'Brighton boys' turned up, via Horsham. Steve Ibbitson enthusiastically marched in and threw a glossy magazine, open at the centre page spread, on the treatment table and excitedly shouted, *"Look at that!"*. A model by the name of Penny Priestley was photographed wearing very little clothing. Little was left to the imagination. Nobody needed a warm-up after that. But, wait a minute, that name was familiar!

It was subsequently understood our new centre-half may not have had prior notice of the photo-shoot, and subsequent publication, but he ignored the 'stick' and got on with the business of the day in an exemplary fashion. Our new central defender was outstanding in our 1-0 victory. Finchley's Iain Denholm, a centre-forward capped three times by Scotland at Amateur level, didn't get a look in. But I seem to recall Roy only remained with us for one match. I understand, though, he returned in 1982 and made several more appearances.

'Ibbo', meanwhile, had settled into the side very well. He made a big impact in our midfield with well distributed short passes and tenacious tackles, sometimes a little too tenacious. And for a player not much more, if any more, at 5'6" he was a good header of the ball, out jumping opponents of taller stature. Although he joined us from Eastbourne United he had started his career as an apprentice at Scunthorpe United where he palled up with another 'trainee' called Joseph Kevin Keegan. Other than tell us about the pranks and mischief they got up to, particularly one story about a Builder's dumper truck they succeeded in wrecking, to which I will refer later, Ibbo spoke little about his friend. I got the impression Steve, like Kevin Keegan, was a proud Yorkshireman. And as Keegan moved on to Liverpool and worldwide fame, Ibbo missed out on a contract with Scunthorpe and moved to Brighton & Hove Albion. When he was released from the Goldstone Ground he ended up, via Eastbourne, playing with me at Horsham. Despite being close friends they had both moved on, but in different directions. I believe Steve felt he now had very little in common with the England star.

After the trek to Finchley we were given a potentially tricky County Senior Cup Semi-Final at Sidley United. The task was made harder by the absence of Malcolm Bailey and Steve Cosham's participation being limited to 'passenger' value before being substituted in the second half. It was, however, reported after the game that, *"Strudwick and Cross played so well Sidley were restricted to only a couple of chances."* Steer opened the scoring for us and Peter Kirkham, a young local Horsham lad, rounded off a 2-0 win. We had reached the Goldstone Ground Final again. Our opponents would be Worthing.

When back in the League, we lost at home to Tilbury 4-3 but then defeated Harwich & Parkstone 1-0. I redeemed an earlier error in the game by heading a Harwich shot off the line in the final action of the match.

A game at Hertford Town followed and disaster struck, as early as the fourth minute. 'Cranky' Cross sustained a double fracture of his right leg, just above the ankle. He was rushed to hospital and under went urgent surgery immediately. All the comment I had heard about a breaking leg sounding like a gun shot was true. I was on the opposite side of the pitch and the crack was as resounding as it was sickening. Keith Cook came on as substitute and opened the scoring fifteen minutes later but something was lost from our mental approach after witnessing and hearing such an unpleasant, but accidental as far as I could see, incident. We lost our lead; we didn't recover; and lost the match 3-1.

But we didn't have time to cry in our beer, three days later we took on Tooting & Mitcham in a Premier Midweek League match. The 2-2 draw kept us at the top of the table but the game was more significant than just the result. Debutants Dave Harding and John Daubney shone. Dave, a Newick Ranger, scored one of our goals. I believe it was at this match a floodlight fell from one of the pylons, grazing Dave's shoulder whilst he recovered the ball for a throw-in. Jokes were obviously made about this extra-ordinary incident but in all seriousness a two inch change of trajectory might have killed him. Meanwhile, John came on as a substitute and possessed such speed I feared for my title as fastest in the Club. Fortunately for my record, John wasn't with us long, his potential was recognised by Maidstone United and he quickly moved on.

By now our minds were starting to focus on the Sussex Senior Cup Final on 12th April, an earlier than usual date. We concluded a spell of four games in ten days with a defeat at home to Maidenhead United, which damaged our promotion hopes, and a midweek Floodlight League victory over Croydon Amateurs. So we headed for the Goldstone Ground for the County Cup Final against Worthing in indifferent form. The Rebels, supposedly being the underdogs, had three former Hornets in their team, Micky Streeter, Ian Dunscombe & Graham Langford. They did their very best to capitalise on our uncertainties. But we held our nerve and, according to the Press, we never looked like losing despite falling behind in time added on by Referee Alan Gunn at the end of the first half. Langford was the scorer with a diving header. After a stirring talk by Manager Osborne during the interval we were more assured in the second period. After playing a 'wall pass' with Peter Medhurst, 'Primrose' set me off on a run deep into our opponents half. I was *"in full flight"* according to the West Sussex County Times when Harry Richardson illegally ended my sprint towards goal with a blatant body-check, for which he was cautioned. It is impossible to remember every tackle in a playing career but I remember this one, clearly. I was crest fallen and left wondering when my next breathe would come. It came soon enough for me to see a cross I sent in towards Worthing's danger zone *"hurriedly cleared to safety by goalkeeper Ian Taylor's right foot"*. We were on a roll. Barry Steer then notched our equaliser before Tasker set up Cosham and 'Coshy' delicately headed home the winner in the 73rd minute.

Alan Gunn officiated the game very well. He kept a lid on a match that, for the raw competitiveness that always exists in a local derby, could have exploded. Being a local lad, and having played for Whitehawk in the County League before taking up the whistle, it must have been difficult to officiate local players playing at a fierce pace. I was delighted to see Alan progress to the Football League and subsequently the FIFA list of Referees. He also controlled the Manchester United v Crystal Palace FA Cup Final in 1994 which needed a Replay, so he got two bites of the 'Wembley' cherry. Sadly he passed away in 2004, far too soon, while he had so much more to offer the game in an administrative capacity.

Our next game was just three days later, on my birthday, away at Carshalton. Our matches against the 'Athletic' were always competitive and close. And they do not come any closer than this one, even though we had the ball in the net twice within a minute during the first half. We fell behind in the 8th minute to a Dave Worby goal and Barry Steer levelled matters in the 44th minute. Almost from the kick-off we regained possession and built an attack which culminated in Newst hitting a 'cross-cum-shot' which curled over the goalkeeper and into the net. The Referee's whistle blew, we thought to award the goal, but he disallowed it saying *"the ball was still in the air as I blew the whistle for half-time."* Neither team could muster another goal in the second half and it ended all square.

A mere three days elapsed before yet another match came along, away at Wokingham. It was a game I enjoyed. After a goalless first half I seemingly showed everyone the way to goal when I scored in the 60th minute with *"a fierce drive"*. We went on to win 3-1. After a 6-0 win over Southall we proceeded to lose our next two League matches the latter of which, against Slough Town, saw Bobby Adam sent off by Referee Alan Turvey. Mr Turvey had booked 'Tanner' three times that season, once for *"Growling"* (ungentlemanly conduct) when trying to distract an opponent. Referee Turvey, another man I got to know well later in my career, dismissed Bobby six times as Horsham's Captain during the '70s. They clearly did not see eye to eye. But Bobby wasn't Turvey's only victim. The Basingstoke Official once cautioned the whole defensive wall, presumably for not retreating ten yards at a free-kick, in a Chelsea v Aston Villa First Division match. I can't remember which team fell victim of Alan's wrath.

We recovered with wins over Carshalton and Staines Town but then got thumped by League Champions Dagenham. We then won 4-0 over Hampton before concluding our first Isthmian League programme with a defeat at the hands of Chesham United. I had a first half shot that hit the post but that wasn't good enough. The final curtain on the 1973/74 season fell after Semi-Final & Final victories in the East Surrey Charity Cup.

We got the better of Redhill in the Final with goals by Steer, Newstead, Terry Stanley and Ricky Kidd. I'm not sure how we came to be in that Competition, probably by invitation, but it meant three or four more games, and ended with a little bit of silverware in the Boardroom.

Since regaining my place in the side on 2nd March I made 24 appearances by 29th May, 10 in April alone. Fixture congestion, no problem. The Club did not actually complete its season until 4 June when it played a friendly against a Polish First Division team, Odra Opole, which boasted 9 full internationals. One of these, Antoni Kot, reportedly thundered in a 30 yard shot in the first minute. We went on to lose 3-1 but I have no recall, nor can I find any record to confirm I played in this game. I may have been in the middle of exams by this date.

When the season was finally over a group of about 20 adjourned to Lloret de Mar on the Costa Brava for eight days. It was hilarious; wall-to-wall sun and minute-by-minute laughter. A match had been scheduled for us against a local team but that didn't materialise, for some reason. So, as we were in the same hotel as Oldham Athletic we trained with the Latics and they offered us a game to make up for our lost match. Rick Summerfield was so impressive against that great old pro Jim Fryatt, Oldham's Manager, Jimmy Sirrell, wanted to take him to Boundary Park for an extended trial. When the prospect was put to 'Snitch' he characteristically whispered to Roy, *"I'm not good enough."* So it didn't happen. 'Snitch' did not have sufficient belief in himself. His beliefs lay elsewhere. We did, though, see a different side of Snitch when he tried alcohol for, seemingly, the first time. I found him in the hotel lift one night going up & down unable to co-ordinate the stop button when it reached the floor he required. Of course, I helped him, but I embellished the story by adding Snitch was complaining that he thought Roy could have booked him a bigger room. That rumour is still propagated today.

I don't know how Rick Summerfield acquired his nickname. He was a very quiet, mild mannered and polite individual. Snitch was the last thing he would do. He was also deeply religious. I never saw him lose his temper, nor did I hear him swear or raise his voice in anger. When at training one night the ball hit Snitch hard, and I mean very hard, in the area of the groin. We all expected a verbal outburst and/or a customary scream of agony commensurately reflecting the pain. But no. After a few seconds spent in a crumpled heap, Snitch stood, bent double, stood upright, took some deep breathes and continued as if nothing had happened. At the end of the session, back in the changing rooms whilst preparing for the shower, Tex tried to goad Snitch into some kind of reaction, reminiscent of similar incidents with other players i.e. one with some colourful language that expressed the pain and agony of the situation. *"Where did that (effing) ball hit you Snitch?"* Tex shouted. Snitch slowly pointed at the bright red crescent shaped imprint of the ball, that was rapidly turning purple, at the top of his thigh. Calmly stating the obvious he said *"Just there, Tex"*. He then pointed to his 'John Thomas' and without any sign of emotion and added, *"And on the end of that, Tex."* Snitch was not for goading. And for once, Tex was lost for words. Snitch was one of the good guys; well loved and with a beautiful demeanour. But he didn't understand how good he was, at football. Or maybe he simply thought stepping into the fiercely competitive world of the professional game was a step too far out of his comfort zone.

As well as the Club's Annual Dinner, another summer 'ritual' many of us tried to support was the Sunday League's Presentation night. Newick Rangers did not finish outside the top two of the League's Premier Division in the 13 years I was associated with the team. We were familiar with the evening's proceedings, held at the Brighton Centre. As Champions we were first on the stage to collect the Club's prize and the players' medals. We were then ushered off the stage and into a small room for a hasty and raucous photo shoot. With winners and runners-up awards to work through, and in those days there were about 20 Divisions, the process was fast and furious. After completing the formalities we retreated to our tables and/or the bar for a celebratory pint. It wasn't a time for particularly clear thinking. Everyone was excited. But one of us did pause, and asked, *"Where's Boo? i.e. Graham Sweet"*. After a while he was spotted. He was seen waiting for the teams to come off the stage with their medals, and with his own award still in his hand, he joined them in the photography room. Everyone was too excited to realise an 'intruder' had joined them for the picture. They posed with huge smiles and thumbs in the air, the camera flashed and they all dispersed to the bar, except for Graham. Sweetie joined the next team to come off the stage and went through the same procedure. He got into every team picture that night, all forty of them! We were all creased up. But the punch line was to come even later, as we assembled for pre-season training. We did not all play for Newick; some of the players played for Sunday teams closer to their homes. Probably six or seven different Sunday teams were represented amongst Horsham's squad. So, when somebody distributed the photos from the Brighton Centre event there were tears of laughter when someone asked, *"What the f**k is Boo doing in our photograph?"* and the same question reverberated around different areas of the clubhouse. Graham had invented 'photo-bombing'. Sweetie was one of the funniest persons I have ever met. I am pleased to have remained in touch with him for many years after he 'emigrated' to Scotland, until he very sadly passed away. I never did get round to asking him, why did he send me two Christmas cards each year? Yes, two.

As we gathered in July for pre-season it was again evident that new faces wished to join Horsham. Martin Rosser, Ray Poole and Dave Gelately all joined their former Redhill colleague Paul Daniels. Former Brighton & Hove Albion midfielder, and Newick Ranger Terry Stanley, sought to bolster our midfield. But without intending any disrespect to these fellows one new signing matched, and in most cases outshone, any defender I had previously had the good fortune to play with. Having been released by Brighton, when Brian Clough and Peter Taylor arrived at the Goldstone, Norman Gall signed for us. Norman had made over 400 appearances in the Football League for the Seagulls and 488 in all competitions. At his first meeting with Brian Clough, Norman explained the pair had met several years ago near Norman's home in the North-East. As a young boy Norman joined his friends outside a hotel to collect autographs from the players of the local team, Middlesborough or Sunderland, I'm not sure which, probably both. Norman approached Clough armed with his pen and notepad but the centre-forward refused to sign. Norman reminded Clough of that brief encounter upon his arrival at Brighton. *"Yes, I used to be a little arrogant in those days"* the England U/23 International advised Norman. Now, at the Goldstone, I imagine Clough & Taylor saw Norman as being in the autumn of his career and they released him. Bad mistake. It became abundantly clear to us Norman still had plenty to offer, especially so at our level of the game. He got height & distance with his headers; he was brilliant in the tackle, especially the 'last ditch' variety; and was totally reliable. Norman made few, if any, errors.

I played in Norman's debut, a pre-season friendly at the highly successful Walton & Hersham. We won 6-1! I even scored a goal!! Thereafter I struggled to make an impression. I was an unused substitute in three of the Club's opening four games of the season. It was the 15th October before I was given a playing role in the First Team, for a match in the Sussex Professional Cup at Hastings United. We beat the Southern League team 1-0. Barry Steer was our scorer.

Four days later it was time for the FA Cup, a Third Qualifying Round Tie at home to Burgess Hill Town. After an early goal by Cosham we huffed & puffed a bit, failed to put the match to bed whilst not being in any danger of losing. Coshy netted again early in the second half but it wasn't until 12 minutes from the end did we secure our place in the Fourth, and final, Qualifying Round. We scored three more. Peter Medhurst side footed home a cross from me and Cosham got two, taking his tally for the match to four. Coshy was a superb player; fast, sharp, powerful and aggressive. But he suffered from what most players would consider minor, mundane or unusual injuries. It became a target for light hearted fun in the dressing room, e.g. Steve couldn't come training tonight as his fridge had broken down. It is dangerous, too, to question a colleagues approach but I don't know of any other player who would find a reason not to accept a call-up from the FA to attend an Amateur International match, as Steve did. Coshy ran his own business in Redhill, a busy hardware shop called The Padlock. Perhaps he was too heavily committed in other directions. Nonetheless, he was a great player for us, and a nice bloke, too. But another we were to lose far too young.

Forty-eight hours after Burgess Hill we won 2-0 at Wokingham. And then came two matches against Sutton United in the London Senior Cup.

Horsham FC 1974/75 season
(left to right – taken prior to the match against Chelmsford, I think.)

Back row – Barry Steer, Norman Gall, Steve Cosham, Dai Mason, Dave Gelatley, Ray Poole, Roy Osborne

Front row – DJS, Steve Ibbitson, Colin Newstead, Malcolm Bailey, Peter Medhurst, Martin Rosser.

We lost after a Replay. Heaven knows how we came to be involved in that but it meant three games in eight days prior to the most important game of our season, so far – Chelmsford City in the FA Cup Fourth Qualifying Round – not the best preparation for a crucial Cup Tie. But we gave it a great shot. We were a goal up after ten minutes. Skipper Colin Newstead played the ball wide to *"put the overlapping Strudwick away and his fine cross was headed home by the leaping Cosham."* Sadly, we couldn't capitalise on our lead and nor could we hold on. We were finally undone by goals from Mick Loughton, a Ray Poole own goal, and John Dunwell. City had several good players, none more so than Billy Kellock. Kellock had previously played for Cardiff City and Norwich City before joining Millwall where Manager Gordon Jago failed to play him so he dropped out of the Football League and joined Chelmsford. After his stint at New Writtle Street he broke back into the League and once changed clubs for a fee of £50,000 during his career. He posed a constant threat the day we played against him. Chelmsford were drawn to play Charlton Athletic in the First Round Proper leaving us to dream of what might have been.

Unusually, we had no midweek fixture following the Chelmsford game so we had a week to cry in our beer. And we also had a new signing to mould into the team. Former Wolverhampton Wanderers, Brighton & Hove Albion and West Ham United striker, Bertie Lutton, came to Queen Street on a one month contract, less than 18 months after he had played for Northern Ireland in a World Cup Qualifying match. He won 6 caps for his Country, between 1970 & 1973 and was a player of exceptional skill but retired from the full-time game, aged 23, because of a serious back injury. He made his Horsham debut in a 3-1 victory at Maidenhead United in which he was cautioned for dissent.

Our next two fixtures were postponed due to inclement weather/unfit pitches so Lutton played his second, and supposedly his final, game at Queen Street against Southall. It was an eventful match, for me anyway, if not entirely successful for the Club. Bertie was subject to a very heavy tackle as early as the tenth minute. In football parlance he became a virtual passenger for the remainder of the match. Shortly after that Dai Mason was involved in a collision and required treatment. With a struggling goalkeeper and only nine effective outfield players we soon found ourselves 3-0 down. Much of the damage, in the football sense, had been caused by a lightweight left winger called Alan Devonshire. (What happened to him? Well, I know. We were to meet several times later on in our careers.) Dai Mason was unable to continue and with only one substitute permitted in those days Manager Ozzie had a decision to make. He chose to replace Dai. Bertie volunteered to take over in goal but having taken off an injured 'keeper Roy chose not to replace him with another injured player, certainly not in such a crucial position. Roy asked me to go in goal and brought Terry Stanley on at full-back. I was delighted to be asked to go 'between the sticks'. Truthfully, I made sure I was in front of Roy when he was making up his mind. His decision meant I played in every position for my hometown Club. I am very proud of that. Besides, even a half fit Bertie Lutton was of greater value to the team as a 'nuisance' up front than in goal. As the game re-started, with me barely visible inside Dai's big jersey, I wondered what on earth I had done. More or less static on the goal line the pace of the game in front of me was astonishing. I began to wonder how I was going to cope. But the team re-shuffle worked as well as it could. We recovered two goals, one scored by Bertie, and I kept a clean sheet, maybe more by luck than judgement. I remember diving at the feet of an advancing forward. I knew what to do, or so I thought, I had seen Dai do it dozens of times. I crashed head-on with the attacker while the ball went loose and trickled wide of the goal. I feared a penalty, our opponents screamed for one, but no – a goal kick was awarded. The local paper reported I had made some saves and one in particular was an effort, *"Dai Mason would have been proud of."* I was, of course, unhappy we lost 3-2 but it was a game I will always remember with a small element of self satisfaction.

Tony Reed deputised for Mason in the following week's League game at Boreham Wood. Once again we were fortunate to have such excellent back-up. As expected, Tony played well in a 1-1 draw. He repeated his efforts in the midweek that followed, against his former club, Crawley, but we were knocked out of the Sussex Professional Cup, 1-0. During my time at Horsham we were lucky to be blessed with several good custodians. Dai Mason was the best goalkeeper I played in front of, without doubt. But he was always pushed to keep his place by Rick Collier and Tony Reed. Before Dai's reign we were fortunate to have Ian Page as a regular 'keeper and Dave Barton as a stand-in. We also called upon Mel Minto, aka Polo, for a few games. A big 'keeper who commanded the penalty area. They were all good guys.

After the Cup exit to Crawley we were able to concentrate on the League. We were still hopeful of grabbing a promotion spot. And between 14 December & 26 April I managed 17 League appearances. The first of these was a home fixture against Hertford Town. We kept our ambitions alive with a 2-1 win after going a goal down when I allowed an opposing forward to go by me and he lobbed in a cross that was headed home. Our search for an equaliser was floundering in the second half according, that is, to the County Times when describing, *"a decent run by Strudwick ended with a mis-hit shot going behind the goal."* I saved my blushes, however, by continuing to support our attack and eventually one of my many crosses was met by Steve Cosham's diving header, in spectacular style. And four minutes later we defied an efficient offside trap and Steer got our winner.

We suffered a set-back the following week at Harlow Town. Harlow played in a municipal stadium with a running track around it. The picture I paint is one of wide open spaces, very thinly populated with spectators. On the day of our visit there was a strong wind; the only weather condition that really spoils a game. On top of this we lost Cosham with a torn muscle after he was stopped, roughly if not illegally, when in full flight towards goal. But even though he was replaced by a class player, Bertie Lutton had re-appeared, we could not get into the game and lost 2-0.

Looking back I am not sure if we were scheduled with a Boxing Day fixture and/or if it was postponed but our only 'Christmas' game was at home to Tilbury on 28th December. Perhaps the Isthmian League didn't believe in local derbies at this time of year but as 'Table toppers' I am sure Tilbury, with former Hornet Ray Major in their ranks, just got on with the business. It seemed that way as they started like a train and took an early lead playing up the slope on the Queen Street pitch. They seemed unperturbed by the heavy ground and fierce swirling wind. But just as Tilbury looked like increasing their advantage Ray Poole ploughed through the mud, lofted the ball into the penalty area for Steer to crash a header home, 1-1. Barry could head a ball harder than many of us could kick it. He was superb in the air, as good as Tony and/or Mark Hateley. Ten minutes later *"Strudwick overlapped to great effect and was rewarded with his second goal of the season. He hit a long ball forward and with the help of the wind it sailed over the goalkeeper's head. A happy Strudwick shook his head in disbelief."* It was a complete fluke. The gusty wind was so strong and unpredictable; it had blown a tree down in a neighbouring garden, it took the ball off its intended course and into the net. But they all count. Steer added two more, to make a hat-trick, and Terry Stanley added a fifth, to make it 5-1 at the interval. Tilbury, though, were not beaten yet. They scored twice in the second period to make it a great game and an important victory for us. As for Bertie Lutton it was to be his final game for us. He suffered yet another injury and was replaced by John Lock. Sadly, that was the last time we saw Bertie. A superb player, troubled by injuries. We all thought he would call it a day but I understand he emigrated to Australia where he played in the Australian Soccer League for Sydney City and South Melbourne before retiring.

Our results continued to oscillate between victory and defeat. Worryingly, we were not showing enough consistency to string together a run of results good enough to challenge for promotion. After Tilbury we lost 2-0 at Harwich & Parkestone despite me finding the net. My 'goal' was disallowed as Coshy strayed offside. We then won at home to Finchley

2-0 but crashed the following week at Carshalton 3-1 in a match that was eventful as it was memorable.

Mickey Stanley, Terry's brother, made his debut at left full-back. We explained to Mick, in defensive situations, we didn't trust Barry Steer to mark any particular player; we just allowed him to 'mark' and/or attack the ball. Anything in the air Barry would challenge for it. Leave it to Barry was the instruction. But as the opposition goalkeeper launched a clearance into our half of the field Micky forgot the advice he had been given. We watched, and then grimaced, as Micky rose to head the ball back when Barry arrived on the scene. He brilliantly headed the ball back on the offensive and knocked Micky almost into orbit at the same time. It happened twice more before Micky got the message. He was quick to listen, just slow to understand. As for the game itself, we started well. I stopped a shot on our goal before having my own attempt on goal at the other end headed for a corner. But we then conceded twice. We got back into the game when John Lock replaced Micky Topping but one of Carshalton's full-backs, a useful and experienced player by the name of Roy Hodgson, then bagged their third. Roy was well known in non-League football around south London but I didn't know him at all. I do remember, though, he had a lot to say for himself, analysing the game, in the communal bath after the match. "*Who's that,*" I asked. *"Roy Hodgson,"* I was told. I was none the wiser. But that's beside the point. We, as a team, were beginning to struggle.

Two more points were dropped in a 1-1 draw at home to Maidenhead United. And what followed was worse; a 5-1 drubbing at Croydon. It was a game in which we started badly, and fell away, in uninspiring fashion and in dreary surroundings. The weather was miserable; the pitch was boggy; and the attendance was reported as being 200. I swear the statistician had double vision. Barry Steer was booked in the 5th minute for arguing, and that set the pattern for the reminder of the game. Bernie Merron put the hosts ahead early on but we equalised midway through the first half when Malcolm Bailey headed home my cross. Thereafter, we didn't get a look in.

Bernie Merron was a thorough nuisance; one of the most difficult players I was ever to play against.

We moved into March without having had a League win since 11 January. And being without a midweek game after the Croydon debacle we had seven days to 'circle the wagons' so to speak. But not even a week's respite and a change of captaincy raised our form. Newst was 'relieved' of the team leadership to help him concentrate on his own game. Barry Steer took over as Skipper and Alan Boorn, a new signing from Hastings, made his debut against Chesham United.

The week of reflection and the changes to the team's composition appeared to work, initially. In the early minutes of the game Steery thundered in a 35 yard shot that crashed against the crossbar with the visiting goalkeeper, R Taylor, beaten. Newst then saw his powerful header blocked by Taylor, who then scrambled the ball away in the resulting melee. Minutes later, according to the local newspaper, *"Full-back Den Strudwick advanced down the flank, received a short corner from Newstead and drove in a shot that would surely have beaten Taylor had right-half Peck not intervened with his head"*. The first half ended goalless despite a long shot from Micky Stanley being pushed wide by the impeccable Taylor, who then comfortably grasped the resulting corner kick. Whilst we tried to maintain the pressure in the second period, we had lost the initiative. Chesham, known as The 'Generals', crept back into the game when Grimwood cleverly stayed on-side and forced the ball home. The introduction of a fresh pair of legs, when Dave Treagus replaced Micky Topping, gave us a lift. But when pushing for the equaliser we were caught out by the pacy Stuart Atkins, another player who could be a thorn in the side of even the best defence. We lost 2-0.

The above match was probably only noteworthy because it was the game, after which we began to think our chances of promotion were beginning to fade. But it was only the 1st March; we had eleven fixtures to go; and we had recruited a new striker. 6'3" Eric Whitington had signed to strengthen our attack.

Eric began his career at Chelsea, as an amateur, and had played for England's Youth team. He didn't break into the First Team at Stamford Bridge and was subsequently transferred to Brighton & Hove Albion. He made just 26 full appearances, plus 6 as a substitute, for the Seagulls and scored 8 goals. He was joint leading scorer, with Kit Napier, in the 1966/67 season but was released in 1968. He went to South Africa and played for Highlands Park whom he helped to win the country's Championship. On returning to the UK he played for Crawley Town, Eastbourne United and Folkestone prior to becoming a Hornet. He made his Horsham debut in our 1-0 win over Harwich & Parkstone. Eric scored our goal. We were back on track and eagerly awaited the visit of Croydon, and that pesky player Bernie Merron, three days later. But the game started badly.

My 3rd minute pass back to goalkeeper Dai Mason got stuck in the notorious Queen Street Wealden mud. Merron pounced and we were a goal down. Eric 'Dick' Whitington equalised two minutes later and Newst put us ahead two minutes after that. But almost immediately after that Norman Gall hobbled off with a badly twisted ankle. Barry Steer, with his incredible heading ability, moved into the back four and John Lock took his place in midfield. Lockie played his best game for the club. Merron, though, continued to be a threat and levelled matters for Croydon just before half-time. Our lead was restored when Croydon's 'keeper could only parry a fierce Lock shot and Newst knocked in the loose ball. Malcolm Bailey then played a perfect ball through to Newst which enabled him to complete his hat-trick and a 4-2 victory for us was sweet revenge for our 5-1 defeat a few weeks earlier.

We didn't get much time to gloat over our victory, though, because eight days later we faced Croydon again, this time in the League Cup. We lost at a near empty Croydon Stadium 2-0.

When we returned to League action, we were away at Finchley, and we paraded another new signing. Vic Bragg, a cultured player in what ever position he took up, mainly midfield or at full-back, joined from

Crawley Town. Notwithstanding Vic's obvious class we lost 2-1 despite having taken an early lead through Terry Stanley. Two days later, on Easter Monday, we lost by the same score at Tilbury. On a muddy churned up pitch, that harboured more stones than grass, we settled after a slow start and Eric Whitington put us into a lead which we comfortably held up to half-time. Tilbury asserted themselves more in the second half but we were still deserving of our advantage. As the game progressed Gary Cross fell awkwardly and on to a stone that gashed his leg very badly. He was taken to hospital for multiple stitches. To make matters worse we eventually conceded in the 85th minute and shortly after Norman Gall inadvertently deflected a wayward shot into our net. Promotion rivals Harwich & Parkstone lost that day so our failure to capitalise on our adversary's defeat meant any hope of promotion disappeared.

Undaunted we travelled away for the third consecutive match, this time at Aveley. And once again we took the lead; twice in fact. Whitington and Steer scored our goals but we conceded on each occasion and drew 2-2. Our first League point in a month. And the first win in nearly a month came three days later when Carshalton Athletic were sent home empty handed. Steer, Whitington and Newstead scored our goals in a 3-1 victory.

Four days later we scored three again, away at Chesham United. We even took the lead twice in the first half but were again pegged back on each occasion before half time. Chesham then notched two in the second half but we could only manage one in reply, very late in the game. Three goals away from home, at Chesham United, and it still wasn't good enough.

In midweek, I spent my birthday enduring a goalless draw at Staines Town in the League Cup before entertaining Staines Town at the weekend, in a League fixture. I was surprised to find myself selected to play 'up front'. But for a few minutes Ozzie's gamble appeared to pay-off. I scored after eight minutes. Playing alongside Newst and big Whit was a good experience but despite several good chances we failed to notch again and the game ended 1-1.

In the following midweek we had two fixtures! Both were at home, and both were in the League Cup. This particular Cup competition must have been played on a League format in small groups as, despite some previous indifferent results, we were still in it. Anyway, we lost 2-1 on Tuesday to Croydon and 1-0 to Staines Town on Friday. I cannot find and/or recall details of the team selection for these games but with a League match at St. Albans City on the Saturday I do not imagine too many of us were asked to play on consecutive days; although we had been obliged to do this occasionally in the past. So, for the second consecutive Saturday we met St. Albans City. And this time, on 26 April, we won. Eric Whitington and Malcolm Bailey put us 2-0 ahead by half-time and we hung on during the second 45 minute period for a 2-1 win.

Eric had proved to be a prodigious asset. His height made him good in the air; he was particularly skilful on the ground; he struck the ball well; and he played with a mischievous/wicked sense of humour. Watching him closely I noticed, even if we took the kick-off at the beginning of the game, as centre-forward he would always line up to take the kick-off at the start of the second half. He got away with it on the odd occasion, much to the chagrin of our opponents. It was Eric's way of asserting himself on the opposition and, of course, the Referee. If gamesmanship was an Olympic sport Eric would be a gold medalist. He was fun, as well as being a terrific player.

Almost inevitably, in our busy/crazy schedule, we had a Tuesday night game in the Isthmian League Cup. Yes, we were still in it!! And it was not an easy one – Carshalton away – and another close exciting encounter. Roy Hodgson was again at full-back for the Athletic but a goal by Malcolm Bailey and an own goal helped us gain a 2-2 draw. Then, with little thought for health & safety and/or the welfare of players, we fulfilled a Southern County Floodlight League game at Tonbridge on the Thursday. I can't remember the score but the result won us the Championship of the subsidiary competition. And although I cannot trace any records for the fixture I am sure I played, as it was the only time I played at Tonbridge's

'Angel' ground. Incredibly, we were then obliged to complete our Isthmian League Cup fixtures with a home game against Carshalton twenty-fours hours later, on Friday 2 May. Three games in four days (or four games in seven days)!! Eric Whitington and Micky Stanley were out injured: Barry Steer sustained an injury during the game and was replaced by Mickey Ansell; and I also picked up an injury during the game but stayed on the field to cause whatever nuisance I could in Carshalton's defence, which probably wasn't much. Roy Hodgson led his team to a 3-1 victory.

That was the end of my season. I was only fit enough to watch from the touchline, the Club's final three games, two of which were in the League – a 3-1 defeat at Hertford Town and a 5-0 victory at home to Aveley. We finished the 1974/75 League campaign in eighth position, for the second year running

I have no reliable recall of what occurred at the Club during the closed season. I think I was engaged in my final College exams. But a lot had gone on by the time we reported back for training ahead of the 1975/76 season. Manager Roy Osborne had left the Club. This was a big disappointment to us all. Roy had been hugely popular. He had a massive personality; had a lot of contacts; and led by example. He was a skilful player so he attracted talented players. He wanted, and expected, his team(s) to play all around the pitch. He focussed his efforts on making sure his team played well. Under Roy's management the Club had enjoyed its most successful period for many years. Something in the memory bank is telling me he left to take up a role at Sutton United.

Tony Elkins-Green replaced Ozzie as Manager for the 1975/76 season, having previously managed Crawley Town. Tony, quite naturally wanted his teams to be successful but I got the impression he placed his attention more towards picking the right players to negate the opposition's strong points. He analysed the opponents closely and passed this information on to his team. He was much more of a tactician. who placed great emphasis on neutralising the opposition's strong points.

As usual, the change of Manager kick started a significant turnover of playing staff. Much of the Brighton contingent, e.g. Newst, Medhurst and Cross were no more. But Eric Whitington, Jimmy Cock, Vic Bragg and Norman Gall were all retained, along with a few stalwarts, including Dai Mason and me. We were joined by a 'new age' group of players:- Micky Fountain; Dave Roberts; Terry Williamson; Paul Holder; Russell Rego and former English Schoolboy International, Micky Cornwell. So there was quite a mixture of the very experienced and the very young. By the time pre-season friendlies began we were half a new team.

The new Manager named me 'Club Captain'. I was delighted with the honour. For me, it seemed to reward my nine years service and it acknowledged I had, for some time, often been the only Horsham born player in the side. But there was no time to stand on ceremony. We lost our first warm up fixture 3-0, at home to a strong Ramsgate team. Next up came another Southern League side, Maidstone United. We fielded a very young side which included Holder and Rego, promoted from the Youth team, and Andy Beer (aka Ginger) between the sticks. Big Eric Whitington scored but we lost 2-1.

Lewes then visited Queen Street and brought with them four former Hornets in their squad, Dave Treagus, Terry Stanley, Ross Gumpright and Alan Clark. They also brought Terry Parris, a Newick Ranger, and their outstanding goalkeeper of many years, Paul Swaysland. Despite most players knowing each other well local derbies of this nature are always quite feisty, in the battle for bragging rights. This game was no exception. And with the start of the season ten days away places in the starting line-up were at stake. It was pleasing, therefore, that we earned our first win of the season, 3-1, with two of the new faces, Cornwell and Roberts, on the score sheet with Whitington.

So, going into our final friendly, we were all buoyant in the race for a place in the opening League game of the season. Southern League Dover Athletic provided the opposition and we sent them home empty handed.

A razor sharp Micky Cornwell scored the only goal of the game. We were ready for the big kick-off.

I always felt the opening week of a football season was a good time to take a family holiday, providing that is, you were not a footballer. The sun was blazing down on Jack Scrace's finely prepared pitch when St. Albans City came to Sussex and found Eric Whitington at his best. Eric scored both our goals in a 2-2 draw. It wasn't the win we hoped for but we were off the mark.

Unusually, our second game was also at Queen Street. Corinthian Casuals were the visitors. The Casuals were a strange outfit; they didn't appear to have a permanent home ground of their own. It seemed they were perpetually in a long term ground share arrangement with another club, most recently at the Grounds of Dulwich Hamlet and Tooting & Mitcham United. They came to Horsham having finished bottom of the Division last season but had avoided relegation as the League sought to enlarge the size of its Competition. We showed them no sympathy. We won 4-0. Paul Holder, who made his League debut the previous week at the age of 17, scored twice. Jimmy Cock and Bob North scored our others.

Even more extra-ordinarily, our third match was also at home. We were humbled 4-0 by Chesham United, who were quickly becoming our nemesis club. Atkins and Bevan did the damage, again!

When finally the fixture list scheduled us to be on the road we earned a point at Hampton from a goalless draw. And four days later we won another useful point away from home, at Tilbury, thanks to another Whitington goal in a 1-1 draw. On a pitch described as *"a terrible dust bowl"* Eric notched after 20 minutes. Thereafter, Norman Gall was outstanding, marshalling the defence as our backs were to the wall for much of the game. As time passed we managed to cause frustration amongst our opponents. Tricky winger Ray Jarman was cautioned when he retaliated against me after I tackled him. I then headed a goal bound shot off the line. But we cracked in the final minute when Dave Barnett found a way through. We were, of course, disappointed to lose two points so late in the game but on the balance of play it was a fair result.

Three days later we were back at Queen Street for the visit of Walton & Hersham, a team in decline after highly successful FA Cup runs a few seasons ago. Such was the club's recent form, it had been relegated from the First Division at the end of last season having won only 8 of its 42 League games and conceding 108 goals. Our optimism approaching the game was justified by a 3-1 win. Whitington (2) and Roberts, a substitute for Holder, were our goal scorers.

The following Saturday we were at home yet again, our sixth home game in eight League matches. Such an imbalance in the fixtures is unhelpful to clubs. It can affect the attendances at clubs with too many home games in a short space of time; it can seriously damage the cash flow of clubs having to find the funding for a disproportionate amount of away travel, i.e. without the income from an equivalent number of home matches. Furthermore, the variance of home & away games misrepresents the true picture of the Competition. But as players, we have to get on with it, and Boreham Wood were our next visitors. Bob North scored our goal in the fourth minute, in what became a 1-1 draw. Thereafter, the local Press found our performance to be our *"worst display of the season so far."* What the media did not, and probably could not, take into account was the herculean effort it took to keep at bay one of the most uncompromising centre-forwards I had faced, Micky Jackson. Jackson did not take prisoners.

We were back on the road three days later for a midweek trip to Wokingham. It was a topsy-turvy game that I was forced to watch from the bench, as an unused substitute. We fell behind when Dai Mason made a rare error; he handled the ball outside the penalty area. Eager to make amends, Dai magnificently saved the resultant free-kick but could only parry the ball into the path of the oncoming Wokingham forwards. We were 1-0 down, but only for nine minutes. Big Eric headed home a Micky

Fountain free-kick. After that, both sides had chances to win but both failed to take any.

It was not a dissimilar tale when we travelled to Hampshire League side, Alton Town, the following Saturday for a FA Cup First Qualifying Round Tie; a game we should have won comfortably. But as the BBC constantly reminds us, *"Anything can happen in the FA Cup."* And it did. We started well enough and an impartial spectator would not have thought Alton had a cat in hell's chance of prolonging their participation in the FA Cup. But football doesn't work with such logical or obvious certainty. The longer they kept us out the stronger their confidence grew. And it was still goalless when, in the 65th minute, Len Phillips, who must surely be a relation of Portsmouth's 3 cap former England International who scored 48 goals for Pompey in 245 appearances between 1946 & 1956, struck an audacious over head shot to put the home side ahead. But don't panic, Whitington scored an equaliser five minutes later. We would surely go on to win now. But no. We gifted Alton a winner in the 90th minute. Without the expletives I can hear Eric's voice even now, *"If we can't get tight in the final minute of a Cup Tie, we never will."* We hadn't got tight and we were out.

We had only three days to prepare our redemption, in a midweek home match against Maidenhead United. And so we did. Dave Roberts notched a brace and Eric Whitington bagged a hat-trick, one was a stunning header from a cross by me! And our defence was water tight, which was more than can be said for the cloud laden sky that dropped its unwelcome load on a soggy Queen Street. The weather reduced our normal attendance to a sparse 230 but they were rewarded for their stoic support with the best win of the season so far, 5-0.

We followed this up with a highly satisfying 3-0 victory over Southern Leaguers Bognor Regis in a FA Trophy Preliminary Round Tie at Nyewood Lane, Bognor. It's always good to beat your local rivals, especially when the opposition contains locally well known names like Jack Pearce, John Sheppard and Malcom Glue. They also fielded a very good goalkeeper in

Vijay. Extensive drainage work on Bognor's troublesome pitch made the surface resemble an American Grid Iron field but neither team was troubled by the unusual surface. We went ahead in the 6th minute when Big Eric capitalised on a poor back pass, intended for goalkeeper Vijay, by Cliff Peach. Thereafter we never looked back. The effervescent Paul Holder scored and the always lively Dave Roberts completed a comprehensive 3-0 victory.

In the following midweek, just seven days after we met at Queen Street we travelled to Berkshire to play Maidenhead United. Whitington scored the only goal of the game in a match I would describe as being as dull as the surroundings. One side of the ground had a low wooden stand that failed to obscure a very imposing railway embankment. The trains that passed, on their way between the west country and Paddington station, all carried more passengers than those who frequented Maidenhead's football ground. I understand a week in politics is a long time; and so it is in football. Ten days after being knocked out of the FA Cup we had won three games, scored nine goals and conceded one. So we were taken aback when, on the forthcoming Saturday, we suffered our first League defeat in over a month, and only our second of the season. Our opponents, that bogey team of ours, Croydon, more than ably assisted by that bogeyman of a player Bernie Merron. Both teams had plenty of chances but we were sunk by a goal from a former team mate, Les Setters.

We recovered our composure a few days later with another win over Corinthian Casuals. Despite a plethora of chances and near misses, our only successes came from Whitington and Cornwell in a 2-0 away win that placed us seven points behind leaders Tilbury. Thereafter we failed to win any of our next four games, to lose ground on the Dockers, before creating a run of five wins.

We drew away at Finchley in a match bereft of chances, let alone goals, before losing at home to Hampton and then away to Gravesend & Northfleet in the FA Trophy. The Kent club, from the Premier Division of the Southern League, was easily the best side we had played in the season so far and we had to battle hard to maintain some credibility. Goals from Woolfe, Angel and Everest gave us a mountain to climb. We were well beaten, 3-1, and a rare goal from Norman Gall was our only consolation. But just like a London bus another Gall goal came along four days later, in an away 2-2 draw at Walton & Hersham. Dave Roberts had opened our scoring a little earlier.

I missed our next match, due to a late Friday evening call-up from the Sussex County FA. I made three appearances for the County Senior side; this one I believe was for an away trip to Gloucester, for my first visit to Forest Green Rovers' hillside ground at Nailsworth. To save travel time and cost I was picked up en route, somewhere in the Horsham area. I was sorry to be missing a game for my club but I was proud to play for my County, albeit a late selection. Any high estimation I had of my new status was quickly deflated when the coach pulled up and I was greeted by a 'blazer' in the front seats with the words, *"And who are you?"*. I was to visit this pleasant Stadium, known as The Lawn, several times later in my administrative career. The Hornets, meanwhile, went to Hertford Town where Big Eric scored a hat-trick and Cornwell also notched in a 4-0 win. To change the team after such a good win would have been risky for Manager Tony Elkins-Green, so despite my selection for the County, I lost my place for a home match against Wokingham Town. Sadly for the team, we lost, 2-1. Norman Gall scored yet again, but this time in our goal, making an error even more scarce than his goals at the other end. Norman was one of the good guys, and an outstanding player.

I was re-instated into the Horsham side the following week for a turbulent trip to Boreham Wood for a London Senior Cup Tie. And it proved to be a day that tested what my qualities as Club Captain were, if I had any, and how I could express these to their full extent. Fixtures against the Hertfordshire side were always physically demanding. But with the 'Wood struggling for form, Bourhinghe Road was not a happy place. Manager Micky Hunter had failed to turn up for a few fixtures, apparently due to work commitments.

The club's form had dipped and the hostilities of the home club's crowd soon turned towards its own players as well as upon us. I do not think we were prepared for the goings-on during an eventful afternoon. We were subjected to very physical tactics; we had tea thrown over us as we left the field at half-time; and after losing a verbal dual with me Micky Jackson took retribution on his nearest opponent, our centre-half John Green, by elbowing John in the face. John lost at least one tooth in the encounter. And, as if to justify his action, Micky stared and pointed at me (from a safe distance thankfully) before satisfying himself with the final words, *"you got him that"*. Despite the torrid tactics and the physical approach of our opponents our very young team remained mature beyond their age and stayed focussed on the match despite a considerable amount of provocation. We won 3-0! It was a game the local Press stated *"Dennis Strudwick would remember with a great deal of pleasure after repelling early home pressure he sent in a series of long free-kicks one of which landed on the goal line and shaky goalkeeper Steve Wyatt dropped the ball and it was poked in by the home centre-half."* Well, it is certainly a game I clearly remember, and not with just a small helping of pride. And it was probably Dave Roberts' best game as a Hornet. Immediately after the game Boreham Wood's Manager, Micky Hunter, resigned. It was not a happy ending for him.

As if we didn't have enough fixtures we were engaged in a Friendly a few days later against The British Police XI. Whilst often seen as a hindrance these games are useful to give non-regular players more game time, and to try debutants. Former Crawley Town, and current Hillingdon Borough midfielder, Tony Goodgame, showcased his abilities as a potential signing and goalkeeper Andy Beer was also drafted into the side. And allegedly, *"Den Strudwick hit a beautiful first goal from twenty-five yards, past the former Welsh U23 goalkeeper Lyn Davies after ten minutes."* We cuffed the Police 3-0.

Beer's midweek appearance proved timely. He was included in the weekend's fixture at Ware, a cold and uninviting ground. 'Ginger' replaced the injured Mason. Tony Goodgame was also included. He signed from Hillingdon on Friday and made his Horsham debut less than 24 hours later when Micky Fountain withdrew with 'flu. Tony was good on the ball, rarely misplacing a pass, and added some physicality to our midfield. Whilst at Crawley we always found him a difficult player to play against. Stockily built, I remember a fixture at Crawley, not against Horsham, in which Tony incurred the wrath of the Referee, following which Tony was cautioned. In an excitable exchange of words, in which Tony was asked for his name, the Referee misheard and/or misunderstood what Tony said and sent him off. Tony left the field and the match restarted amid some dissent from the Crawley bench and fellow players. The Referee's response was to explain Tony had remarked in disparaging terms how good a game he (the Referee) was having, or not having. No, no, no, the protests grew louder. He was giving you his name; you asked for it. The Referee called for a Match Programme. On seeing the name Goodgame he recalled the player from the dressing room. But back to the Ware match, Eric Whitington opened the scoring with his 19th goal of the season, and it was only 1st November! Dave Roberts and Jimmy Cock also scored in our 3-1 win.

Seven days later Dave Roberts singlehandedly won our home match against Harlow Town by bagging a hat-trick in another 3-1 victory. Four wins on the bounce set us up nicely for another local derby clash against Lewes in the Sussex Senior Cup. As usual for these matches competition was fierce. In Clark, Jones, Medhurst and Graves the Rooks fielded four ex-Hornets. And in Paul Swaysland they had an excellent 'keeper. As if to prove the point, 'Sways' saved Eric Whitington's 5th minute penalty. Thankfully, Dave Roberts scored in the 72nd minute and we looked to have the game won. But Lady Luck was not on our side. My Sunday team mate from Newick Rangers, Terry Parris, grabbed an equaliser with two minutes remaining to book a Replay at The Dripping Pan.

The second match was a 'humdinger', as my Dad would have said. Although goalless after 90 minutes chances had been created and missed by both sides. With the Tie deep into extra-time, and a further Replay looking to be on the cards, Micky Cornwell snatched the winner in the 112th minute. An excellent away win that tasted even sweeter at 'The Pan'.

We approached the end of November with an unbeaten away record but faced two further games on the road before the month was over. Both games were winnable. Our record, however, looked under threat in the first of these fixtures against Bromley. The Kent club had been relegated from the top Division the previous season and were just about treading water above the relegation zone this season. But we travelled to Hayes Lane without Dai Mason and Norman Gall. We fell behind after two minutes and then lost Vic Bragg with a cut head after seven minutes. We were in trouble. The impressive Dave Roberts, who was improving with every game, bagged two goals. And although we were pegged back by an equaliser an unfamiliar figure appeared in our opponents penalty box, that of John Green, who rose to head home a Roberts' in-swinging corner for a 3-2 victory.

A trip to Aveley came next. We were optimistic against a side that had found goals hard to come by. Although we had to wait until the 45th minute for our goal, a shot by Micky Cornwell that bounced on the uneven surface and deceived the home 'keeper, we looked on course for another win. But football is not as predictable as it seems and we ended up hanging on for a 1-1 draw after the Essex side scored its first goal in 697 minutes play!

I missed the next game. I left work early for the match, another away game, this time at Imber Court the home of Metropolitan Police for a London Senior Cup encounter. Imber Court is/was an impressive stadium with good facilities and an excellent playing surface. It was a ground I had not previously visited and, subsequently, was destined never to visit. I was taken unwell on the journey and became unfit for play. I was obliged to retire to bed, instead. Nevertheless, we won 2-1 thanks to goals by Terry Williamson, his first goal for the Club, and almost inevitably, Dave Roberts. We were through to the Third Round.

After ten games unbeaten we returned to League action at home to Hornchurch feeling quietly confident about our chances of promotion. Team Captain Micky Fountain was anything but quiet. His customary pre-match wind-up contained its usual quota of table thumping, fist pumping, foot stamping and motivational encouragement all delivered at the speed of a hurricane in a loud voice that was populated with expletives. In the lull after the verbal hurricane someone quietly said, *"Mick, you can't say three words without swearing."* As if still high on octane Mick screamed, *"I can, c**t!"* The dressing room collapsed in laughter.

The mood quickly changed on the field. We began badly. Starting without key defenders Terry Williamson and Norman Gall we looked a mess, defensively. Our ineptitude saw us struggle and we were a goal behind at half-time. It could have been more. The interval provided another opportunity for a Churchillian speech from the Team Captain but it was more likely the controlled and determined words of cunning Team Manager Tony Elkins-Green that helped us turn the tables in the second period. The local newspaper reported on an *"immediate improvement"* in the second half in which *"John Green's header was blocked on the line and Eric Whitington forced home the rebound."* And *"after a three man move Whitington nearly scored again following a fifty yard burst upfield by full-back Den Strudwick."* We were on a roll. Our winner came in the 75th minute when a Whitington shot took a deflection. The visiting 'keeper managed to tip the ball onto the crossbar but Roberts forced it home. The game had swung full circle. Billy Patterson hammered a shot inches wide as the visitors realised their initiative was lost. Frustration set in and their goalscorer Tony Wimpory was booked *"for shaking Den Strudwick"* after I stopped him in full flight. Our promotion hopes were growing until...

One week later we met genuine Championship chasers Carshalton Athletic at Queen Street. I had never met a poor Carshalton side. The 'Maroons' always moved the ball about well and the player in possession was never without support. It was always a delight to play a match against

Carshalton even though you knew you may spend long periods with your backs to the wall. And this mid-December day proved to be no exception. We kept pace, though, for 75 minutes, enjoying periods of success along the way, but no goals. So it was a huge disappointment to fall behind with 15 minutes to go. We did our utmost to get back into the game but, inevitably, left gaps at the back. A side as good as Carshalton did not look 'gift horses in the mouth' and despite chasing the match we eventually lost 3-0. It was a devastating blow for us and it showed us where we had to be if we were going to be serious contenders. We had a week to reflect on matters.

The British winter imposed itself on the Queen Street pitch for the following week's game at home to Harrow Borough. A deep frost had got into the ground but the surface began to thaw on the morning of the match. This made for a wet slippery surface on top of hidden ice. The only suitable choice of footwear was to have studs, but would there be sufficient give in the surface to take a stud. There was no other option. Whatever, we found it difficult to get to grips with our opponents despite their relatively mediocre League position. We showed only glimpses of our normal performance level before falling behind in the 55th minute. I then, reportedly, *"almost jinked"* my way through the visitors' defence before hitting a free-kick that Norman Gall headed home for the equaliser. But that was the best we could do, in a poor performance. We failed to take the chances we created and then dithered in the final minute when our opponents took a smart free-kick and scored. We were sunk 2-1. A disappointed son, Benjamin, watched from the warmth of the grandstand on his second birthday.

Our festive fixture, the day after Boxing Day, was a visit to our friends at Boreham Wood. The game was as competitive as usual, so not much 'goodwill to all men', but it was unusually goalless. After two home defeats, to extend our unbeaten away record into the New Year was very satisfying. So too was the pleasing debut of 15 year old Peter Ranson, a Crystal Palace Junior. Peter had been coached in Horsham Youth team by workhorse

John Laker, a wonderful fellow. Peter progressed to Crystal Palace and was a member of Palace's FA Youth Cup winning side, in a back four that included Kenny Sansom, Peter Nicholas and Terry Fenwick. All three subsequently became internationals. Peter had been brought up in good company so he easily coped with his baptism of fire at Boreham Wood.

The fixture scheduling at the start of 1976 was odd. But we could not have begun the year with a more difficult encounter. In these times County Football Associations were 'all-powerful' in football administration. If a County FA said clubs would play in a local County Cup Tie, the club was obliged to do so. A scheduled League fixture would be postponed and re-arranged, often imposing difficult midweek issues, e.g. travel. And so, I guess, it was on Saturday 3rd January. Instead of a tasty local derby in the League we faced Ilford in the London Senior Cup Third Round. They didn't come much harder than Ilford who boasted England Internationals in the shape of Tony Bass, Peter Deadman and John Butterfield alongside that most impressive of characters, John Still, again. But we gave it a good go.

Of course, against such a power-house, we had to defend tenaciously. Norman Gall and I made clearances off our own goal line. At the opposite end Norman and Eric Whitington both had headers similarly repelled. We gave as good as we got for 84 minutes until Tony Bass, another amongst the most accomplished forwards I was to play against, netted. Another cup run bravely ended.

In our return to League action the following week, at home to Bromley, we fielded the youngest team ever to represent Horsham. Peter Ransom, at 15, retained his place, and Paul Holder, at 17, was back in the side. Ian Brown, at 18, and a young Terry Williamson were in the heart of the defence. With such youthful exuberance, the task ahead did not look too daunting, on paper. But as we always had to remind ourselves, we didn't play on paper! Bromley were still struggling at the wrong end of the table and they were prepared to scrap to maintain their place in the competition. And scrap was the operative word. In a most memorable match, but not entirely for all the right reasons, Great Bookham based Referee Ray Lewis cautioned nine players; seven from Bromley and two Hornets, Eric Whitington and me! I was cautioned in the 40th minute for reportedly seeking revenge against an opponent who had earlier fouled me. I didn't see it like that and subsequently won an Appeal against my booking. This was a great source of amusement between Mr Lewis and I as we frequently met later, and became firm friends, during our administrative careers. Eric was cautioned when he stopped in his run up to take a penalty, to point out the goalkeeper had moved. Mr Lewis disagreed and cautioned Eric for ungentlemanly conduct. Bromley's plethora of cautions was not without just cause; to incur seven bookings in a match in those days was unheard of. And although we could only manage a 2-2 draw the visitors could not match Peter Ranson's class and Paul Holder's flamboyance in midfield. I still hold the image in my memory of Paul terrorising his opposite number, McCarthy, for the umpteenth time. As he rode yet another reckless McCarthy tackle Holder turned, placed his thumbs in his ears; wiggled his fingers; poked his tongue out: and shouted *"Nah, Na, Na, Na, Na. Na, Na"* Juvenile, yes, but at 17 with no small ability and the world at your feet, you can afford to be less than serious once in a while. Besides, the cheek of it made us all laugh. McCarthy was booked for his treatment of Holder but saved the best of his unorthodox defending for a challenge on Terry Williamson. Left flat footed and helpless by Terry, McCarthy grabbed whatever he could of the speedy Hornet, and that happened to be Terry's shorts. They were torn from his torso as he continued his run passed McCarthy in his jock strap. Inexplicably, McCarthy escaped further sanction. It was an extra-ordinary scene. The following Friday's headline in the West Sussex County Times was a specific reference to the Referee, *"Mr Bookham from Lewis!"*

After that hiatus whatever happened in the following week's County Cup Tie at Burgess Hill would be tepid by comparison. But it was no push over. Games against Sussex County League sides were always a 'banana skin' for us as the 'local' teams looked to upset the club perceived to be at a higher League level. The Hillian's had some good players, ex-Hornet Kenny Swallow amongst them, so proved to be tough opposition. Goals from Whitington and Cornwell steered us into the 4th Round but I limped off in the second half forcing me to miss the following week's League game at Harlow Town.

The Sports Stadium in Dag Hammarskjold Way, Harlow was one of my favourite away grounds. It was a large stadium with the pitch being surrounded by a running track. The playing surface was always in good nick but it was, I imagine, like playing on the moon, i.e. large stadium; pitch surrounded by grass banks; very few facilities; minimal crowd (about 100 if you were lucky). There was never any atmosphere but there was something I liked about the place. My disappointment at missing the game was exacerbated by a 1-0 defeat.

The weather took a turn for the worse during the forthcoming week. The temperature fell dramatically and by Friday we all felt our home match against Finchley the following day was unlikely to go ahead. There was, however, no indication of a postponement prior to match day so everyone arrived early for what we thought would be the obvious outcome of the Referee's pitch inspection. We guessed wrong. After careful consideration the Referee said, despite the frozen ground, the surface was flat. The match would go ahead and he didn't mind what the players wore provided their kit was on top. To say we were surprised would be an understatement. Some players wore track suit bottoms & tops to protect knees and elbows. I decided, rather foolhardily under the circumstances, that if the Referee judged the pitch fit for play, I would wear the usual attire. But, I would have to quickly reconsider my footwear. I rushed to Tony Smith's Sports shop, long gone now, at the junction of Park Street & East Street, the 'go to' place for the hopelessly ambitious player, to see Les. I cannot remember Les' second name but I recall how popular the enthusiastic and knowledgeable sales assistant was. Whatever Les recommended must have worked. I kept my feet on the flat icy pitch and managed to hit two *"accurate free-kicks that found Eric Whitington"*. Eric scored directly from one and forced a defender to deflect the ball into his own net for another. We won 2-0 in a one of the most enjoyable games I played in. Due to the rock hard surface nobody was interested in over zealous physical contact. Everyone's first objectives were to stay upright and play football. A good game was had by all. The Referee had made a brave decision and it came off.

We were at home the following week, too, and defeated Hertford Town 2-1 before losing to our bogey side, Croydon. We had only beaten Croydon once in seven previous meetings and the last three encounters at the lifeless Croydon Sports Arena had all ended in defeat. It was like playing in a vacuum. This particular Monday night followed the same pattern and Bernie Merron stuck to the script and scored against us again.

We bounced back on the Saturday with a 2-1 win over Hailsham Town in the Sussex Senior Cup Quarter Final. It was a game we were expected to win comfortably but after falling behind in the 19th minute we were rescued with two goals by Dave Roberts and were happy to complete the game in one piece, against a team clearly intent on not taking any hostages.

A little more than 48 hours later we were on our way to the Goldstone Ground, Brighton to face the Seagulls in the Semi-Final of the Sussex Professional Cup. It was always a delight to play at such a stadium and a privilege to play on the surface that was always prepared outstandingly well by Frankie Howard. South African born Frankie was an incredibly popular outside-left for the Albion in the 1950s. He made 200 League appearances and scored 26 goals before becoming Groundsman when his playing days came to an end. Devoted to the Albion, Frankie once told me, when we met later in my career, he turned on the floodlights very late one freezing Christmas night when the weather forecast predicated a thaw enabling him to roll the pitch to ensure the Boxing Day fixture went ahead. What a character. When Frankie was made, the mould was broken. God bless him. I would like to think we did Frankie proud and justified our place on the Goldstone. The Albion team included an ultra slippery winger called Peter Ward, who was soon to become an England International. But our own former Brighton players also shone. Eric Whitington scored our goal, which brought us back into the game after going behind 2-0, and Norman Gall's outstanding performance must have made Albion aficionados wonder if they had let the centre-half go too soon.

Having resurrected our season with four wins in five matches the defeat at the Goldstone on 16th February proved to be the catalyst for a poor run-in to the end of the season. We lost eight of the remaining 14 games in which I featured to the end of the season, winning only four. Only two of these victories were in the League, so that saw the end of our promotion hopes. The other two were in the County Cup, so that afforded us some consolation.

Five days after losing narrowly to the Albion we were thumped at Hornchurch 3-0. We were dreadful. It gives me no satisfaction to say I had been left out of the starting eleven and viewed matters from the bench. As a team we are all in this together. Furthermore, although I was a 'used' substitute I was unable to do anything to influence the result. We were so bad our opponents were rewarded with a bonus payment from the League sponsor for winning by a three goal margin; the first to be awarded in a match against Horsham.

A fixture free week followed, giving us time to sort ourselves out. We went into the next game, at home against a high flying Harwich & Parkeston, in a positive mood. A rude awakening awaited us. The visitors were aggressive, uninterested in taking anyone captive. We went a goal down in the first minute and fell further behind on the half hour. Half-time could not come soon enough but we avoided conceding a third. I do not recall a stirring speech or dressing down by Manager Elkins-Green but the break in play changed the course of the game. The local paper reported we were a completely different team in the second half. Norman Gall shored up the defence; Dave Roberts came alive up-front: and *"Den Strudwick gave the signal for all-out attack with a great run in which he slipped past two defenders."* Unfortunately, for the sake of this memoir, the reporter has omitted to record what I did, or did not achieve. But collectively we rallied. Roberts, Goodgame & Whitington all scored to put us into the lead. We had snatched victory from the jaws of defeat, or so we thought. We let our guard down in injury time and allowed our visitors to equalise and gain *"an undeserved point."*

Next up, our friends at Boreham Wood, for a League Cup Tie. We had already played the Wood three times this season, winning one and drawing two. Such familiarity breeds contempt and this fourth encounter in one season was no exception. Micky Jackson was his usual 'difficult' self and Ricky George, famous for scoring a goal for Hereford United that knocked Newcastle United out of the FA Cup, demonstrated his pedigree – and the power of his shooting. Dai Mason was outstanding, saving several goal attempts by George. I recall getting in the way of another George shot that left the brand name of the ball on my leg. The only other contribution I remember making was to take *"a measured free-kick"* that enabled Ian Brown to head home on his Isthmian League debut. But we lost 2-1.

So, with our interest in another Cup competition ended we returned to League fixtures, at home to Ware on Saturday 13 March. Having gained only one point from the last 9 available we were desperate for points if we were to coattail on the final promotion places. But the weeks were ticking by; opportunities were running out quickly. The season was behaving like a toilet roll – the closer we got to the end the quicker it ran out. Having won convincingly in Hertfordshire, here was our chance to keep up with the pace setters. We fell behind as early as the 8th minute and despite Cornwell's equaliser we lost 2-1. The local newspaper wondered if our young guns were feeling the pace of a long competitive season. Norman Gall was proving there is no substitute for experience, as he returned to the team after injury. But whilst I would never doubt my own commitment I was currently being selected to play in an attacking midfield role, supporting the front two. This was not where I was most effective and/or comfortable. But at least I was regularly in the team, getting game time. So get on with it is what I did; we had Carshalton away in three days time and matches didn't come much harder.

With Dai Mason returning in goal we managed a spirited performance. The League leaders were held to a single goal, but it was enough for them to win. There was, however, more optimism in the team ahead of our longest trip to Harwich & Parkstone on the following Saturday. We incurred some late team changes. We were without master goalscorer Eric Whitington and Andy Beer was thrust into our goal when Dai Mason became unavailable. None of the changes were to blame for two errors that put our opponents two goals up in the first ten minutes. We steadied the ship and put Harwich under a great deal of pressure in the second half. Jimmy Cock pulled a goal back and an equaliser was on the cards when Tony Goodgame hit a post. But it wasn't to be. Somehow, Harwich survived and our hopes of League honours were finally dashed. We now had a week to prepare for our last chance of a meaningful reward for the season's efforts, the Sussex Senior Cup.

Eastbourne Town stood between us and a place in the Final. Our opponents had incurred a shed load of injuries and could field only eight fully fit recognised first team players. To make their predicament worse, the club had lost its place in the Athenian League due to an administrative error. It took Eric Whitington only two minutes to rub salt into Eastbourne's wounds, and he went on to score a hat-trick, his third of the season. Jimmy Cock and Dave Roberts completed our scoring. We were going back to the Goldstone Ground for a Final against Hastings United of the Southern League.

I missed the next fixture, an East Surrey Charity Cup Semi-Final against Merstham, which we won 3-1 but I was back for our next League fixture at St. Albans City. The afternoon started worryingly and got worse. John Green and Micky Cornwell arrived only minutes before kick-off, causing concern before the match began. Then, within minutes of the start a back pass to Mason by Whitington was intercepted and Mason brought down the attacker now in possession of the ball. Dai made amends by saving the resultant penalty. We recovered and maintained our composure until well into the second half when Paul Mayles struck for the Saints. Undeterred, we pressed for an equaliser and Cornwell and Whitington went close. And with three minutes to go a long throw-in by me, was nodded on by Whitington to Roberts whose shot on goal was deflected in by a home defender. An element of luck, maybe, but it was well deserved on the day.

For whatever reason(s) we did not then have a match for 13 days. But the forthcoming 48 hours told a different story. On Good Friday 16th April we played at home against Wembley. After 80 minutes of goalless unexciting and uninspiring football we won with three goals in the last ten minutes. The first came from *"a flighted free-kick from Dennis Strudwick onto Whitington's head and the tall striker nodded it wide of the 'keeper"*. The second came five minutes later when Terry Williamson rode a fierce tackle before hitting the ball over the 'keeper from an acute angle. And in the 90th minute *"Strudwick wrapped the game up when he side-footed the ball home from a fine Goodgame chip."*

Less than 24 hours later, on Easter Saturday, we were on the road for another League fixture at Harrow Borough. I can't be certain whether I played or not in this one but I can be fairly sure fatigue would have played a part in our 2-0 defeat. And believe it or not we were scheduled for a third League fixture in two days when we entertained Aveley on Easter Monday. I was definitely not included in the team for this game, which we won 2-1 with goals from Gall and Whitington. But with a record of having made almost 50 appearances during the season, and the Senior Cup Final six days away, I sought some reassurance about my place from Manager Tony Elkins-Green. I was told not to be concerned, I was definitely in the side. And it was a comfort to return to the line-up four days later for a home game against Champions designate, Tilbury. The Dockers won 3-1, giving them the points to claim the title with two games to spare. We fell behind in the fifth minute but it wasn't 'backs to the wall' stuff for us. *"Micky Cornwell equalised when Dave Roberts flicked on a Dennis Strudwick corner kick"*, the County Times reported. Although we conceded again we took the game to our opponents in the second half. And *"Roberts, Cornwell and Strudwick all went close to levelling the score again."* But it wasn't to be. As tiredness set in Tilbury made it 3-1 in injury time, in a match closer than the score suggests.

We then had only one day's rest before our biggest game of the season, the Senior Cup Final against Hastings United at The Goldstone. After an afternoon at Dora Bryan's seafront hotel, as we always did prior to the County Final, we took the short journey to the stadium. Once gathered in the dressing room the Manager announced the team. I was named as a substitute. After the Manager's assurance given just six days ago, I was shell shocked. What a devastating blow. And to receive it, in the Dressing Room an hour before kick-off, hurt. I don't remember much/anything about the game other than I did get on the field and I recall hitting a shot that travelled meekly across the face of the goalmouth. The main thing is, we won, 2-1. Whitington opened our scoring in the first minute of the second half. Hastings equalised with an own goal by Vic Bragg but our 'Player of the Year' Dave Roberts struck the winner with seven minutes remaining. I didn't know then, but with three matches of our season left, my appearance at The Goldstone was to be my last for Horsham. Not a bad place to finish off 300 odd appearances for your home town club.

CHAPTER FOUR

Into Administration (But not Insolvency)

Part One – The Sussex Sunday Football League 1976-1981

The 1975/76 season drew to a close leaving me with a bitter/sweet feeling. I had been bitterly disappointed at not being named in the starting line-up for the Sussex Senior Cup Final especially after Manager Tony Elkins-Green had given me a clear understanding my place was safe. Having made 50 appearances during the season, including each round prior to the Final, my angst was exacerbated by what I considered to be a lack of veracity by the Manager. But so be it. My upset was, of course, compensated by remembering I had made a considerable contribution in getting us to the Final, and to the season as a whole. I had got onto the field for what amounted to little more than a cameo appearance, and above all, there was sweetness in the team's victory. It was my fourth appearance in the Final of the most senior County competition. One loss and three victories was not a bad collection of medals. I've no doubt that I continued to train properly and made myself available for the final three games of the season; I just wasn't selected. I had no thoughts of not being at the first training session for 1976/77. And I did not realise at the time, my cameo at the Goldstone was to be my last appearance in the Lincoln Green & Amber – at this stage of my career, at least.

As I was about to enjoy the summer break, following a long and difficult season, the change in climate produced one of the hottest and prolonged spells of sunshine ever. In the relative calm a job opportunity came on the horizon. And it was one I found too tempting to let pass by. The Sussex Sunday Football League was looking for a new Secretary. On the basis of 'nothing ventured – nothing gained', and with more hope than expectation, I threw my hat in the ring.

Following the Competition's inauspicious beginnings, i.e. playing under the radar in an unaffiliated capacity, through the determined offices of Tom Foster and Ron Pavey the Competition had officially affiliated in 1960 and had subsequently gained authority and respect. It had also grown in size as well as stature. Sunday football had become a serious pastime in Sussex. For example, it gave people like my brother unavailable to play on a Saturday due to work, the opportunity to play organised football at the weekend. Sadly it came along too late for Derek; his playing days were long over. But it gave the football maniac an additional opportunity to play. Like many of my Horsham team mates I had frequently played a second game over a weekend (for OBJ and then Newick Rangers) for the sheer love of the game, and to share more time with friends. It was also helpful to regain match fitness, at a decent level, after recovering from an injury.

So, I responded to a 'sits-vac' advertisement in the Brighton Evening Argus. I was invited to meet the Committee at the League's headquarters in Queen's Square, Brighton. I knew the building well, having attended social functions there. It comprised offices on three floors, for the football activities; meeting rooms, which several club utilised; a large function room and a licensed premises. There was always something going on. A few days after the interview process I received good news and a question, when can you start? I gave one month's notice to T&E Homes and exchanged my commute to Reigate for one to Brighton. I started on the 1st June 1976 and ran into difficulties, but not of my own making, almost straight away.

I was the fourth person in the position of Secretary. The first, Ron Pavey, had moved on to become Commercial Manager at Brighton & Hove Albion Football Club. Ron was followed by Alan Gunn who left as his Refereeing career began to blossom and take priority in his list of commitments. Then came my predecessor, a gentleman (I'm sorry his name escapes me) who retired from a full-time career in the military. I am told he had difficulties coping with civilian life and, as I found out, it was clear football was not his first love. So, one of my first jobs was to change the culture on the football side of the business, e.g. the player registration system required better controls and governance; the referee marking system would be monitored and tightly controlled; and clubs that relied on the use of a Council owned pitch (which was the vast majority) would, wherever possible use only that pitch for their home league games. Having played in the Competition for several years I was also aware the fixtures needed more regulation. Wherever possible I would endeavour to ensure all clubs, or as many as possible, had a fixture each week. I quickly discovered this was an impossible aim as not all pitches were available from the beginning of the season so a full fixture list was not feasible until the season was in full swing. I also encountered the occasional withdrawal from use of some council pitches as the venue was required for another purpose. On one occasion I could not use a park in Eastbourne which contained three pitches for one whole month, as tree fellers were required to use the changing room area as living accommodation while they undertook major forestry work during the weekends. As best as I could I tried to maximise the number of games I could schedule each week and maintain, as closely as I could, an equal number of matches played by each club. It wasn't easy. But I needed to try.

The Competition had to be commercially cognisant, too. It could not rely on club subscriptions alone. To achieve this it ran a weekly lottery and member clubs were obliged to sell a specified minimum number of tickets. Whilst some clubs found it a burden to sell the minimum requirement each week (40) others easily exceeded the basic number, making the club a greater proportion of profit. The licensed side of the business was also financially helpful. It was available for functions and many clubs frequented the premises after their Sunday morning matches. A part of my contract involved becoming one of the named license holders. I did not have a roll to play in running the bar on a day to day basis but the title 'licensee' carries with it much responsibility. So I had to learn. In terms of time, the football office was my main domain. Overall I had a lot of balls to juggle. And worse was to come. Before that, though, I had a Management Committee to get to know and between us we had a good deal of work to complete, i.e. closing down the 1975/76 campaign with a Presentation Evening at The Brighton Centre and an Annual General Meeting. These events were followed by the election of new clubs for the forthcoming season.

Tom Foster was the League Chairman. I am not sure what Tom's profession was when I joined but he certainly seemed to have a lot of time on his hands; and he gave much of it to the Competition. Tom was a leader and as a founder member of the League he had a strong personality who didn't suffer fools gladly. I guess his strength was an asset when chairing a meeting of more than 200 people. Well, it worked for him. And if chain smoking was a martial arts sport Tom would surely have been a black belt.

Co-founder, Ron Pavey was Vice-Chairman. A proud Whitehawk man born and bred who had played and managed his local team in this particular area of Brighton before moving into the administration side of the game. He was a Council member of the Sussex County Football Association and was to serve two terms as Chairman during his career. He had a brilliant 'football brain' which I tapped into on many Sunday mornings during the early weeks of my tenure.

I cannot remember all the members of the Committee but some names remain in the memory bank with affection. I remained in contact with Rod Lynn for several years, using his insurance broker business. George Millyard, another man from Whitehawk, watched his team every Sunday wherever they were playing before finding a bus or cadging a lift to our headquarters in Queen Square in the centre of Brighton. After a liquid lunch he kept me company in the office while I collected the day's results. George was a good man but not always great company; he fell asleep within minutes every week! Peter Hiscox was another Committee man who also sat on the County FA. I don't think Peter was attached to a particular Sunday club but he served on the Committee at Lewes FC. He was a most enthusiastic fellow and resembled a bottle of pop about to explode. We had two Referees on the Committee, George Rees and Bob Curtis. I hope he will forgive me for saying this, George was quite advanced in years, but he took an appointment from me to officiate a match every week without fail. As the League was short of Match Officials, people like George were like gold dust. Similarly, Bob turned out 'in the middle' every week wherever I sent him. And despite being a Referee Bob was very popular. His home was on Goldstone Lane and his back garden overlooked the Goldstone Ground. On the rare occasions I watched Brighton & Hove Albion I could recognise several faces in the small crowd on Bob's rear lawn, all enjoying Mrs Curtis' hospitality and a free view of Albion's match.

The summer of 1976 was one of the hottest and driest on record. Hose pipe bans were introduced at an early stage of the summer and with water levels in reservoirs sinking to their lowest known records alternative methods of supply had to be introduced. In many places, particularly in rural areas, stand pipes and deliveries of bottled water were introduced. The affect on football pitches was devastating. Much of Sussex comprises an area called The Weald which rests on clay. Without water clay shrinks, creating huge wide open cracks in the ground. One, for example, was featured in the Brighton Evening Argus. Burgess Hill based, (now) Football League Referee Alan Gunn was photographed very carefully holding his son over a crack in the ground on a local football pitch. The gap was visibly large enough to engulf Alan's son. This pitch, like most others in the County, was clearly not fit for play. So, from the beginning of the season I faced immediate and widespread postponements. I discovered one exception, the Goldstone Ground, sadly not available to the Sunday League. On a visit to see Ron Pavey, now Brighton & Hove Albion's Club Secretary as well as Commercial Manager, like any football nut I couldn't resist a walk on the pitch. It was in immaculate condition and was being watered! Groundsman Frankie Howard explained he had been advised to carry on as normal as, despite the drought, there was plenty of water in "them there hills", pointing at The South Downs. I guess the Albion's business depended on it. I looked on in envy and waited for a break in the weather, hoping my first season in administration would get underway as soon as possible. And so it did, eventually, in a fragmented way. Scores of matches were lost before pitch surfaces, and the grass, recovered. But within six weeks of this dreadful start to the season's the fixture list, clubs incurred even more postponements – due to frost and snow! Snow and frozen pitches in October. I couldn't believe my bad luck. A backlog of fixtures had built up before the season was fully up and running. Such issues caused by the regular British winter proved to be synonymous with all efforts to complete the season, let alone completing it on time.

Law number 1 in Ron Pavey's book was "always get the Cup matches played". To assist this the League had a rule which 'pooled' the use of all pitches. In other words, the Competition had the power to postpone a League fixture and move a Cup Tie, which had otherwise been postponed because of an unfit pitch, to a pitch that was declared fit. So some Sunday mornings were extremely busy rescheduling the venue of games, which meant redirecting teams and Match Officials, too. This was not a frequent task but it was certainly a regular one which made for some hair raising moments. The secret was to assign the Cup Ties to be played on the best pitches, in the first place. As for the League campaigns, these often suffered due to inclement weather and the poor state of grounds. It didn't take me long to fall out with quite a few Local Authorities who charged significant hire fees for pitches but then, in poor weather, insisted on postponing games by noon on a Friday – for a Sunday morning fixture! I argued that on many occasions the pitches would be, or were, fit for play by the time kick-off came along almost 48 hours later. This problem was mainly confined to the mid & north areas of Sussex, e.g. Crawley and Horsham, in the Weald, where management closed down on a Friday afternoon despite providing a service for an amenity to be used at the weekend. My repeated moans about this policy made me very unpopular in two or three Council Offices. But I am pleased to say, my complaints worked; policy was changed to a more workable solution. Conditions on the chalk based pitches of Brighton,

Hove, Worthing and Eastbourne were much more favourable, so too were the Authorities. Unless conditions were totally unsuitable, or unsafe, with 6 inches of snow for example, these Authorities would not postpone matches until the day of the games. Generally, they left the Match Referee to make the decision upon his arrival at the ground.

In one particular season the pitches in Horsham Park were deemed unfit for football for sixteen consecutive weeks. As we scheduled as many as four matches each week in the park this added up to a considerable loss of fixtures. Coming from Horsham, and knowing the Park well, I reluctantly accepted the pitches would be in a very poor condition. But after such a long period of inactivity I began to worry whether the Horsham based teams would be able to complete their season. So I ventured into the Park to take a look for myself, accompanied by my 'toddler' son Ben. Much of the Park, not just the football fields, was a bog. There were some areas better than others but in the main the whole area was totally unfit for football and/or for even just a walk in the park. Indeed, I do not remember seeing another soul during my unofficial inspection. Two of the pitches were either side of the fine wildlife pond so having established football was out of the question I took Ben to see the ducks and geese. We spotted more than we expected. Seeing some material or cloth floating in the water, from which what I believed was hair floating on the surface, I climbed the barrier fencing and eased my way down the bank. I prodded the object. It moved very much like a log, or something equally stiff, would move if immersed in water. It was a body. And it didn't take any time to assess there was nothing I could do to save it. It was very dead.

I picked up Ben and ran to the nearest telephone box on North Parade, about 250 yards away. There were no mobile phones in these days. I dialled 999, reported what I had found to the emergency services and made my way back to the distressing scene. By the time I arrived at the scene about 15 to 20 people had gathered. Where had they come from? Seemingly, some had seen me pick up Ben and make off at great speed. They were re-assured by my return, with Ben, and I explained what I had found. It wasn't long before Police and Medical personnel were on the scene. I gave a brief statement and explained why I had not attempted a rescue operation by getting the body up the bank and out of the water. I was told it was a good job I had not made such an attempt as I would have pulled off the limbs. First impressions were, the body had been in the water for at least three weeks. It had gone unnoticed due to the Park's lack of use. A little later the Police helpfully followed up my sad discovery by advising me the body had been identified and close relatives had been informed. The lady had been in a care home about ten miles away before going missing. How she got to where she was found was unexplained. Whatever, my helpless and sad experience wasn't in the job description but it indelibly stained my memory.

Anyway, back to my first season in full-time administration. It was a baptism of fire, or more accurately; drought, rain, frost & snow, and more rain. The weather, and the poor quality of some of the pitches in use, meant completing the season on a conventional basis was impossible. On a very few occasions 'double headers', a match scheduled with two shortened halves followed by two similar periods or a normal 90 minute game played for 4 points had to be employed. And the Cup competitions were all completed authentically by the transfer of ties to pitches where the games would get played. I wasn't comfortable with these unusual measures but there was no other way to fulfil the fixture list and complete the campaign. But 'we' got there each season thanks to the support of a strong Committee and a diligent staff.

The geology and geography of Sussex is wide ranging, in terms of the soil on which many of the football pitches were sited. Playing fields in the north and middle of the county, whilst generally being level, were plagued by clay and/or soil that just refused to drain quickly, or in a timely manner. And those that suffered most from postponements were likely to be the pitches that received least maintenance as it was frequently impossible to get machinery onto the playing area. Some were better than others, it is true, but many in the Horsham/Crawley area, and mid-Sussex, suffered from many & successive postponements. Pitches along the coast were generally in better condition, due to good natural drainage. Some had the added benefit of being positioned on the slopes of the South Downs. The picturesque Preston Park in Brighton, for example, had two pitches on a serious slope. There were two pitches (possibly three) in Hollingbury Park, Brighton, that were better suited to mountain goats. Rarely was it necessary to postpone games on these grounds. And I cannot resist mentioning a pitch that was in regular use prior to my stint as Secretary, Wrights Farm, Brighton. It was on land in the middle of the City's Horse Racing Course, at one of the highest points of the Downs. But use of the pitch was decommissioned by the League and/or the Local Authority, just before my tenure after a match was abandoned due to inclement weather and one of the players was taken to hospital suffering from exposure!

The rock in the Office was a lady from Leeds, Audrey Hadfield. If anyone upset Audrey they did so, and I say this with tongue in cheek, at their own risk. Audrey looked after all the finances. She was scrupulously honest, reliable, efficient and tidy, everything I needed for someone looking after the financial tiller! I was fortunate to have the company of three Secretaries during my five year spell at the Sunday League. The first I recruited upon my appointment was, I think, Sue but I have to apologise for being unsure of her name, and entirely forgetting her surname. Upon her departure Lynne joined me from BBC Radio Brighton. Lynne was very sports minded and during her tenure she met and teamed up with one of the League's Referees, Alun Tucker. They married and subsequently moved away, towards East Anglia, if my memory serves me correctly, where Alun became an Undertaker. The third Assistant cum Secretary to work with me also came with a Radio Brighton connection. Janet Brackley was the wife of Peter, the station's Sports Editor.

I had met Peter briefly during my days with Horsham FC, when the station covered the County's senior football clubs, in particular the Sussex Senior Cup Finals. I was now to meet the broadcaster on a regular and frequent basis. BBC Radio Brighton, which became Radio Sussex and thereafter Three Counties Radio, featured a 30 minute programme called 'Sunday Soccer' every Monday. Being the largest Competition in the County in terms of the number of teams, indeed the largest League in the Country we understood, coverage of The Sussex Sunday League occupied most of the airtime. Peter was assisted on the programme by Stephen Rooke, a journalist on the Worthing Gazette & Herald as well as being the club secretary at Worthing FC and a Referee. I supplied information for the programme every week and 'appeared' on-air at least fortnightly, to provide stories and updates relating to clubs and players. Occasionally, I was invited to read the results, alternating the Divisions with Peter & Stephen, and sometimes Neil Coppendale. Whilst I enjoyed this new role, I guessed I wasn't too good at it when Stephen suggested they could find me a permanent job in broadcasting – but it would be *"with the other side."* Obviously this conversation was just banter. The Station relied on volunteer contributors like me; Stephen was supplementing his journalistic work; but Peter was the consummate professional in the early days of a budding career. He was a coy fellow, not naturally outgoing or over confident, until that is, the red light outside the studio went on signalling 'on-air'. It was literally a light bulb moment – Peter came alive, fidgeting in his seat as he enthusiastically gave his listeners all the latest news on whatever sporting story he had prepared.

As well as his own broadcasting Peter was also responsible for programming and ensuring all the County's sporting events were covered. So Saturdays were always extremely busy. And this is where Peter excelled. After a morning of regular bulletins to update sports enthusiasts with the latest news, assisted by a team of volunteers, he orchestrated a programme throughout the entire afternoon covering the live action of whatever sport and/or event was occurring in Sussex. Peter was in his element. And the extent of his professionalism and will to always do well was evidenced at the end of one particular programme.

These exhausting afternoons always concluded with a thirst quenching adjournment at a nearby pub, The Volunteer, I think. On one such occasion Peter overhead his two voluntary Rugby reporters discussing the events of the afternoon with one, for example, saying, *"Was it Billy Bloggins?" "No."* came the reply. *"Was it Wally Woods?" "No"* again. Peter's curiosity was piqued. *"What are you doing?"*, Peter asked harmlessly. He was given a response in equal sinless innocence, oblivious to any concern it may cause the professional broadcaster. The two volunteers took it in turns each week to share the tasks of compiling and reading the report on air. Whoever compiled the report inserted a fictitious name and whoever read the report, on air, had to guess who was the rogue insert. Peter hit the roof metaphorically, and verbally. *"Don't worry, Pete"* his colleagues replied, *"we have done it each week for the past two seasons and nobody has ever complained, queried or corrected us!"*

Elements of the job, as highlighted above, were great fun – not really like work at all. But with over 260 teams to manage and control in 22 Divisions covering virtually the whole of the county, the demands on my time were immense. I was in the Office full-time each day from Sunday to Friday and half day on Saturday. Not even these hours met all the demands, the phone at home was rarely quiet in the evenings. Sundays were always the most demanding. I needed to be at the Queens Square HQ by at least 8.00am; even earlier on days when the weather was unkind. But I was working in my hobby. I was lucky.

There was little time for me to continue a playing career but I occasionally turned out for Newick Rangers on a Sunday morning before racing back to the Office to take the scores of all the other matches. Clubs had until 5pm to report the result of their match, after which I would update the League tables and prepare any fixture changes for the following weekend's programme. Where necessary I would also book the pitches with the local authorities for the following weekend before driving home after a long day.

Upon completion of my first season, feeling comfortable I could manage the job, I allowed myself to be persuaded by Dave Hutchings to join him playing for Steyning Town in the Sussex County League Second Division. Saturday afternoon was the only time I had for myself so with family support, and a large degree of selfishness, I agreed.

The Manager was Ray McCarthy, a former player I knew from my time with Newick Rangers. Ray had a good knowledge of the game for which he was well respected. His warm outgoing personality had won him many friends and had built him an inexhaustible supply of contacts. He used these assets to assemble a formidable group of players, none I had played with before, except Hutch, and only some I knew of. Ray then used his own skills and made us into a decent team.

A pair of the best locally known players were two of the Watts brothers, from Whitehawk. I had previously played against eldest brother Dicky, no

Ron puts on the frighteners

SUNDAY SOCCER — By Jamie Baker

THE SECRET of Newick Rangers' success over the years is finally out, and it's all down to their hard - hitting manager, Ron Eastwood.

Nicknamed Ron Who? after an article in this column last season, which suggested he was one of the least - known managers in Sussex soccer, Eastwood is probably the longest serving and certainly the most successful.

He is now in his 17th season with the club he has cultivated and inspired to great things year after year and been responsible for hitting the headlines.

It has taken 17 years for the bruising truth behind the success story to be revealed. In a week when Rangers smashed last year's premier division champions, Whitehawk Martlets, 6-1, the secret is out.

Apparently, it's all down to fear. The players just dare not lose, or heavyweight Ron dishes out the punishment in no uncertain terms.

"If we're not winning in the last five minutes, the players are scared stiff to come off the pitch," one ex-player told me.

The boss has been known to lay into the most hefty of centre halves and get away with it.

Newick's latest success was quite a shock, considering Rangers fielded three reserves and are still missing the services of suspended midfielders Steve Ibbitson and Bruce Aitken.

But it was no surprise to Ron. "We've been threatening to do this to Martlets for a long time. Don't take anything away from us. They had a good side out," he said.

The men who fired Rangers to victory were Davie Harding, Pip Harris and one of the reserves, Dave Thacker, who all scored two apiece. Thacker also put through his own net for Martlets' reply.

Chances still went begging for Rangers, however, and the culprits had to face the manager, who dished out fines. "They can't get away with it. I catch them some way. I fine them. It all helps club funds," he said.

Indeed, if you turn up at the team's headquarters at the Rosehill Tavern, you get fined. Why? "Because you should have come before," explains Ron.

Eastwood reckons the team's new pitch at Waterhall is responsible for the good results recently.

"It's probably one of the best pitches in the county. It certainly helped us and gave us all the room we wanted to play football," he added.

Newick are now four points clear at the top, having dropped just one point in seven starts.

Newly - promoted Snipe are second, but they let slip their first point of the season after drawing 2-2 against Brighton Ramblers.

It was an ex-Snipe player who stopped their 100 per cent run, Dave Stevens scoring both Ramblers' goals. Snipe had Graham Bailey (penalty) and Kevin Murray to thank for their point.

Martlets are now in third place with seven points from as many games.

St. George won 1-0 against Whitehawk Athletic, the only goal coming in the last minute through an own goal by Micky Packham.

Crawley Traders gained their first point of the season in a 1-1 draw at home to Hangleton, Steve Welch getting the all-important goal.

Last year's runners-up, Alpine Rovers, were held to a 3-3 draw by PDWT. Alpine's goals came from John Patten, Alex Siveyer and an own goal.

Ron Eastwood (Manager of Newick Rangers FC) probably the most successful Manager in the history of the Sussex Sunday Football League.

longer playing, and second eldest, Dixie. I had not previously made Dixie's acquaintance as a team mate, nor that of youngest brother Stevie. I was surprised neither had ever tested their abilities at a level higher than the County League. Stevie was a tenacious midfielder who never recognised when the ball, or a game, was lost. Dixie was a natural goal scorer who possessed exceptional skills. From my position at the back Dixie was a joy to watch and I remained astounded he never attracted the attention of clubs further up the football pyramid. Any good Coach would have found him a joy to work with, and I am convinced Dixie would have been successful. He was good to play with and was certainly successful in the 1978/79 season for Steyning Town FC.

With Ray's commitment to attack, and Dixie & Hutch's obsession to get goals, we needed to be strong at the back. We were well served by Goalkeeper Keith Cheal. Keith was a superb shot stopper with a safe and solid pair of hands. I would wager 10p on him in any one-on-one situation. We had a contrasting pair at full-back. On the left side Phil Turner was strong and steady; not the quickest perhaps but rarely beaten by anyone prepared to challenge him. At a late stage of the season Phil sustained a very nasty leg injury that forced him to wear a calliper as part of his recuperation. I have seen him since and I am pleased to say he returned to playing having made a perfect recovery. Thank goodness. Our other full-back was, and I say this with the utmost respect, the most unlikely looking footballer I have ever met. But John Ansbro's rag-tag appearance belied an efficient effectiveness that annulled any

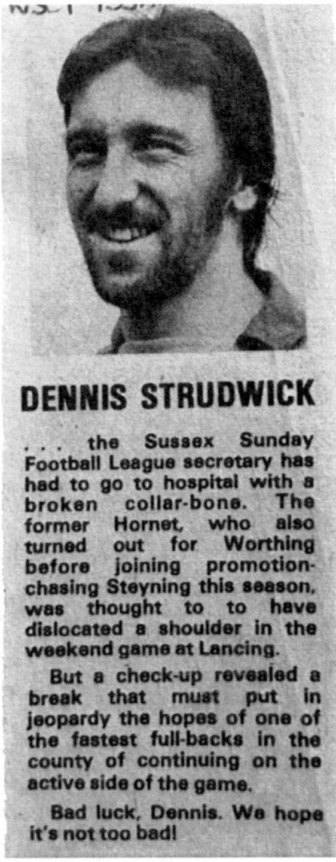

DENNIS STRUDWICK

. . . the Sussex Sunday Football League secretary has had to go to hospital with a broken collar-bone. The former Hornet, who also turned out for Worthing before joining promotion-chasing Steyning this season, was thought to to have dislocated a shoulder in the weekend game at Lancing.

But a check-up revealed a break that must put in jeopardy the hopes of one of the fastest full-backs in the county of continuing on the active side of the game.

Bad luck, Dennis. We hope it's not too bad!

attack from our opponents' left side. Our midfield was held together by 'steady as a rock' Butch Reeves, who was probably slower than Phil Turner, but rarely outmanoeuvred. As for our own attack, Hutch and Dixie were well supported by Jimmy Collins. These three were a thorn in the side of any defence and chased lost causes all over the pitch to create chances. A loss of concentration in the opponents defence was often fatal for it.

Obviously I have not remembered all of the team. I hope I will be forgiven for not recalling them all, particularly as, collectively we were good enough to win the League by a considerable margin and earn promotion to the County's top Division.

There's nothing like success to breed goodwill, and there was plenty of that around The Shooting Field, Steyning. I think it was the Club's first League Championship success. Everyone at the Club worked for each other and shared the responsibilities equally. Training under makeshift floodlights, albeit not good enough to stage a game under, was fun. In near darkness on the outer fringes of the playing area the ball often disappeared into the adjacent gardens. On one occasion the athletic Jimmy Collins boastfully hurdled the boundary hedge which formed the border between the Ground and a row of houses. Not realising the hedge was fortified by a wire fence in the middle he dragged one foot lower than the other and was brought down when in full flight. The sight was greeted with raucous laughter from about 20 witnesses and the image of Jimmy emerging from a cabbage patch, trying to appear as if nothing untoward had happened has not faded despite the intervening years. As for me, I was also the butt of the squad's sense of humour. Every Tuesday evening I was tested on how many Sussex Sunday League results I could remember from the previous weekend. With as many as 140 games each weekend it was quite a challenge but it was all good fun until the Manager's patience finally cracked as he tried to regain everyone's attention and shouted, *"Leave him alone!"*

My time at Steyning FC was happy, albeit comparatively brief. It unexpectedly extended my playing career by a further year and provided relief from an intense non-stop work schedule. Intense to the point of having callers at home, in person and/or telephone, often after a day's toil in Brighton. One club secretary, who I recall visiting my home, said he was happy to wait to see me while I finished a bit of household maintenance. I was painting fascia boards at the top of a ladder! He waited at the bottom!! But what the heck? I was working in my hobby; I had a commute through the Sussex countryside, followed by a fabulous view of the English Channel from the top of the South Downs, which is now a National Park. My Office was in beautiful Brighton, within walking distance from the beach, and I had a good team around me.

I also enjoyed the company, nearly every day, of sporting fanatic Martin Bodenham. Martin John Dale Bodenham, actually, but he never revealed the Dale bit otherwise I am sure he would have taken a bit of ribbing. Professionally, Martin worked for Prudential Insurance. Whatever his role was, it seemingly gave him a lot of down time. He frequented our Office most days and made himself useful by fulfilling any task we needed help with including making the tea. He was very good company. He was also engaged in a blossoming football officiating career. At the time I met him he was a Referee on the Football Combination, which comprised the Reserve teams of Football League Clubs, and soon to become a Linesman on The Football League. The journeys and commitment involved in fulfilling these appointments meant he was not often available to officiate in the Sunday League, but he did when called upon as he knew the League was short of Officials. In return I drove him to his matches on a couple of occasions and watched the game from a privileged seat as his guest. The first, one of Martin's first assignments as a Linesman, if not the first, was to Watford, a stadium I had not previously visited. Another, as 'Bodders' experience and stature grew, was to Highbury for an Arsenal v Southampton First Division fixture. And as well as affording me the opportunity to see a 'top' match the occasion provided me with a lasting moment. And please bear with me on this one; I am a total anorak where football is concerned!

During my spare time in Brighton I had frequented The Lanes, an area of quaint independent shops. On a visit to a tiny bookshop I found a copy of Kevin Keegan's first autobiography. I had a quick 'lunchtime' browse and found a couple of references to a 'Nobby' Ibbitson. Yes, my tenacious team mate at Horsham was known at Scunthorpe as 'Nobby'. KK recalled a night out when, as apprentices, the pair camped out and found themselves the next morning to be in the centre of an island in the middle of a road. In another tale the twosome were joined by another apprentice and they constructed an obstacle course amongst the materials & machinery on an area of construction work at the Club's ground. They each took it in turns to drive the contractor's dumper truck around their makeshift course to see who could do it the quickest. KK won the event but wrote off the dumper truck at the same time when he crashed over the finishing line.

Anyway, having chauffeured Martin to Highbury in good time I waited inside the Stadium's main 'Marble Hall' entrance. After a short while the coach transporting Southampton FC pulled up in the road outside and the players hurried into the Stadium. As they sped by I spontaneously called out, *"Mr Keegan, Nobby Ibbitson sends his regards."* KK stopped, looked around, and asked *"Who said that?" "I did",* I replied. We had a brief conversation during which I explained how I knew 'Nobby' and KK's last words before disappearing towards the dressing rooms were, *"Tell him to contact me. He was my best mate."*

I told 'Ibbo' of my brief encounter and passed on Mr Keegan's message. I also mentioned KK's book and the story about racing a dumper truck around an improvised race track. Steve was amused and said, *"I'll tell you how that story finished."* Steve regaled as follows.

Club Manager Ron Ashman called all three into his office. He gave them a collective rollocking and then proceeded to address them individually. Steve mentioned the name of his other 'partner in crime', but sorry I've forgotten it, but for the sake of the story I will call him Harry. The Manager appraised Harry's skills and told him what he was good at, adding words to the effect he could make a living in the game. Steve advised, Harry is now driving buses in Huddersfield, or similar. Steve/Nobby was next in the Manager's sights. You pass the ball well, you are strong in the tackle and good in the air, for your 5'6" height. You too, will do well in the game. Steve ended up playing with me at Horsham. Mr Ashman then turned to Kevin Keegan and, making reference to a well worn phrase about a backside and an orifice said, *"You'll never make it all the while you have..."* I can only imagine KK did something about that orifice to have enabled such a glittering career.

As for Martin, it wasn't long before he attained promotion to the 'middle' of the Football League, in 1978. He was subsequently selected by the Premier League for its Referees' List when it was formed in 1992. During his time at the top of the Match Officials' tree he was 4th Official at the 1974 European Cup Final in which AC Milan defeated Barcelona 4-0. Three years later he refereed the League Cup Final in 1997 at Wembley between Leicester City and Middlesbrough. The game was drawn so he got a second bite of the Final cherry in a replay at Hillsborough. He refereed two FA Cup Semi-Finals before retiring in 1998. He then pursued what I believed to be his 'first love', cricket. He became an Umpire and made his way to the County Cricket list of Officials to become, in 2009, the first person to officiate at the highest level of football and First Class cricket. That's one heck of an achievement, and career. I am delighted he shared a few of the early days with me.

Back at Queen Square, Brighton, Jan Brackley was more animated than usual when she came into work one day and said Peter had landed a three month secondment at the BBC National Network on Radio 2. There was no indication this was an audition for a permanent assignment but we all tuned in, particularly on a Tuesday evening, when Peter hosted and evening of football. With stories coming in from all parts of the globe, from every sport imaginable while featuring live coverage of a top game, concentration levels needed to be at their highest. Peter explained, whilst monitoring everything happening around him he received instructions from the Producer in one earpiece and heard what was being broadcast in the other ear. It was hardly surprising, therefore, when winding up a programme one evening, Peter became tongue-tied when a late result was fed into his ear. Amongst a reprise of the evening's events and issuing thanks to all who had contributed Peter reported, " I have a late result from Scotland. East Four five – Far Five four. No, sorry, East Fife five – Forfar four. No, pardon me, East Fife four – Forfar five. Goodnight!"

Peter returned to Radio Brighton having made his presence felt and better for the experience. I felt this first secondment was a test; another opportunity would arise, and Peter would be successful. And so it proved. But in the meantime, Peter surprised us all. Despite being of a quiet disposition, unbeknown to any of us, Peter had built an inner library of mimicked voices from the interviews he had conducted with various sporting personalities. So one evening, unannounced to everyone, except Janet I suspect, Peter entered a talent contest at Butlins Hotel at Saltdean. Armed with only a few props, e.g. a towel and a cap to enhance the sound of Henry Cooper's voice, he won the contest. This led to him receiving several commercial offers. He was that good. But his head was not turned. He was a superb broadcaster. He continued on the radio before moving into television with ITV, Channel 4 & Football Italia and Sky. 'Brackers' covered 20 plus FA Cup Finals, European Competitions and World Cups while continuing to write a weekly article on his favourite club, Brighton & Hove Albion, in the Evening Argus. Sadly, he fell seriously ill and passed away prematurely due to a heart attack in October 2018, aged 67. He was pre-deceased by his wife Janet. Two immensely popular people who populated my career in a lovely way.

The stature and growth of Sunday football in Sussex continued apace. The League's relationship with the County FA was sound and with two or three Clubs, including Newick Rangers, entering the National Sunday Cup the Competition was becoming known at Lancaster Gate. I felt things were progressing sufficiently well, at least well enough for me to respond to an advertisement in early 1979 for a League Secretary at a new Competition called The Alliance League. I received short shrift. In a staggeringly blunt letter from the League Chairman Jim Thompson, also Chairman of Maidstone United FC, I was told my application fell short of the high standard expected for this prestigious position. Although Mr Thompson put it less kindly. After the shock of receiving such a terse response Mr Thompson's letter went straight in the bin. I dwelt only on the thought, Mr. Thompson had never been tutored by John Kendall. Little did I know at the time, we were to meet frequently several years later, and I would get a second bite at this "prestigious" cherry.

By the start of the 1980/1981 season membership of the Sunday League had risen to just over 220 clubs. With reserve teams and, in some cases, a third team that meant the League comprised 297 teams in 22 its Divisions. The Competition at its peak was, in terms of membership numbers, the largest in the Country. But something, and I am not sure what it was, made me call it a day at the end of the campaign. Maybe, after five years, I saw no visible career path along this preferred route. Whatever, I just decided it was time to change. Looking back, it was a 'poor choice' decision to give up a job in my hobby, and a role I certainly loved. I would surely come to miss it and perhaps I would not get another chance to work in football.

I returned to accountancy, with Horsham Building Society. The Society's Secretary was Rod Taylor. Rod was a Committee Member, and Treasurer, of Horsham Football Club (HFC). That association certainly helped me settle into my new position, along with helpful mortgage terms and the lack of any necessity to commute. It was three miles from my home in Southwater to Horsham. What could I possibly do with the extra time I suddenly found on my hands? I returned to Queen Street to help take the training at HFC!

Taking the training also embraced assisting with the management of the Reserve team. The arrangement was helpful to me in respect of keeping fit and guiding young players at the beginning of their careers. It was satisfying to monitor the progress of some players and push them in front of the First team Manager with a recommendation for selection. I saw the Reserve team's major role was to create and supply players to the First Team. In the first few months of the season, with First team results being indifferent, eleven players were given their debuts in the First XI. They were 'on their way' in senior football. On the other hand, the Reserve team's role was also to accommodate and rejuvenate 'off form' or 'out of favour' players. Whilst not being any less satisfying, if successful, the role had an alternative aspect that had to be dealt with, i.e. the player discontented at not being in the front side. In one particular instance I asked one such player, disillusioned at being 'dropped' by the First team Manager, to sit and help me on the bench for a forthcoming midweek Reserve fixture. He was not in a good frame of mind to play; besides, I already knew of his capabilities. I was surprised by the instant and unexpected response. *"I would rather watch Coronation Street."* After suggesting he might want to consider watching each week, I never saw him again. Maybe I was a little harsh, but I believe in the saying, *"When the going gets tough, the tough get going."* And with a bunch of youngsters playing their hearts out trying to achieve a First team place I didn't want anyone in the group likely to adversely affect the performance of others. Coupled with commitment it was essential for everyone to pull their weight, and preferably all in the same direction.

One other thing slightly troubled me. I had not played at Isthmian League level for five years, and apart from one season at Steyning, I had not played regularly at any level for three years. Despite this lack of serious game time I ended up in Horsham's First team. By 1st December I had played five matches and had been selected as a substitute twice. I was not convinced I had maintained my standard of play that well. The additional unexpected games did, though, afford me the opportunity to play with Marvin Hinton who had joined Horsham during my absence. Marvin had commenced his career with Charlton Athletic before being transferred to Chelsea where he won the League Cup and the FA Cup amongst his 344 appearances for the Blues. Again, I was lucky and privileged to have played with such an accomplished player. Marvin was a top guy, too. Sadly, this team picture was taken the week before he joined.

My final team picture.

Back row left to right:- Peter Beaney (Physio), John Laker (Manager), Micky Fountain, Tommy Barden, Stuart Heywood, Gary Elphick, Stuart Reed, Mark Tidy, DJS, Fred Stenning (Assistant Manager).

Front row:- Ricky Holder, Martin South, Tony Bollingbroke, Dave Harding, Martin Elliot, Lee Mobsby, Paul Toms, Glen Geard.

Part Two – The Southern Football League 1982-2007

Just a few weeks prior to the fixtures referred to above, about the beginning of November (1981) I had either been alerted to, or I spotted, a newspaper advertisement inviting applications to become the Secretary of the Southern Football League. It was only a part-time position but if I was to get back into the football industry it was an opportunity I couldn't afford to miss. Although much maligned by 'Isthmians' the Southern League was acknowledged as a highly regarded football competition comprising professional Clubs and players. It had, during its long history, supplied many clubs to the Football League, indeed, more than any other Competition. Member Clubs covered the whole of the South & Midlands ranging from Dover and Folkestone to Merthyr Tydfil and Barry Town as well as Gosport and Salisbury to Nuneaton and Kidderminster. The likes of Bedford, Cambridge, Witney and Cheltenham filled in the middle. The task looked big. So I began by researching who and what I needed to know about the Competition and who, within my range of contacts, could brief me on the personnel I was likely to meet. I discovered the League's current Secretary, Bill Dellow, was a former Referee. I also discovered he was a very hard taskmaster, a strict disciplinarian. So among those I contacted first was the Sussex FA Referees' Secretary, Sid Vicars, also a former Referee, from the same era. Sid was a huge help and unbeknown to me at the time he submitted a reference on my behalf. In the meantime, I consulted Rod Taylor about my plans and, helpfully, received his approval and co-operation. So, as soon as I was ready, I drafted my letter of application and posted it with my CV to arrive two days before the closing date. The next two weeks were tense but a letter eventually arrived. I was asked to attend an interview at the Heathrow Holiday Inn, adjacent to junction 4 of the M4, an uplift to what I had been accustomed to.

I was vaguely familiar with the area having played at several west London clubs, so I found the venue in good time. But that is where my 'comfort zone' ended. The Hotel was enormous and very busy. I felt like a grain of sand. I am not sure how many applicants were interviewed but I was to learn the League received 85 applications. When my turn came I met a sub-Committee formed to make the appointment to succeed Bill Dellow following his imminent retirement after 26 years service. I quickly realised Bill was leaving some big shoes for his successor to wear. As well as being Secretary, Bill had also been Treasurer for the past 11 years. The sub-Committee comprised David Setterfield (Chairman); Dick Etheridge (Vice-Chairman); Derek Sharp (Director) and Bill.

Like all such nervous first meetings, coupled with the passing of 40 odd years, I cannot recall any finite detail of our discussion. No doubt my time and involvement in football was close to the top of the agenda along with the financial 'safe hands' security provided by my accountancy training. One week later I received notice I had reached a short list and was required to attend a second interview, this time at The Cafe Royal, Regent Street, London. Bloody Hell!! This is a place I had only seen on the television. A venue frequented by Oscar Wilde and Winston Churchill. If only my Father could see me now. He had passed away almost a year ago to the day. But I knew he was watching as I climbed the steps and pushed my way through the revolving doors.

Upon arrival I was encouraged to find the competition was not vast, not in numbers, anyway. There was just one other candidate. The other contender, though, was a seriously high calibre person and existing football administrator – Peter Hough, the Secretary of the Dorset County FA. We met and wished each other luck. Peter was called first. When my turn came I was unaware, whether or not, Peter had left the building. After nervously doing my best, in front of the full Board, I thanked the Directors and bade farewell. As I reached the meeting room exit door I was joined by the Chairman, to 'see me off the premises' so to speak, I presumed. Instead, Mr Setterfield said, *"Would you like to stay for lunch."* It was a moment I have clearly not forgotten. I believed it was a signal I had made it. And I felt elated; so elated I crossed Regent Street and spent £50 on a new maroon leather brief case that had brass like reinforcement on all its corners. After coming down to earth I quickly realised the shortest serving Secretary had 'reigned' for 12 years. The big shoes I was about to fill just got a bit bigger.

I now had a lot to think about. How could I accommodate my new role within my full-time job? I had a lot to learn about how the League was organised and exactly what the full working itinerary comprised. A

Job Description was one thing; the reality of the role was something else. Furthermore, I was expected to work from home meaning a few adjustments were required, e.g. the loss of, and the adoption of, a spare bedroom. I was determined to make it happen. I was back in the game. And at a professional level, too. I did not underestimate the luck I had been bequeathed. There was, though, one sacrifice I had to make.

New man in 'hot seat'

League appoint Bill's successor

It's nostalgia time for Secretary Bill Dellow and the Southern League.

For he has just entered his last month as Southern league Secretary — and at the end of April his long and illustrious reign will be over.

Stepping into his shoes will be Dennis Strudwick, who was chosen from a staggering amount of 85 applicants.

However, Bill Dellow, who has done a magnificent job for the league over the last 27 years as Secretary will not be stepping out of the spotlight completely.

"I will carry on as Chief Executive, and will still be the treasurer," explained the Southern League "legend".

"So I won't be cutting all my ties with the League. But it is time a younger man took on the role of Secretary," continued Dellow.

It took the League several meetings to finally choose the new man to step into the hot seat.

"There is no doubt about it, it is a popular job," explained Dellow. "But I am sure the new man will do well."

Strudwick, has a difficult task, following in the footsteps of Dellow.

However, he proved himself to be a top class administrator in the Sussex Sunday league where he was general secretary, and has also been a more than useful player in the past.

"It is a complex and difficult job to do, and I will be only too willing to pass on any advice I can," concluded Dellow.

SOUTHERN LEAGUE NEWS | SOUTHERN LEAGUE NEWS | SOUTHERN LEAGUE NEWS

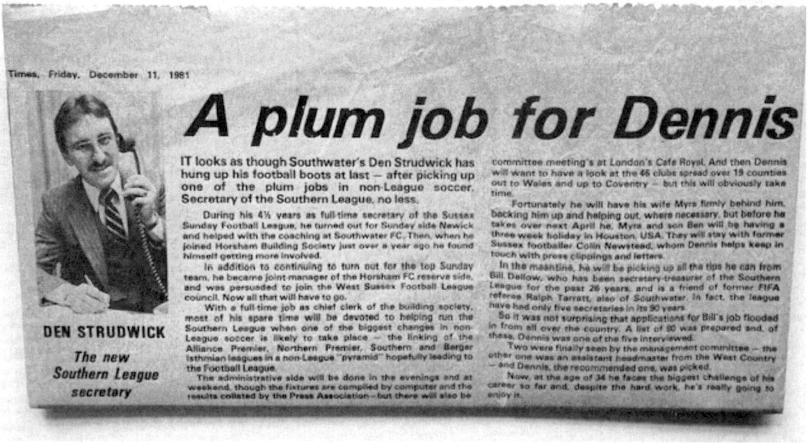

Times, Friday, December 11, 1981

A plum job for Dennis

DEN STRUDWICK

The new Southern League secretary

IT looks as though Southwater's Den Strudwick has hung up his football boots at last – after picking up one of the plum jobs in non-League soccer, Secretary of the Southern League, no less.

During his 4½ years as full-time secretary of the Sussex Sunday Football League, he turned out for Sunday side Newick and helped with the coaching at Southwater FC. Then, when he joined Horsham Building Society just over a year ago he found himself getting more involved.

In addition to continuing to turn out for the top Sunday team, he became joint-manager of the Horsham FC reserve side, and was persuaded to join the West Sussex Football League council. Now all that will have to go.

With a full-time job as chief clerk of the building society, most of his spare time will be devoted to helping run the Southern League when one of the biggest changes in non-League soccer is likely to take place – the linking of the Alliance Premier, Northern Premier, Southern and Berger Isthmian leagues in a non-League "pyramid" hopefully leading to the Football League.

The administrative side will be done in the evenings and at weekend, though the fixtures are compiled by computer and the results collated by the Press Association – but there will also be committee meeting's at London's Cafe Royal. And then Dennis will want to have a look at the 46 clubs spread over 19 counties out to Wales and up to Coventry – but this will obviously take time.

Fortunately he will have his wife Myra firmly behind him, backing him up and helping out, where necessary, but before he takes over next April he, Myra and son Ben will be having a three week holiday in Houston, USA. They will stay with former Sussex footballer Colin Newstead, whom Dennis helps keep in touch with press clippings and letters.

In the meantime, he will be picking up all the tips he can from Bill Dellow, who has been secretary-treasurer of the Southern League for the past 26 years, and is a friend of former FIFA referee Ralph Tarratt, also of Southwater. In fact, the league have had only five secretaries in its 90 years.

So it was not surprising that applications for Bill's job flooded in from all over the country. A list of 80 was prepared and, of these, Dennis was one of the five interviewed.

Two were finally seen by the management committee – the other one was an assistant headmaster from the West Country – and Dennis, the recommended one, was picked.

Now, at the age of 34 he faces the biggest challenge of his career so far and, despite the hard work, he's really going to enjoy it.

I had to relinquish my position with Horsham FC; I had played my final match for my home town Club. Twice each week, until the end of March, my evenings were spent at Bill Dellow's house in Reigate learning how he had run the Southern League for the past 26 years. In one early meeting Bill demonstrated his style. Upon arrival he asked me to wait while he replaced a Referee on a match the following evening. He dialled the number of his chosen Match Official, Ken Leach. *"Leach?"* said Bill. *"Bilston tomorrow, 7.30 kick-off."* The phone crashed down, leaving Ken to get his kit prepared. Bill's modus operandi was, if the Match Official's availability was open absolutely no excuse not to fulfil an appointment was acceptable. Needless to say, Ken Leach went to Bilston the following evening. Bill took no messing. He did not stand fools at all, let alone lightly. Ken knew the score. And I was to find he was one who knew you had to be committed at this level of the game. Ken was on his way to the Football League, like many others I came to work with. I was to find not everyone understood the rules and/or showed the required level of respect and/or commitment. Those who did, had a future – depending on ability. Those that did not could not expect to have a lasting career, unless they 'saw the light.'

My long evenings with Bill were punctuated by interruptions from his friendly wife, Laura, many of which were accompanied by tea and home made cake. Laura was a good cook but, to say she was also garrulous is an understatement. I found Bill's blunt call for Laura to be quiet, delivered as abruptly as he delivered his instruction to Ken Leach, embarrassing and awkward to deal with. But Laura was unperturbed. Despite Bill's bluster, Laura was the Boss in the house.

After a few weeks I met Bill's Assistant, Jimmy O'Brien. Rightly or wrongly I quickly formed the impression, Jim's background was in the Services. Everything he did was with military precision. His personal appearance was always immaculate and sharp; his record keeping unimpeachable; his hand writing was flawless; and his respect for Bill was beyond dutiful. As Bill wanted to pass to me one of Jim's biggest roles, i.e. the appointment of Linesmen to matches, I was concerned about how this would be received. I need not have worried. Jim accepted the handover in his stride, professional as always, prepared to help and share his experience. He was to become a huge ally to me and someone I could rely on for assistance. And I did just that, frequently.

I was also soon to meet another extraordinary fellow, and close associate of Bill's, a Mr F Jess-Lay, another with copper plate hand writing skills. I don't think I ever discovered what the 'F' stood for; he was know only as Jess. In these pre-digital days Jess was famous for his photographic artistry. What that entailed I am not wholly sure but I discovered much of his time was consumed by editing photographs, by hand. He was regularly, and frequently, called upon to adjust wedding photographs where an unsuspecting groom or prominent guest appeared with an open fly on his trousers and/or a bride whose bra-less gown revealed a little more than expected. One of his most difficult assignments, he told me, was to adjust the frontal appearance of a man wearing a bold checked suit who appeared overtly proud in the front row of his matrimonial pictures. He once told me agents acting on behalf of the Royals were amongst his clients.

Anyway, I was soon to discover these three wise men had established a Referees' Assessment Scheme, believed to be the first in world football, to help monitor the current and future progress of Match Officials. They also established the first known Match Officials' Association enabling Referees & Linesmen to meet regularly to discuss interests and issues that arose when officiating, and to meet socially. The Association's first Secretary was Jim Hill, a popular and successful Southern League Referee who was on the national list of Linesmen.

These people and their successors, the likes of Laurence Jones, Steve Tincknell, Dave Shadwell, Roger King and Mark Ives successfully nurtured the fine careers of colleagues e.g. Andre Marriner, Phil Sharp, Andy Woolmer, Keith Stroud, John Singh, Trevor Parkes, Simon Hooper and many more. As my role entailed selecting these fellows from football's junior Competitions and subsequently promoting them through the Southern League and making recommendations to The Football League, I am proud of their successes and pleased with the small part I played in their careers.

Another strong ally emerged unexpectedly from within the Southern League Board. I was to learn Doug Gillard, a League Director, also applied for the Secretary's role. When advised at a subsequent Board meeting he had not been successful I understand Doug's disappointment manifested itself into a few tears. But I need not have worried about any animosity Doug might harbour for Bill's successor. Doug proved to be my biggest supporter, along with his wife Pat. They were both particularly helpful during some difficult personal times. And Doug proved to be a strong and great leader. Another meticulous man with honesty and integrity at the top of his agenda.

As the 1981/82 season drew to a close, and my official start date of 1st April approached, I managed to take in a couple of matches amongst Bill's training sessions. At this point the League comprised of two Divisions, South and Midlands and a part of my job was to manage the transition of the Competition into three Divisions, a Premier and South and Midlands. So I went to see two of the teams most likely to gain a place in the newly formed Premier Division, i.e. Wealdstone v Fareham Town. Wealdstone were running away with the Southern Division; they had an exceptional team. Up front they had the Cordice brothers, Alan & Neil, who were consistent scorers. Alan was quick enough to catch pigeons for a hobby. In the defence Paul Bowgett and Dennis Byatt were rocks. At full-back they had a player whose style, my conceit tells me, had a slight resemblance of me. He was aggressive; strong in the tackle; quick to see any opportunity to attack; and was not without pace, especially when getting back to defend. But there, any vague similarity with me ended. This lad became a great player; captain of England! It was Stuart Pearce. Wow! I was taking charge of a seriously strong competition.

The clamour was on to finish in the top eleven of each Division enabling the formation of the new Premier Division, comprising 22 clubs. Interest was so great a match during February at Bedworth, against Nuneaton, attracted a crowd of 5,127. At the end of the season Wealdstone won the Southern Division by a single point from Hastings United and were promoted to the Alliance League. They were accompanied by Nuneaton

Borough, winners of the Midland Division ahead of Alvechurch. 'Church then sold their top scorer, Alan Smith to Leicester City for a fee of £15,000. Smith joined Gary Lineker in the Foxes front line. Thereafter, it was full steam ahead into the 1982/83 season, my first in the hot seat, alone.

The Competition had reverted to three Divisions with an overall membership of 65 Clubs; the top ten in each of the previous seasons regional Divisions were accompanied by two clubs relegated from the Alliance League to form a top Division of 22. This enabled a definitive Champion Club to be crowned. The remaining balance of Clubs, along with several new members, formed two regional Divisions, as before. The first Champion Club of the new era was AP Leamington. After a shaky start Manager Graham Alner's 'Motormen', with two 'stand-out' players, Kim Casey and Graham Mackenzie, finished three points above Kidderminster Harriers. But it was the Harriers who were promoted as Leamington's 'Windmill' ground fell short of the grading criteria. This decision came as a huge surprise. AP Leamington FC was a founder member of the Alliance when it was created just four years before. To discover the Ground was not now acceptable was a shock.

In the Regional Divisions, like a breath of fresh air, newcomers made an instant impact. Sutton Coldfield Town, newly promoted from the West Midlands Regional League, finished second in the Midland section and joined Cheltenham Town in winning promotion. In the South, newly promoted Fisher Athletic finished as Champions and were promoted along with second placed Folkestone.

A black cloud descended upon the League early in the 1983/84 season. Bill Dellow passed away on the 8th November, aged 73. I was to discover Bill had received an unwanted diagnosis concerning his health back in 1981. He bravely acknowledged it was time to stand down, and thinking of the League, prepared the trail for his successor. I visited him in Redhill hospital during his final weeks and his last words to me were, *"Is everything alright boy?"* I assured him it was.

As the season progressed I was re-acquainted with an old adversary, John Still. John had left Leytonstone/Ilford to take over at Dartford. The 'wise owl' built a sterling side and won the League at his first attempt, losing only 6 of their 38 fixture programme. But they were only 3 points ahead of Fisher Athletic who had continued their progress up the football pyramid whilst gaining a notable reputation for treating their guests like royalty, at the new Surrey Dock Stadium.

There was a surprise winner of the Midland Division, in Willenhall Town, who scored 100 goals in the League campaign, and finished 5 points above Shepshed Charterhouse. The South was won by a team that joined the League from Sunday football only the previous season, RS Southampton. They topped the table by 9 clear points, above a Crawley Town team managed by my good friends, and former opponents, John Maggs and Dave Haining. The Newtowners goalkeeper was a former team mate of mine, Ricky Collier, aka Shirley, because of a mop of curly blond hair that resembled Shirley Temple.

As if to emphasis the impact and importance of the League I had joined as chief administrator, it is worthy of note, Alvechurch sold yet another forward, David Kelly to Walsall. Kelly was subsequently transferred to West Ham United and Newcastle United and became an Eire international. And Fareham Town sold David Leworthy to Tottenham Hotspur for a club record fee of £51,000. The League was full of talent.

My third season in the 'hot seat' was eventful, but not all recollections necessarily made my life any easier. On the contrary, in fact. Juggling full-time employment with the Horsham Building Society which joined in a 'Transfer of Engagements', a merger by any other name, with Bradford & Bingley became a little harder as my role changed with the new masters. I was appointed Assistant Manager of the Horsham Branch. My accountancy responsibilities were exchanged for day-to-day interfacing with the general public, talking about investments and mortgages. Far less invigorating and/or stimulating than my existence in the football world.

The 1984/85 season began with a change of name for the League Cup to The Bill Dellow Cup, in order to remember the long serving Secretary. I was dealt a significant headache when compiling the fixture list. Aylesbury United, in the Midland Division, declared it had to vacate its Turnfurlong Lane Ground, the Club's home since 1935, by mid-February. This meant its final eleven games were all 'away' as its new venue would not be completed. The same situation prevailed all season at Cambridge City, in the Southern Division. Cambridge was obliged to play all their matches away as the pitch at their new stadium was not ready. Hillingdon faced similar tenancy problems. The Club's season seemed to bounce from one crisis to another during a period of uncertainty about being able to continue life at The Leas Ground. And despite building a credible promotion challenge it was clear at the beginning of April the club's already 'borrowed time' on its tenure would not be extended. Hillingdon's last game at home, against Chatham Town, ended in a 1-0 defeat and their promotion hopes went 'kaput' too.

There were no such problems in the Premier Division, not visibly, anyway. The season climaxed like no other I had experienced so far in my career. With three weeks to go three points covered the top nine Clubs. There seemed to be no prospect of being able to be in the right place at the right time with the trophy and medals, not with any certainty anyway. As the games were ticked off Cheltenham began to emerge from the pack. I took a chance one Saturday and loaded the car with the spoils of a Championship victory and hid in the crowd. Unfortunately for me, compared with other scores in the Division, The Robins' result did not prove decisive. I had to leave the ground under the gate, metaphorically speaking, hoping my presence had not been noticed. I cautiously re-appeared a fortnight later for Cheltenham's home match against Alvechurch. As 'Church had Directors Don Pedley and Brian Nevett on the Southern League Committee, I could not hide. But Cheltenham won 2-1 and took the Championship, along with the enormous shield and medals, with it. Job done at the second attempt.

But the drama was not over for Cheltenham. The Alliance League, as it was known in those days, rejected the Club's application because of a shortfall in the Ground Grading criteria. The Alliance delegation decided the club's Wadden Road Ground was not up to scratch; a decision that would have saved Worcester City from relegation from The Alliance. As I recall it, however, Worcester City's Chairman, Gerald Turner, was on the Alliance's Inspection Committee, sent to assess The Robins' suitability for the Alliance League. Whilst casting no assertions upon Mr. Turner, his presence at the inspection was a startling and obvious conflict of interest. So, on Cheltenham's behalf, the Southern League lodged an Appeal against the decision in support of its Champion club. The Appeal was upheld by the Football Association and Cheltenham Town FC was promoted.

Several new clubs continued to make their mark elsewhere in the Competition. Willenhall Town and RS Southampton, for example, finished in 4th & 5th positions respectively. Fisher Athletic, aka 'The Fish', continued to stamp their authority on the League. Although finishing only 8th in the Division they won the inaugural Bill Dellow Cup, defeating League Champions Cheltenham 6-2 in a two-legged final. And this, despite losing last season's top scorer, Paul Shinners, to Gillingham. The Fish then joined King's Lynn on a trip to Italy to play in the Anglo-Italian Cup, an annual four team tournament originally arranged by Bill Dellow and his friend Luigi (Gigi) Peronace. Bill had made friends in high places. Gigi, an Italian Football Agent had, in his working life, brokered the deals that took John Charles, Denis Law, Joe Baker and Jimmy Greaves to Italy. The Fish and the Linnets lost to their Italian opponents, Pescara and Teramo, leaving the Southern League clubs to play for third place. Fisher won the play-off. The memory of my first trip to Italy is still very pleasing but it was not without its difficulties. The cultural difference between a club from the Capital and one from the Norfolk coast was marked; so significantly marked, my colleague on the sojourn, John Eastment, and I were forced to share our time between each club making sure they were always apart. In all other respects it was a wonderful trip. Our hosts' generosity and hospitality was excessive. For example, the Fisher boys who played in regular black & white stripped shirts decided upon arrival they wanted a new kit in the Juventus style. After all, we were in Italy. But it was Easter; the shops were shut. No problem said our hosts. By the end of the day a new kit was delivered and cash changed hands. But to Fisher's surprise and dismay the shirts were not numbered so the kit was returned. The following day, as we gathered at the stadium to prepare for the match, the same Fiat 500 we saw yesterday screeched into the car park, sending dust and shale everywhere. Almost before the car had stopped an excited gentleman jumped out with a basket full of Juventus style shirts – with numbers. A little more cash was handed over. I think it was this kind of financial flamboyance that was alien to King's Lynn. But all's well that ended well.

I believe that was the last Anglo-Italian Tournament for non-League clubs which was a shame. The Tournament had provided great opportunities for clubs and they were, in the main, happy occasions. On an earlier Anglo-Italian trip, couple of years before I joined the League, Bill Dellow and David Setterfield accompanied the clubs. I cannot remember who the clubs were on the occasion to which I now refer but football obviously came second to some of the travelling guests. Being in the home of the profiterole Bill & David decided to have a profiterole eating contest. Italian profiteroles are not the size of golf balls; they are at least the size of a baseball stuffed with cream and ice cream. With the score at 38 profiteroles each they agreed to call it a draw! Now, I love a profiterole but I feel ill imagining eating 38!!

Amid all the positivity of the cracking season just ended there was a negative. Chairman David Setterfield exceeded his authority by transferring some of the League's funds into a portfolio within the investment Company at which he worked; thereby compromising his position. The Committee called for David's resignation; its was given unhesitatingly. As Treasurer I, too, felt compromised. But I had no part in the transaction and there was no evidence to suggest otherwise. We all moved on, with Vice-Chairman John Eastment taking over the Chair. When the dust settled the investments proved to be remarkably successful. But I was hurt to have been placed in such an invidious position, and one that could have been damaging for me, personally. Conflict of interest had raised its ugly ahead again. I felt it was something I must be aware of at this level. Lessons were learnt.

Financial controls exercised by Leagues upon member Clubs, at this time, were few and far between. But alarm bells began to ring about the perilous condition of some members' fiscal state following the demise of Addlestone & Weybridge, Bridgwater Town and Milton Keynes. This meant no Club was relegated from the Competition's Regional Divisions at the end of the campaign. Then, in June, Hastings United surrendered its lease on the Pilot Field Ground, at the same time revealing debts amounting to £95,000. Through the Offices of the Joint Liaison Committee, a group comprising the Southern League's feeder competition, the Sussex County League allowed Hastings Town to fill United's place. There was an irony about this transaction. United had controversially secured the lease on the Pilot Field, from Town, when they were called Hastings & St. Leonards FC in 1948. What goes round comes round.

The 1985/86 season was remarkable for Welling United. Known as 'The Wings' the Club had been formed in 1963 by two brothers, Barrie & Graham Hobbins (Secretary and Manager, respectively), along with their father Syd. At that time the Club was a Youth set-up playing on Sundays. Development enabled a move to adult Saturday football playing in the London Spartan League. After a while, a few seasons in the Athenian League preceded election to the Southern League Southern Division. An 8th place finish at the end of 1981/82 won the Club a spot in the League's Premier Division following the re-structure of the Competition mentioned above. Welling United now won that Division by an astonishing 23 points, meaning promotion to the Alliance, now called the Gola League for sponsorship reasons, followed. The family Club remained there for 14 years.

Bromsgrove Rovers, managed by former West Bromwich Albion & Scotland midfielder Bobby Hope, won the Midland Division – 17 points ahead of Redditch United. And Cambridge City, now on their new pitch at its Milton Road Stadium, pipped Salisbury for the Southern title despite a fixture backlog caused by drainage problems. City had to cram in 17 games in the final six weeks of the season.

Following the building of a formal structure by The Football Association, to manage the movement of Clubs at the end of each season, eight Leagues were assembled beneath the Southern League from which clubs would be promoted from and/or relegated to at the end of each season. The process included an extension to the Ground Grading system to ensure player and spectator amenities were maintained to a good standard. The gradual increment of the standards at each level also ensured compliant clubs were always in reach of the League above, to enable promotion. The expansion of the Southern League meant quite a few clubs had already advanced, so following the demise of a few clubs, as evidenced above, greater pressure was put on the Feeder Leagues to provide clubs for elevation. Notwithstanding their angst at having more work to do, there was no shortage of clubs wanting to pursue their ambitions. Some had good credentials but not all clubs ticked all the required boxes. This occasionally made for difficult times.

I recall visiting Holbeach Town FC., accompanied by Doug Gillard, representing the League's Board. It was impossible to understand how its League considered the Ground worthy of recommendation for promotion. The 'Ground' was merely a pitch in the corner of a large park, not enclosed, at all. It was not fun to have to say, *"No."* to a club but it was the club's responsibility to ensure compliance with the document published by the FA on the required Ground Grading standards. It helped, too, if its League managed the club's expectations which wasn't the case in this example. At the end of a pointless visit, as we said our farewells, Doug and I were asked to advise the club it had nice Dressing Rooms! Our subsequent report, albeit negative, gave encouragement.

V.S. Rugby, on the other hand, were promoted in 1983 from the West Midlands Regional League (WMRL) as holders of the FA Vase. So when

Halesowen Town, the club they defeated at Wembley to win the Vase, won the WMRL I imagine it had a reasonable expectation it would follow VS Rugby into the Southern League. The club had been successful for a while and was clearly being well managed by its legendary former player, Treasurer, and now Secretary/Chairman, Harry Rudge. There were, however, several non-compliant issues regarding the Ground on which it had played since 1881, some of which could not be remedied quickly. For example, following inspection the Southern League described the playing surface as "undulating". To create a true surface on a level plane was more than a summer's work. So having had its application turned down Harry gathered around him a team of volunteers to tackle the task. And after a second application was rejected independent specialist advice was sought to ensure the pitch now qualified. It was, however, discovered that whilst the pitch remained slightly sloping end-to-end, and the surface flat & true, the playing area was shaped like a parallelogram to enable it to fit on the site. It was necessary to purchase a slice of land from a neighbouring garden to rectify the conundrum. I believe everyone was pleased and relieved when the club's fourth application for promotion in 1986 was successful. It was certainly not easy to say *"No"* to a club with such a high profile but looking back it is not unreasonable to believe the club would not have the Ground it has now had the League not insisted the required work be completed to enable entry. Indeed, in subsequent years, The Grove was awarded a Football Conference Ground Grading standard. And perhaps more pleasingly the old saying, 'adversity breeds strange bedfellows' has prevailed.

So, the 1986/87 season got underway and proved to be a memorable year. Halesowen, now holders of the FA Vase for the previous two seasons, made its debut in the Midland Division. Former Crystal Palace, Tottenham Hotspur and England International, Peter Taylor, left Chelmsford City and took charge of, and revitalised, Dartford following the club's relegation from the Gola League. All three Championships remained undecided until the final day's fixtures, making my job almost impossible but incredibly exciting at the same time. And Fisher Athletic realised its ambition to win the Premier Division. But its promotion hopes looked to be in vain when its purpose built Surrey Dock Stadium, completed just five years ago, was initially turned down by the top competition, now known as the Vauxhall Conference. Only considerable investment and a major effort, which involved contractors working overnight to get the job completed in time, persuaded Jim Thompson and his Conference colleagues, Fisher was 'over the line' in terms of ground grading.

It was Fisher Athletic's fourth championship win in ten years. All had been achieved under the leadership of Chairman Terry McCarthy and the team management of Dogan Arif, a Turkish-Cypriot former player who moved to England as a young boy. The success immediately raised the club's profile. There was suddenly a great deal of interest in the club. For example, I was frequently asked, *"With such small crowds, how has the club funded its success?"* and *"Where is Fisher?"* By that, I mean people wanted to know where a town or district called Fisher was situated. Well, there wasn't one; not one that I knew of. I was only aware the Docklands/Bermondsey area was well known for a famous and successful amateur boxing club, so I had to do some homework in order to satisfy the inquisitors. The club had been formed in 1908 when the John Fisher Catholic Society, whose aim was to provide football facilities for the under privileged children in the district, formed a team. Consequently, the club is named after the Catholic martyr, John Fisher who was Bishop of Rochester and principal tutor to Prince Henry. The Prince became Henry VIII and ordered John Fisher's execution for refusing to accept Henry was head of the Church of England. Fisher Athletic is the only football club known to have been named after a person. Even more interesting information about Fisher was to emerge in the coming years.

The 1987/88 season began with a huge announcement. The League had attracted its first title sponsor, Beazer Homes, the Bath based house builder. What's more, the Bill Dellow League Cup attracted sponsorship from Westgate Insurance and Advance Sports agreed deals to support the Manager of the Month Awards. The League was on a high and the clubs responded by providing a fantastic competition. These were, however, busy and difficult times for me. Despite remaining professional in all aspects of my business life I lost my way domestically. Looking back I find it impossible to recall these matters in a clear and accurate chronological order.

I had become totally absorbed with my fabulous role in football and busy holding down a full-time job at the same time. I neglected my responsibilities at home and became distracted. This led to Myra and I ending our 15 year marriage and going our separate ways. Professionally I continued to do alright, sufficiently well in fact, for Bradford & Bingley to ask me to take over the management of its Branch in Worthing. The change in career direction led to a relocation to the coastal town and I was accompanied by Wendy Basson, a friend and work colleague with whom I had become close. The relocation enabled me to renew many friendships from my playing days at the seaside town, in particular, Wilf Hugill. Wilf transformed a large extension room at my new home into an office by using his carpentry mastery. This gave me space, shelving galore and room for equipment which enabled me to develop my football administration role even further. The job already demanded work on all seven days of the week but the extra space allowed me to extend the service I provided to clubs even further by extending my hours. I was totally immersed and committed to my work. In the long term, Wendy could not cope with my obsession with football, to which I devoted many unsocial hours, in addition to full-time working hours. She also missed Horsham, her family and friends in the town and a broader social life. She decided to return home. It was a very difficult time for us both but matters began to stabilise for me when the League was in a financial position to make my appointment a full-time role. I was, of course, very excited by the prospect of being back in football as a full-time administrator for the second time. I had struck lucky, at least in this aspect, again. But when I left the Manager's job at Worthing's

Bradford & Bingley it was not without some sadness. During my three years in the Worthing branch my team and I had successfully tripled the Branch's lending. I had called in a lot of football contacts looking for business leads. Brian Gregory (ex-Crawley Town) and Ross Gumpright (ex-Horsham) and his partner in business Trevor Still (ex-Worthing) gave me magnificent support. Thanks fellas. To deal with the level of business we achieved in such a relatively small branch required great assistance. I had that with my no. 2, Barbara Sopp, brother in-law to Ricky Sopp – ex-Brighton & Hove Albion and Worthing, and Sally Klesnil, who followed me from the Horsham Branch. Thanks Ladies.

Meanwhile, Trevor Gould's Aylesbury United set the pace in the Premier Division by remaining undefeated until the end of October 1987. Aylesbury's momentum was interrupted by a controversial defeat at the hands of Bobby Hope's Bromsgrove Rovers and The Ducks were subsequently caught by the chasing pack. They emerged, however, to regain top spot by the end of February and needed only three points from their last four matches to claim the title. Two 1-0 defeats, at Alvechurch and Leicester United, piled on the pressure and then Aylesbury managed only a draw at Cambridge City. With other results going in United's favour they needed only a draw in their final match to win the Championship on goal difference. Despite falling behind on two occasions at VS Rugby, Aylesbury recovered with a final equaliser by Cliff Hercules to finish above Dartford and win the League by a goal difference superior by just four goals. Both had scored 79 goals but Peter Taylor's Dartford had conceded four more than Aylesbury.

There was, however, considerable consolation for the Darts. Despite losing the First Leg of the Westgate Insurance League Cup Final at Bromsgrove, 3-1, Dartford won at Watling Street 3-0 to lift the Trophy, shrugging off a penalty miss in each game by the Player/Manager. Notwithstanding those transgressions the former England International was in a class of his own, several rungs above the best around him; a sheer delight to watch. My son

Ben, who accompanied me whenever we were both free to see a match, appreciated Peter's silky skills and became a Dartford fan!

In the absence of English clubs in European Competition Merthyr Tydfil did the League, and its new sponsor, proud. Having won the Welsh Cup the previous season The Martyrs qualified for the European Cup Winners Cup, where they drew their Italian counterparts, Atalanta in the First Round. Merthyr won 2-1 at Penydarren Park but lost the return in Bergamo 2-0. Atalanta went on to reach the Semi-Final where they lost to eventual winners, Mechelen. Domestically, Merthyr walked the Midland Division, winning by 8 points from Moor Green. Their goals tally of 102, included victories over Bilston 8-0 and Rushden 11-0, and won Lyn Jones' men the Merit Cup for most goals scored in the League campaign.

The Southern section was more hotly contested. The top two sides, Chris Kinnear's Dover Athletic and Ernie Bradwell's Waterlooville, lost only five matches between them throughout the whole of the League programme. But it was not until the final game of the campaign between the top two, which ended in a goalless draw, that finally decided the destiny of the championship. Dover won the title by 3 points.

Amid the hub-bub of a season winding down I was offered a little gem, in footballing terms. As I had no opportunity of attending the FA Cup Final I was given the chance of two tickets for a Semi-Final. As the Semi was often a better, and more competitive, match than the Final I jumped at the chance. And as Liverpool were scheduled to take on Nottingham Forest, Ben, a Liverpool fan like most of his mates of the same age, came too. We had a great day out at Sheffield Wednesday's Hillsborough Stadium from the safety & comfort of the main stand in 'privileged' seats immediately behind the Directors' box. Lucky, or what? It was an adventure to the FA Cup Semi-Final we were to repeat for the next four years, with varying degrees of experience.

So another super season drew to a close. But there was some icing on the cake to come. For the first time any where in the world the National

Football Association sent its full international squad to play a friendly against a non-League club. Seemingly, Frank McGee, a Sports Reporter for The Observer and Aylesbury resident persuaded the England Manager, Bobby Robson, to send a team to play the Ducks as part of the Three Lions' preparation for the forthcoming European Championships. And so it happened, on 4th June 1988; an England side finely tuned to play an International Tournament played against an Aylesbury side called back from their holidays. England were 2-0 up after ten minutes and went on to win 7-0, after changing their entire line-up at half-time. Aylesbury's record goal scorer, Cliff Hercules, 301 goals in 669 appearances, said, *"We couldn't get near them."* Sadly for England, the game didn't appear to boost their performance level. They returned from West Germany winless, losing all their group matches against the Republic of Ireland, the Netherlands and the Soviet Union. As for the friendly at Buckingham Road, where 6,031 fans squeezed into a ground with a registered capacity of something between 4,000 to 5,000, it made memories for many, the like of which cannot be bought. It brought great publicity for the League, too.

Lyn Jones continued to improve his Merthyr side for the 1988/89 season. But the Martyrs started the campaign indifferently. A run of 21 wins in their final 28 games of the season, however, enabled them to overhaul Dartford to win their first Southern League Premier Division Championship for 35 years. Dartford looked to have gained the initiative with a 2-1 win at Penydarren Park in April but a victory over promotion rivals VS Rugby put Merthyr back in the box seats. A final day win over a Crawley Town team, weakened by the loss of Northern Ireland International Gerry Armstrong, in front of 3,341 Welsh fans, clinched the title. Peter Taylor's Dartford finished second, for the second year running but enjoyed consolation, of sorts, by winning the Bill Dellow League Cup for the second successive year.

Interest in the Competition's players still abounded. Burton Albion, League Cup finalists, sold Steve Cotterill and John Gayle to FA Cup holders Wimbledon for a combined fee of £30,000. Waterlooville had earlier signed Guy Whittingham from Oxford City and Paul Moody from Fareham Town. Both were destined for the full-time game; Whittingham joined Portsmouth and then Aston Villa; Moody moved to Southampton before enjoying huge success at Oxford United.

In the Regional Divisions Gloucester City, under the Chairmanship of Geoff Hester, benefitted from its move to a new Stadium at Meadow Park and finished on top of the Midland section, ahead of Ron Bradbury's Atherstone United. In the South, Chelmsford City celebrated its Jubilee season with the Championship, scoring a prize winning 106 League goals along the way. Gravesend & Northfleet finished runners-up, to return to the top table.

Amid the climax to the season Tamworth added icing on the Competition's cake by winning the FA Vase. The Lambs were held to a 1-1 draw at Wembley Stadium by Sudbury Town from the Eastern Counties League. But a 3-0 Replay win at London Road, Peterborough enabled the Southern League to boast of becoming the only Competition to have a member club win England's three major national competitions, i.e. the FA Cup (Tottenham Hotspur 1900/01); the FA Trophy (Telford United (1970/71) and now the FA Vase (Tamworth 1988/89). I think I can say that is an achievement unlikely to be repeated. I wish, too, for another event I experienced never to be repeated.

Just prior to the end of the campaign, Saturday 15th April 1989 was set to be a happy day, a day to be remembered. It is remembered alright, but for all the wrong reasons. The morning began brightly; the sun was shinning; Benjamin and I were going to a football match; and it was my 42nd birthday. We set off for Sheffield to see our second FA Cup Semi-Final, again at Hillsborough, and again Liverpool v Nottingham Forest. Having seen a super match last year we hoped for another good game. Ben wished for a Liverpool victory, but I wouldn't let him wear any colours; we knew what to do and where to go. We were well prepared and we knew what to expect; or so we thought.

Needing to leave early from the south coast, the train journey to London was relatively quiet. The journey from the Capital to the Steel City was much noisier, with many more travelling football supporters. But everyone was in good heart. By the time we arrived at Sheffield the train was packed, almost exclusively with football fans. As the first choice colours of both clubs was red it was impossible to discern where respective allegiances rested but as we had travelled from the south the majority of the crowd at this point followed Forest. But a club the size of Liverpool has fans everywhere so there was a mix. Everything was very orderly, however, and everyone's focus was to grab a place on one of the courtesy buses waiting to take us all to the Stadium. The caravan of buses snaked its way out of the city centre and turned northbound on the A61 towards Owlton. Ah, so that's how Sheffield Wednesday got its nickname, i.e The Owls. We were delighted when the bus came to a halt on Parkside Road, immediately opposite the central entrance to the West stand. Perfect. We had just 40 yards to walk to the main Stadium doors of the south stand.

As we approached the outer gates/boundary of the Stadium we showed our tickets to the patrolling Police. *"You can't come in this way with those tickets, you need the entrance back there"* pointing towards the East Stand. As, wisely, the crowd was being strictly segregated we asked for guidance on the recommended route to our entrance. The only route available to us was to continue along Parkside Road, walking away from our intended destination; turn right into Leppings Lane and take the first available street towards Penistone Lane North, the A61. We were instructed to turn right again, walk the length of the East Stand and then right, over the River Don behind the South Stand where the entrance we required was sited. In a nutshell, we were ordered, albeit politely, to circumvent the whole Ground, passing through the segregated areas of both sets of supporters. That 'order' seemed strange given the strict procedures in force on the day. But we did as we were told, and despite it being a little discomforting the nervy experience gave us no clue of what was to come. We very excitedly found the Guests' lounge and subsequently our seats immediately behind the Directors' Box. We sat and watched the Stadium fill up.

I imagine it was geography that determined Liverpool fans would be housed in the Leppings Lane end of the Ground, now to our left. Access to this Stand, at the north end of the Stadium, was best suited for the direction of, and accommodation into, travellers from Merseyside. This Stand, though, was the smaller of the Stands behind the goal at each end of the pitch, despite Liverpool FC having a far larger following of the participating clubs. Forest fans occupied the East Stand, to our right.

As 3.00pm approached it was noticeable the Leppings Lane end was becoming more densely populated, particularly the central enclosures. The two enclosures, or pens, either side of the 'penalty area' were more thinly populated; spectators were visible from the waist up, standing casually in comfortable space. As time passed, this increasingly contrasted with the central pen where only red faces could be seen. Eventually, people were being lifted out of the enclosure by supporters leaning dangerously over from the tier above and hoisting them up. Some attempted to climb the pitch perimeter fence to escape the overcrowding but this aspect was being controlled, and prevented, by the Police.

The fear of 'trouble' percolated throughout the stadium. This was, after all, only four years after the Heysel Stadium disaster when a wall collapsed and Liverpool fans surged towards Juventus supporters. Thirty-nine supporters died in the ensuing clash which led to fourteen Liverpool supporters being found guilty of manslaughter and jailed. But at Hillsborough the situation was different; these fans all supported the same team. So when Ben said to me, *"Dad, what do you think has happened?"* Not seeing any hostility, all I could say was, *"I think something terrible has happened."*

After what appeared to be a great deal of uncertainty Referee Ray Lewis got the game started. Almost simultaneously the number of fans being lifted into the upper section of the stand increased. And, as if recognising this was not the kind of 'trouble' to which we had become accustomed to in the '70s and early '80s, Police began assisting fans escape over the perimeter fence. Many collapsed on the red cinder surface surrounding the playing area but it wasn't long before scores of fans were laying on the pitch. Mr Lewis had no alternative to stop the game and take the players off the field. Only four minutes had been played.

By this time many fans had encroached further onto the pitch, out of necessity. Many had just sought the safety in the open space the pitch provided; many helped by carrying others to reach this sanctuary; and others tore down the advertising hoardings and used these as makeshift stretchers to ferry fellow supporters to safety. It was utter chaos, the severity of which was becoming apparent as each minute passed. There were casualties all over the west end of the pitch. Thoughts of the game restarting faded fast as medical help, in the form of an ambulance, could not penetrate the traffic and/or get into the Stadium. I believe it was at least fifteen minutes before an ambulance entered the Stadium but its progress was impeded by the number of bodies spread over the playing area. Ben and I watched helplessly, like forty-thousand others, as the match was inevitably abandoned. In the coming days we learned ninety-six spectators had died. A ninety-seventh Liverpool supporter died of his injuries thirty-two years later. We had witnessed the worst disaster in English sporting history.

Such dreadful memories overshadowed the excitement of a passing season. A new campaign, therefore, could not come quickly enough. Besides, 'the show' must go on. So, soon after the formalities of the AGM were complete I prepared for another fortnight in isolation to manually compile the fixture list for the 1989/90 season. And it was to become a season that left one of the Competition's most convincing Champions crestfallen.

Dover Athletic won the Premier Division by four clear points having conceded only 27 goals and losing only four of their forty-two League matches. But promotion was denied them due to a shortfall in requirements at The Crabble Ground, enabling Runners-up Bath City to return to The Football Conference. Dartford were once again in the running for honours throughout the season but they finished third in the League; lost to VS Rugby in the League Cup; and then lost Manager Peter Taylor, who joined Enfield at the end of the season.

After their Herculean efforts to qualify for membership of the League, and three subsequent near misses in the Midland Division, Halesowen Town finally topped their regional section, despite selling an important player, Stuart Cash, to Nottingham Forest in September. It had not been an easy passage as the newly relaid pitch suffered several postponements due to drainage problems. But Manager John Morris overcame fixture disruptions and built on the previous successes of Paddy Page to assemble a team containing several outstanding players. Although work commitments prohibited me from seeing a match every week, after many earlier visits to see the Ground works, I managed to take in a Halesowen fixture. Three players stood out; Defender, Andy Pearce; Midfielder, Sean Flynn; and Striker, Dean Spink. Consequently, without intentionally meaning to disarm Halesowen of three good players, I felt compelled to 'promote' these players with the occasional Manager who called my office. Colin Murphy, Lincoln City Manager at the time, was looking for a centre-forward. I suggested he looked at Dean Spink. *"Is he big?"*, Colin asked. Big enough to challenge for anything, and he knows where the goal is, I proffered. Andy Pearce was a huge centre-half; not the quickest on two legs, by far, but he used his physic to great effect. Then there was Sean Flynn, a dynamo in midfield who knew how to tackle and distribute the ball. I contacted Barry Lloyd, Brighton & Hove Albion's Manager. Not all Football League Managers were prepared to 'take a chance' on a non-League player but having got to know Barry on my trips to the Goldstone, and living in the same area, I was confident Sean could do a good job for the Albion. I am certain my prompting carried little weight but I was delighted when these three were given a break in the full-time game. Spink was signed by Aston Villa, and subsequently became a folk hero at Shrewsbury Town; Pearce moved to Coventry City, then Sheffield Wednesday and finally Wimbledon; and

Flynn joined Coventry City. I Phoned Barry Lloyd again to tell him the Sky Blues had taken Sean for £20,000. *"I haven't got twenty f*****g pence, Dennis"*, said Barry. Times were hard at Brighton during this period and Barry knew that was a missed opportunity. Flynn went on to play in the Premier League for Derby County and West Bromwich Albion before spending time at Tranmere Rovers. Terry Angus, at VS Rugby, was another defender that caught my eye. I don't know if anyone I spoke to about Terry followed up on my prompts but he eventually moved to Northampton Town and Fulham. I'm under no illusion I did anything to advance their careers. On the contrary, speaking to Managers at this level I was impressed at how much they already knew of the players. Their knowledge and network was enormous. In the case of another player about whom I talked to a Football League Manager, I was puzzled why the lad had not been 'discovered' earlier. *"He's already had opportunities"* came the reply from one Manager I spoke to, followed by a whispered description of some anti-social behaviour. I ceased to mention the player's name to anyone again but I noted later he was given a second opportunity by a League One club and subsequently made over 200 appearances in the Football League for various clubs.

As another season ended, and the Annual General Meeting wrapped up the year's affairs, whilst also setting up the Competition for another campaign I sneaked off for an unusual 'working' holiday. I joined Wilf Hugill on one of his trips to Romania. Accompanied by a mutual friend we flew from Gatwick to Bucharest where we were met by one of the network of local people Wilf had built up on his previous visits. I didn't know what to expect but the experience of the next ten days is indelibly etched in my memory.

Along with our host we were four adults crammed into a modest, far from new, vehicle loaded with luggage, gifts and practical items Wilf required to extend his work on the school he discovered a few years before. Bucharest was no London but its wide streets were very busy. It was a relief to reach the countryside. But the condition of the roads was poor, a danger in many places. This made the three hour journey seem twice as long. Our first stop was in Tecuci where we met a family Wilf had befriended and helped on a previous trip. Gheorge, Connie and their six year old daughter (sorry, I have forgotten the young lady's name) lived in an apartment block on the outskirts of the city. The welcome we received could not have been warmer but times were hard for the young family. George spent days away looking for, and hopefully finding, work wherever he could. The apartment had no heating, that I recall; Connie switched the gas cooking hob on to keep warm. Hot water was only available on Wednesday and Saturday. These people were diamonds. And although we only stayed one night in Tecuci I am pleased to say we were to meet a few more times on the trip. During one meeting Connie was thrilled to tell us she had studied and passed some exams to improve her status at work. When collecting her certificate the Adjudicator demanded a bribe before handing over the accreditation papers! As if times were not already hard enough.

The following day we moved on to the focal point of our journey, Ghidigeni, and the school full of abandoned/orphaned boys Wilf had discovered following President Nicolae Ceausescu's downfall. The lads went wild when they saw Wilf, or *"Ulf"* as they called him; they couldn't pronounce the "W". Wilf deserved his 'Hero' status. Following the execution of Mr & Mrs Ceausescu on Christmas Day 1989 Wilf had organised successive teams of friends to raise funds and visit the school. It will take too many words to explain the conditions in which these children had been living. When first found the building was ridden with damp and infested with rats. Subsequent cleansing and repairs undertaken by Wilf and his teams had made the school habitable. It was now clean and dry, thanks largely to Wilf having re-roofed the whole building.

We worked, played and ate with the boys. About 120 lads 'lived-in' and I soon met one particular boy who, through Wilf, I had helped. I could not afford to fund the whole complement of the school so I asked Wilf to nominate a boy who needed help, the problem being, they all needed help.

Over a series of visits made by Wilf and his teams I had sent 'T' shirts and other light clothing for the summer, some sports gear e.g. sweat shirts and a track suit and, for the winter, a pair of Doc Marten boots. To meet Kostel at last was a special moment. He was wearing his Tottenham Hotspur branded track suit and I eventually got around to asking about the DM's. After a while we discovered Kostel had traded them for cigarettes. He was a rascal of the highest order. I couldn't be disappointed, they were his to do with what he wanted. I accepted someone else was benefitting. To be frank, they were all rapscallions. Whatever kindness you showed them, we had to make sure our watch and/or bracelet was still on our wrist after shaking hands. Most were capable of stealing from any source, simply to survive.

During our time in Ghidigeni we were hosted by more of the acquaintances Wilf had made on previous visits, a Romany family in their mud brick house. We were warmly welcomed and cared for by this family of four, who had very little yet they were willing to share. Their house had no electricity or water supply. They cooked with gas bottles and water had to be fetched from a standpipe beside the road. Their nearest tap was over 100 yards away. I recall their most prized possession was a magnificent looking horse that was kept in the front garden, with the unmentionable toilet situated at the bottom of the back garden!! We then spent our last two nights with a family in Tecuci, sleeping on a stone floor. This house was of a more conventional structure and it had its own water supply, to a standpipe in the garden; so cold water only.

Looking back, this trip remains a humbling eye opener for me. With one notable exception* the people we met had very little, but we were

---

* The notable exception, by the way, was found when visiting the 'owner' of a local distillery. His home on the edge of Ghidigeni, his possessions, the car he drove (a Mercedes), and his outlook on life were in sharp contrast to the villagers who worked at his factory. I concede, his presence did provide a source for existence and survival to many local inhabitants but I had trouble reconciling his wealth with the theory of communism, in a classless society.

welcomed, even encouraged, to share what they did have. But they seemed to be living with fear; a hangover of fear from the dictatorial regime that had just ended and a suspicion that anyone might be 'working' for a secret police force. Although despising Ceausescu his successor, Ion Iliescu, supported a communist state. So despite overthrowing its leader, Romania merely changed the face of communism. Our driver, who had previously been in the Romanian army, constantly informed us, I think for his own safety, he *"had papers"* that would protect him. He never enlarged on what these papers contained but he clearly believed they gave him some security. I often wonder how these people are now, and what happened to Kostel. I know Connie and her family managed to 'escape' and settled in Canada. I received an unexpected call from her, from Montreal, saying they were all well. But that's the last I heard from her. Wilf eventually drew a close to his personal aid work after twenty-nine trips in eight years. He deserved an honour.

The 1990 AGM welcomed Farnborough Town, following the club's relegation from the Football Conference. Eight months later it was farewell to the Hampshire club as Ted Pearce guided Farnborough back to the top flight. Last year's Champions, Dover Athletic, began well but fell away before the end of the season despite, once again, having the meanest defence in the Division. Elsewhere, Southern League players continued to attract the attention of full-time clubs in The Football League. Cambridge City sold Kevin Wilkin to Northampton Town for £10,000. And after the end of the season Waterlooville sold their 25 goal striker, Paul Moody, to Southampton for £50,000. Notwithstanding all the trials, tribulations and delight of completing another season the 1990/91 campaign has a bitter-sweet memory for me. After the very difficult times managing the three failed membership applications from Halesowen the club had responded well and had been successful since joining the Competition. The Ground was now looking good, and continued to improve, and its facilities frequently hosted meetings of the League's Match Officials' Association. Any hatchets, if they were any, had been firmly buried in the past by the club's newly formed Board, masterfully managed by its Chairman, Harry Rudge. Harry, a former player and Secretary, had single handedly kept the club alive after the Second World War and led it to multiple successes throughout the years. He was a character of immense integrity and stature. At times I felt it had not been easy for me to appear in control of the League's affairs at the same time as working with this hugely popular and effervescent personality. Harry was a giant in Non-League Midlands football. And I was pleased to have got to know him in the way I did. It was impossible not to like and respect Harry. So when I received a telephone call on 18th December 1990, to say Harry had suddenly passed away, my true feelings for this loveable fellow manifested themselves in quite a few tears. One week later I filled up again when Mrs Margaret Rudge, Harry's widow, asked me to compose and read a eulogy at Harry's funeral. I was frightened and proud. It was an honour that could not be purchased.

The 1991/92 season saw the return of Fisher Athletic, relegated from the Football Conference and now without their ambitious Chairman, Terry McCarthy, and prolific team leader Dogan Arif. I had met Terry only a couple of times. Dogan, I got to know well, having met at meetings and matches many times. We enjoyed a good football friendship. Sadly, for reasons I would neither have imagined nor make up, I was not to meet them again. Terry, I was told, was found guilty of defrauding the Post Office and was given a custodial sentence of four years. Dogan, who I had come to know as a sophisticated operator of businesses including a jewellers; a restaurant on The Old Kent Road, at which I had eaten on a evening out; and the football club, had been convicted at Maidstone Crown Court of charges involving drugs. He was ordered to serve a long sentence in prison from where, it was claimed, he continued to control the family's fortune. I was staggered. I could not believe what I was hearing and reading. And the story did not end there.

The National Press published stories of 'the notorious Arif family' comprising seven brothers, including Bekir, Mehmet, Deniz and Dogan who, it alleged, had taken over the London crime scene after the Krays and the Richardsons. Dogan, it reminded readers, had been charged in the early 1980s for being involved in a plot to kidnap Iranian diplomats and military officers. The conspirators, it alleged, also planned to swindle the Iranian government in an arms deal, charging them £26m for 8,000 missiles that did not exist. Dogan walked free after being acquitted of conspiracy to imprison. But in November 1990, it reported, Mehmet and Deniz took part in an armed robbery at Woodhatch near Reigate, a scene I passed each day on my commute to the Offices of T&E Homes. The unsuccessful robbery, during which Deniz wore a Ronald Reagan face mask, and Mehmet, dressed as an old man, was shot and wounded by Police also saw fellow accomplice Kenny 'Bum Face' Baker shot dead. And in 1999 Bekir, known as 'The Duke', was jailed for 23 years after Police detected a heroin plot.

The above events were, of course, happening in a parallel universe compared to my mundane existence as a football league administrator. But Fisher, and Dogan in particular, was an integral part of my story. So, too, was the Club's Secretary, Les Rowe. A quiet professional man who, I believe, lived on his own and who took off to his second home on the Isle of Sheppey at the glimpse of any sunshine. And then there was the Treasurer, Bert Kyte. Bert had the loudest voice I have ever heard. When at full blast, cheering on 'The Fish', Bert could break windows. In a quieter moment upon Fisher's return to the Southern League he said to me, *"I've just spent some time down your way, Den."* Being curious, *"Where?"* I asked. *"Ford"* replied Bert. *"There's an open prison down there, Bert, where a road passes through the middle." "That's right"* said Bert, *"That's where I stayed for a while! I still go back occasionally, to throw a few 'lardys' out of the car window for the boys." "Lardys?"* I inquired. *"Lardy-dah's, cigars!"* said Bert. I had definitely led a sheltered life. But the characters at Fisher had all been good to me and had opened my eyes. The guys I got to know will always have a place in my tale, and the tale will not be without affection for them.

Unfortunately for the football team, Fisher could not stop the rot and, come the end of the season, they were relegated for a second successive time. At the end of November life didn't look much better for Bromsgrove. But the Rovers, still managed by former Scotland International and West Bromwich Albion player, Bobby Hope, lost only two of their final thirty games to lift the Championship. Last year's Champions, Dover Athletic finished second, six points adrift. Elsewhere, Southern Division Hythe Town resigned its membership and subsequently folded. And in the Midland Division a revolution began in Northampton. Rushden Town vacated its deteriorating town centre Ground and moved to Ithlingborough where it merged with local rivals Irthlingborough Diamonds. We were to hear more of the newly formed Rushden & Diamonds very soon. Meanwhile, the League continued to demonstrate its quality by its players attracting the interest of clubs further up the football pyramid. Sean Flynn (see above) became the third Halesowen player to sign for Coventry. He scored on his Boxing Day debut and held a regular place in the Sky Blues First Division side for the remainder of the season. Dave Busst also moved to Coventry, from Moor Green. His former team mate Ian Taylor moved to Port Vale, and subsequently Aston Villa; and Redditch United trousered £40,000 from the sale of Dave Farrell, also to Aston Villa.

The 1992/93 season proved memorable for many reasons. Dartford, a formidable member in past years, collapsed in September following the demise of Maidstone United who were tenants at the Darts' Watling Street Ground. The Stones had sold their own Ground in the centre of Maidstone but had failed with a planning application to relocate elsewhere in the town. To gain and/or retain its recently earned position in the Football League the club entered into a ground share with Dartford. After consuming much money on a land purchase, and a subsequent failed bid for planning Maidstone was forced to withdraw from the League in August without kicking a ball in the new season. I cannot remember any intrinsic links between the clubs that prevented Dartford from continuing its fixtures at

Watling Street but a financially embarrassed Dartford ceased to trade the following month.

There was, however, brighter news for another Kent club. Dover Athletic won the Championship for the second time in three years and this time its Crabble Stadium was deemed acceptable to the Football Conference. The Lillywhites lost only 4 of their 40 games and finished a massive 13 points ahead of Cheltenham Town who had been relegated from the Conference at the end of the previous season.

The entry of Gresley Rovers into the Midland Division brought with it memories of Halesowen Town's ground grading experiences. Gresley's very compact 'The Moat' ground had failed to meet the required grading criteria on a series of occasions. Upon the third occasion the club had erected what appeared to be a fine looking Stand with more than the needed number of seats. A major improvement, or so it seemed. What had gone unnoticed amid the construction work was, the roof of the Stand extended over the touchline. A ball could hit the Stand without going out of play! It was back to the drawing board once again and I was labelled a megalomaniac by a Sports Reporter in the local newspaper. One year later, having corrected the construction error, the club qualified for membership, won the Midland Section and earned promotion to the Premier Division.

Salisbury, now with City attached to its name to reflect its City new status, won the Southern section but was denied promotion, despite an Appeal to the FA, as its Victoria Park ground was deemed unsuitable. Elsewhere, Gravesend & Northfleet's Steve Portway broke the League's goalscoring record with 58 League & Cup goals. Margate's Martin Buglione, with 31 goals, attracted the attention of Scottish Premier Division side St. Johnstone, where he scored on his March debut. Halesowen sold yet another player in March when hotel Porter cum Waiter, Frankie Bennett moved for £7,500 to Southampton. Frankie subsequently made 19 appearances for the Saints, mainly from the bench. My own personal highlights of the season was a visit to Burden Park, Bolton for Sutton Coldfield Town's FA

Cup Tie against the Wanderers where I was introduced to Nat Lofthouse. On another working 'day out' I was invited to the opening of The Hand Stadium, Clevedon where I met Sir Stanley Matthews. Sir Stanley kindly signed my copy of Barry Hugman's book which recorded players who had played in The Football League.

The day I met Sir Stanley Matthews

I was fortunate to meet Sir Stanley, by now into his eighties, on a second occasion about two years later. Upon our hosts' introduction Sir Stanley said, *"Oh! You are the bloke with the big book."* To be remembered, for whatever reason by such a football 'Great' like Sir Stanley, made a magic moment for a football nut like me. I balanced this memorable moment with Sir Stanley with my brief meeting with another Knight of the Realm, Sir Alf Ramsey. When I invited him to sign his entry in my book I received a curt refusal, *"I don't think so"*, accompanied by a dismissive hand gesture. Not such a memorable moment, not a nice one, anyway.

As the League approached its 100th birthday, in 1994, the Board engaged with 'Paper Plane Publishing', a Midland based company, to produce a book to mark its centenary. To enable this we were introduced to a most remarkable football historian called Leigh Edwards. What Leigh didn't know about football clubs; players and stories, particularly at 'our' level of the game wouldn't have merited inclusion in the book. He knew all there is to know about 'our' level of the game, and more. Names and tales rolled off his tongue. He had an encyclopaedic knowledge of football and its participants. Thanks to Leigh's astonishing work over the next twelve months, and Phil Walder at Paper Plane, the League successfully published a hardback book, appropriately, albeit oddly, priced at £19.94. Thank you Leigh and Phil.

Another part of the League's celebrations included a Luncheon at The Cafe Royal where over 400 guests enjoyed an excellent meal, entertainment by my friend Peter Brackley and his pal Mike Osman and a valedictory speech by former footballer & television personality, Jimmy Hill. When Mr Hill discovered he was due to speak immediately after the entertainment he expressed considerable disquiet. *"I can't follow those two"*, he protested. His fears were well founded. Peter and Mike 'brought the house down' with their mimicry of famous voices. Jimmy did his best with a truncated professional address congratulating the Competition on its 100th birthday, but his was an impossible task such was the hilarious brilliance of the Brackley/Osman performance.

Farnborough, having been relegated from the Conference twelve months earlier, won the Championship in the League's Centenary year, and its 91st season in competitive terms. The newly formed merged club of Rushden & Diamonds, under the stewardship of Dr. Martens owner Max Griggs, immediately made its mark by winning the Midland Division. Mr Griggs then, through Dr. Martens, agreed to sponsor the League Cup, whilst undertaking a massive redevelopment of the Club's Nene Park Stadium. And what a job he made of that over the next few seasons.

As for the Competition, following the success of lengthy sponsorship arrangements with Beazer Homes, Westgate Insurance and Larchimage Windows, the Board strengthened its financial stability by entering into an agreement with British Telecom to transmit all news, fixtures and results via a telephone information service. The service, called Clubcall, was highly successful. Working with a resident journalist it raised significant sums enabling an increase in funding to member clubs. Notwithstanding the performance of the service, after a few successful years, BT found reason to carry out a fact finding exercise in relation to its editorial performance. Two senior members of its management, one of whom was Mike Hendrick the former England cricketer, descended upon my home unannounced. Something was amiss, they said. I was only able to report on my daily contribution of news, information & interviews with and by BT's journalist, which was all operating to our satisfaction, as well as the future development of the service. Shortly after this meeting the League was advised 'our' journalist had been replaced and a new operative, Mike Tranter, had been assigned to our account. Normal service was seamlessly resumed. The outgoing journalist was clearly aggrieved. Relying on the support of his Union he attempted to take action against me and/or the League. It took him quite a time for him to realise that such actions against his intended targets were groundless. After months of lengthy legal exchanges I received the letter my lawyer said I would never get, an unequivocal withdrawal of any proposed action, supposedly *"in the interest of football"*. In the interest of seeing sense, more like it. The sorry saga was happily drawn to a close and it was, unknowingly at the time, to have an even happier lasting legacy for me. I had called on my friendship with Halesowen Town Chairman, Harry Rudge. Harry's daughter, Janet, was a Court Manager and I sought her guidance throughout, what was for a while, an unpleasant experience. Janet had access to Judges' advice. The advice I was given, that the journalist's case was futile, and without grounds to the point of being vexatious. This gave me great comfort. Without knowing it at the time, my acquaintance with Janet was to become a longer lasting friendship.

Back on the football front the seasons continued to roll on. Whilst from the 'outside' one season's work must have looked like any other, the reality was quite the opposite. Each season threw up its own issues. Hednesford Town won the 1994/95 Championship but promotion to the Football Conference was in doubt whilst the club's excellent new Stadium remained incomplete. Fortunately for the Pitmen good sense prevailed when it was established the grading and safety criteria had been met within the finished parts of the construction, enabling the final touches to be completed prior to the start of the new season. Newport, formerly Newport County, continued its resurgence in the football pyramid by winning the Midland section. After years of hard work by David Hando, following the collapse of the former Football League club and several seasons playing in exile in England, soccer success was returning to South Wales.

The 1995/96 campaign saw Rushden & Diamonds continue the development of its team, under the Management of Roger Ashby, and the completion of its magnificent Stadium. The glorious Nene Park proved to be a worthy home for the giant Championship Shield. And the Diamonds didn't hang around. They went on to win the Football Conference to earn promotion to the Football League. On the other hand, the well respected Stafford Rangers suffered its second consecutive relegation, plummeting from the Conference to the Southern League Midland Division. At the end of the season Beazer Homes chose not to renew its title sponsorship of the League after nine fine years. Negotiations in the summer months saw the mantle generously taken up by Dr. Martens.

My own closed season around this time was disrupted by an injury far worse than anything I suffered in my active playing career. It was, I believe, to mark it being 20 years since Manager Roy Osborne brought to an end his successful period at Horsham FC, that former colleagues at the Queen Street Club decided to stage a match between the Club's teams of 1966 and 1976. As a member of the team during both those years I made an appearance in both teams. Everything was set for a joyous Sunday afternoon amongst friends and the mood was set when some of the players asked their 2 inch striped shirts to stretch over their slightly larger than 'playing days' torsos. *"This shirt was pin striped when I picked it up"* exclaimed Jimmy Wond from inside his shirt cum tourniquet. The atmosphere, like the weather, was magical and the game progressed well. No doubt everyone had lost a bit of pace over the years but not an ounce of enthusiasm or competitive spirit was missing. As I chased a ball in the second half, ahead of Terry Williamson, I felt what I thought was a kick in my right calf. From my position, now on the ground, *"What did you do that for?"* I asked Terry. *"I didn't do anything; I wasn't close enough to you"*, Terry replied, which was quickly confirmed by all around. I was immediately sorry for my misplaced thought. As I was helped to my feet the evidence was clear, my right foot was hanging limp. My achilles was ruptured. I was driven home to Worthing, and after getting cleaned up I was taken to the hospital. A&E was relatively quiet and I was seen almost immediately. One squeeze of the calf confirmed the Doctor's diagnosis, *"Your achilles tendon has gone up your calf like a roller blind. If you are not doing anything for the remainder of the day we will operate this evening."* I left the hospital five days later, after crutch training, and spent the next seven weeks, with my right leg in plaster from toe to knee. Prior to this incident I had broken my nose twice, surgery was required each time, and had dislocated my shoulder incurring a fracture. The NHS has never let me down. And it didn't on this occasion. I hope we can all support this great institution during it current testing times.

Moving on, having satisfactorily addressed many issues at its 'Moat' Stadium, Gresley Rovers gained promotion to the Premier Division at the end of April 1997. After three years in the top Division, under the management of Paul

Futcher and Assistant Garry Birtles, they won the Championship. But the Ground fell short again and the Rovers were denied promotion once more. As a consequence, Futcher and several players left the club. Within three years Gresley Rovers was relegated and shortly after, liquidated. Runners-up Cheltenham Town benefitted from Gresley's misfortune. After making a huge decision to sack their Manager Chris Robinson in January, when third in the table, the Robins appointed former player Steve Cotterill. Cotterill led the team into second place, and the Football Conference, once again.

Notwithstanding the good days, living and working in football, I worked hard with many clubs that had to fight hard to maintain their existence. The well established club of Dudley Town had, a few seasons prior to this period, to vacate its Ground after subsidence at the adjacent cricket ground exposed gaping holes in the earth; the consequence of mining in the area. Sudbury Town withdrew from the League after finding the cost of travel at the higher level of football too much. Trowbridge Town folded after a fire burned down the club's grandstand; the heat wilting the two floodlight pylons either side of the building so the light fittings at the top bent over and rested on the turf. The sight was extra-ordinary and devastating for the club. And two Hampshire clubs, Havant Town and Waterlooville saw the benefits of a merger.

The Competition, however, remained strong. There was no shortage of clubs seeking to win promotion and move up the football pyramid which, with assistance from the Football Association and Liaison Committees between Leagues throughout the country, had become a formal and regulated structure. 'Fourth Officials', or 'Reserve Match Officials' had been introduced at Premier League and Football League level and Leagues equivalent to the Southern League were requested to make these assignments from their list of Match Officials. It was another task, but one that brought about an uplift to my duties and a role the League's complement of Officials enjoyed. I was asked to appointment Fourth Officials to the home matches at twelve clubs, which included Arsenal, Birmingham City, Brighton &

Hove, Queens Park Rangers, Portsmouth, Southampton, Tottenham Hotspur and Wimbledon. It was good to work with full-time professional clubs and build new relationships. Arsenal were particularly friendly and helpful so I asked if they could help me launch a League sponsorship at one of the club's home matches. The Gunners accommodated representatives of the League and Westgate Insurance to make a pitch side announcement at half-time of our new commercial agreement. Our story was also articled in the match programme. The game they allowed me to choose – a European Cup Tie against Benfica! And during preparations I literally bumped into Eusebio, in the tunnel. Another magic moment for a football nut like me.

Times, however, were not always as good as this. Whilst I always blessed my luck to be working within my hobby, this seven day-a-week job had its perennial problems. The worst of these was the poor weather generously provided by the British winter. It caused havoc with the fixture list. The quality of pitches, and their ability to cope with inclement weather, varied throughout the Competition. The programme was disrupted many times during every/any season. Occasionally, a whole weekend's schedule would be wiped out which led to intense debate amongst the affected clubs when trying to reach agreement for a re-arranged date. Sometimes, the debate boiled over and I was called upon to be Solomon. A fixture congestion towards the end of a season was frequent. One year, I recall, Redditch United played eleven League fixtures in twelve days! On day twelve they played a County Cup Tie!! Thankfully that case was a 'one-off', and nobody could influence the weather.

Another aspect of the administration was a constant source of frustration, and the problems it caused needed to be tackled at some stage almost every week. I experienced too many match officials not understanding the level of commitment required for football at the step on which they operated. As a player I was expected to travel to wherever I was required and be available every week and/or every day on which my club's matches were played. If I was not available on any particular match day, and/or missed training twice each week, I would lose my place in the team. And I did not want that. I discovered too many Referees & Linesmen on the League's List of Officials lacked a disciplined and professional approach.

Each month my job entailed making several hundred appointments of match officials to the games. Officials could, at any time, let me know in advance any date on which they were not available. Inevitably, changes would be required due to priority fixtures and/or unforeseen circumstances. But, for example, when match officials returned assignments because they were going on holiday and, in more than one occasion, it was his/her wedding anniversary, I was not happy. I would have expected anyone to know of such an event well in advance. And on more than one occasion my phone rang at 10.00pm on Christmas Eve, and even Christmas Day, to be told by a parent and/or partner, my son and/or partner cannot do his game on Boxing Day morning as he had been unwell all day. What could I do at such late notice? I was left with no option but to trouble other people on a Christmas Day looking for a replacement. Those episodes were unhelpful and I could not avoid being a tad annoyed, even suspicious on occasions.

On the other hand, I did have my moments of fun especially when games were scheduled on April Fools' Day. On these occasions I attempted to lighten the mood when publishing the otherwise unexciting monthly Match Officials Appointments List. Recording the Referees surname first, followed by his two Linesmen, now known as Assistant Referees, I managed to assign, amongst other examples, a Green; Black and White to a match, mixed with a Brown and a Gray on another match, followed by a Castle, Bishop and Rooke to another match and then three Singhs (Jarnail, Gurnham & Sanghera) to another. Jarnail, aka John, was the first Sikh to become a British football Referee. John was an exceptional Match Official, with a matching personality, who progressed to the Football League. His two sons have since followed in their father's footsteps.

With the help of the League's Match Officials Association we collectively set about changing the culture. The Assessing scheme, now run by Jim Hill, was enlarged making sure more Referees were monitored and coached each week. The Association arranged regular meetings and Training days, which included visits from Club Managers to make sure lines of communication between all parties were open and convivial. I do not recall missing any of these meetings and I was accompanied whenever possible by a League Director, more often than not, Doug Gillard. The Association also held an annual Conference weekend for members and their families, frequently staged in Bournemouth. It all worked. It was a super bonding process. The arrangements were the envy of the Southern League's contemporary Competitions. I do not suggest there wasn't the occasional disagreement between Clubs and Match Officials over a decision or two on match days but bridges were built and a better understanding of each others issues was created. I believe we managed to create, what I like to refer to as a 'Dressing Room' atmosphere between the 66 Clubs and, at any one time, the League's 300 Match Officials. An example of our creation came to light after Mrs Margaret Hill, Jim's wife, mentioned to me that her husband was spending so much time on his football activities with the League that he had failed to repair a broken toilet cistern in their home. The closet had been out of use for the past two years. Happily they had another one! But to help Margaret with her plight, and to galvanise Jim, I asked all the Match Officials and Clubs to send a 'Get Well Card' to Jim's loo. Within ten days the Hills received 600 cards, 3 bouquets of flowers, a few boxes of chocolates and a brand new pedestal from a member who worked at Armitage Shanks in the West Midlands. Such was the community we created. As for the new loo, Jim returned the compliment; it turned up at my house for my 50th birthday!!

The day I met a former player of Stockton Heath.

Meanwhile, the show rolled on, so too did the friendship between Janet and I. We had begun to see each other at weekends, i.e. enjoying a bachelor existence between Monday & Friday and having each other's company in Worthing or Halesowen on alternate Saturdays/Sundays. The Southern League, at this time, regularly supplied a handful of its fixtures to Littlewoods for the Football Pools Coupon. On one occasion I was invited by Littlewoods' Phil Watkins to have lunch with the Pools Panel at the Midland Hotel, Manchester. On duty that day were Gordon Banks (formerly of Chesterfield, Leicester City, Stoke City & England), Tony Green (Blackpool, Newcastle & Scotland) and Roger Hunt (Liverpool, Bolton Wanderers & England). Phil introduced Janet and I to the Panel and we were warmly welcomed. Implying Janet could hold her own in any conversation about football I added she was a former Director of Halesowen Town FC. Without hesitation Roger Hunt said, *"Oh, you beat us in the semi-final of the FA Vase."* Nobody understood. Roger was asked to explain. Roger articulated, he began his football career in the Mid Cheshire League with Stockton Heath Albion FC, which was renamed Warrington Town FC in 1961. Halesowen Town defeated Warrington 6-3 in the Vase semi-final in 1986. So, we spent lunch in the company of three Internationals, two with World Cup winners medals in their pocket, and the main topic of conversation was Halesowen Town's FA Vase successes, in particular a match against Warrington Town. With so much more they could have talked about, we were humbled by their knowledge and interest in 'our' level of the game. Three wonderful footballers and three wonderful gentlemen who gave Janet & I a wonderful memory. Thanks. Gordon Banks, by the way, was affectionately known by his Pools Panel colleagues as "One Save"! Why was that, I wonder?

After spending three hours in such illustrious company we went on to Maine Road where Portsmouth were playing Manchester City. Unfortunately my accent betrayed my origins and a couple of supporters around us turned ugly. I was abused for being an *"Effing Southerner"*. We left the game at half-time feeling a sharp contrast with the company we had kept two hours earlier.

Back to business, having gained promotion to the Premier Division in

April 1997 Forest Green Rovers, now under the Chairmanship of Trevor Horsley, won the 1997/98 Championship at the first attempt. Trevor was a Top Man whose Company was heavily involved with the installation of services at the new Wembley Stadium. We were to meet again, and work together, a few years later.

But prior to the start of another season Jan & I reviewed the weekly pilgrimage we were undertaking between the south coast and the West Midlands. Whilst we were both committed to our careers we could not deny the 350 mile round trip was time consuming and costly. We decided to sell our respective houses and look for a new home somewhere equidistant between West Sussex and the West Midlands. Middle England proved to be beyond our means so when broadening the discussion to include other circumstances we settled on Worcester. The Faithful City was close to the motorway network and was on railway lines serving Birmingham and London. It wasn't long before we found the house we would call home. For the first time in our respective lives we left 'birth area'; Jan left her hometown and I left my home county. Twenty-seven years later we are still here, loving life together and still following football. So...

Nuneaton Borough, who led a chequered existence from one season to another, succeeded Forest Green as Champions in 1998/99. The 'Boro endured a traumatic departure from its Manor Ground, close to the town centre, before putting roots down at Liberty Way, on the outskirts of town. Nuneaton, managed by former Cambridge City and Northampton Town striker Kevin Wilkin, finished an astonishing 23 points ahead of Boston United. The Pilgrims, however, were not to be denied for long. The following year, led by the charismatic Steve Evans and his Assistant Paul Raynor, Boston topped the table 14 points clear of Burton Albion, and celebrated exuberantly in a unique way.

For the Millennium the League's Board arranged for its Annual General Meeting and Presentation Dinner to be held on board a ship. After the formalities of the AGM on the morning of a Saturday in June the ship set sail from Harwich to Hamburg. The weather was perfect; the North Sea was calm; the passengers were all very relaxed before eventually retiring for the remainder of the crossing. The fine weather continued the following morning enabling everyone to enjoy the stunning cruise along the River Elbe followed by several hours in Hamburg's attractive city centre. The scene was set. Upon returning to the ship dinner suits were donned by the men and posh frocks by the Ladies and everyone gathered in the Dining Room for Sunday's evening dinner. And the moment the Master of Ceremonies announced the arrival of the Chairman and his Lady, Doug and Pat Gillard, a metaphoric champagne cork exploded. As the sun set on the North Sea the most fantastic celebratory night of this kind erupted and continued long into the night. Something/Someone looked after us all that weekend. It was an event that is still talked about, over twenty four years later, at least by those who can remember. By that, I recall finding Jason Turner, the hugely popular Bath City FC Secretary wandering aimlessly around the boat as we disembarked on Monday morning. Jason had not slept the whole weekend. Jason became a loyal friend. He went on to spend time as Secretary of Plymouth Argyle, Newport County and Cardiff City before spending seven years as Chief Executive of Notts County FC. Jason passed away suddenly on Thursday 30th March 2023, aged 50. Two months later, when the Magpies won the National League Play-Off Final at Wembley the players included Jason in their celebrations by holding aloft a framed photograph of him as well as the trophy. A thoughtful and very touching gesture.

Margate took over Boston's mantle as League Champions in 2001 and won promotion to the Football Conference. But there were no celebrations at Witney Town and Baldock Town. Both clubs folded at the end of the season. Baldock's demise came only a few years after it launched the career of Kevin Phillips who left to join Sunderland, with whom he won eight England caps. The League, however, suffered the saddest news possible with the passing of the Chairman's wife, Pat Gillard. Pat defined the word stalwart. Almost single handedly Pat ran the family business, a general store in the village of Charing, near Ashford, enabling Doug to service all his roles in football. To say I was flattered when Doug asked me to read a eulogy at Pat's funeral would be an understatement.

Kettering Town suddenly revived its fortunes in 2002. A long period battling for survival, with its existence at its London Road Stadium uncertain, followed the heady days of Derek Dougan's presence at the club. Dougan revolutionised the club when he engineered the first shirt sponsorship in British football. What followed was a less glamorous period but, nevertheless, ended with the League Championship in May 2002. Elsewhere, clubs continued to come and go. New clubs were promoted from the Feeder Leagues but at the end of the season Bilston Town resigned from the Competition and Bloxwich ceased to trade. My own season ended with a personal gem.

Match Officials, like clubs, also joined and left the Competition. Some retired; some decided officiating at this particular level wasn't for them; while many earned promotion along their career path towards the Football League and some acquired FIFA status. The Southern League's Phil Sharp, for example, progressed along this route and had earned a placed on FIFA's list of Linesmen. Sharp by name and sharp by nature Phil ventured even further; he was selected to participate at the 2002 World Cup tournament in Japan. Everyone I know was delighted for this popular Match Official. As the end of June approached I began to snatch some 'down time' during the comparative quiet of the closed season, whilst preparing for the next campaign and watching the World Cup on television. Unusually, for the time of year, the phone rang during early evening. I answered. There was a pause, suggesting this wasn't a local call, before a voice said, *"Den, it's Sharpy. I'm on the Final."* The excitement was electric; the cheers explosive. The person I had promoted to the Lineman's list of the Southern League; then upgraded to the Referees' List before recommending him for promotion to the Football League had included me in the long list of people he sought to thank and inform of his latest assignment. For Phil, it was 2.30am in

Japan; for me it was another magical moment in my career. Upon Phil's return, he gave me a signed copy of the World Cup Final Match Programme and Team Sheet – Germany v Brazil 30 June 2002 which was immediately framed and has since hung on my office wall at home.

The League's 100th competitive season, 2002/03, was won by Tamworth. The Lambs had enjoyed much Cup success and after completing some major ground works the club took its place at Non-League football's 'top table'. The year, however, was consumed by much talk and debate about the Football Conference's ambition to construct a second division. There were countless meetings at a 'Joint Liaison Committee' which comprised of members of the Conference and its Feeder Leagues, i.e. The Southern League, The Northern Premier League and The Isthmian League. There was, understandably, considerable resistance given the Feeder Leagues would be required to provide the 22 clubs to make up the proposed new Division. My personal view was the Country's Football Pyramid, at what was effectively the sixth tier, could not sustain another nationwide Division. I opined, if such a re-structure beneath Non-League's national Division was to be successful it should comprise two regional Divisions, e.g. North and South, with it three feeder competitions below, thereby creating a pyramid. This would, I acknowledged, entail the Feeder leagues giving up more clubs to the Football Conference so the idea wasn't universally popular. But it created a logical structure and subsequently prevailed. As in the past The Southern League provided the most clubs to create the new Divisions including moving some clubs to support the structure in the north.

The 2003/04 season, therefore, began with the announcement of what would happen at the end of the season. It also began with the sad news of the passing of Crawley Town legend, Stan Markham. Stan had started his football career as a goalkeeper at Tottenham Hotspur. He played many games for Spurs' Reserve and 'A' teams before injury ended his playing time prematurely. He subsequently spent 41 years at Crawley Town in just about every position possible, from Secretary to Chairman. Nine months later The

Newtowners were crowned Champions. What I would have given to see Stan's face on the final day of the campaign. But I have no doubt he watched his team lift the trophy, from wherever he was, with the broadest of smiles.

The season had not, however, been an entirely happy one within the League's Boardroom. Four Directors, one of whom helped source and then propose the acquisition of a new Office for League's administration, but then inexplicably voted against the planned move, expressed some differences of opinion to the Chairman. It was unclear to me precisely what their grouses were but whatever they were they were not shared by the remainder of the Board and the League's Officers. Nevertheless it made for an uncomfortable couple of months for the League's administration, in particular Chairman, Doug Gillard. With backing from his Board, Doug sought and received support from the Clubs on the direction of travel. He requested resignations from the four Directors concerned. These were all forthcoming in March 2004. Business seamlessly returned to normal. I had not been accustomed to such disagreement with a group supposedly working together, for the same end. Doug was a man of good character. He was always scrupulously fair and he dealt with a tricky situation with probity.

To accommodate the introduction of the Football Conference Regional Divisions, i.e. North and South, major surgery was required for the three Leagues that fed the top echelon. The Southern League Premier Division for 2004/05, for example, contained only six clubs from the previous season. Ten clubs were elevated from the East and West Divisions and six were moved from the Isthmian League. The loss of thirteen clubs inevitably impacted on the strength of the League, but not on its competitive nature. An emerging Cambridgeshire club, Histon, narrowly won a fiercely contested Premier Division by three points ahead of Chippenham Town. But the introduction of Play-Offs enabled fourth placed Hednesford Town to defeat Chippenham in the Final and join Histon in the Football Conference.

Salisbury City featured often during my career. I had spent many hours in the company of Manager Geoff Butler discussing issues with the club's

Ground at Victoria Park before its relocation to the custom built Raymond McEnhill Stadium in 1997. I followed the club to Yorkshire in 2003 for its match against Sheffield Wednesday in the FA Cup. Wednesday won 4-0. It was an eerie return to Hillsborough for me. In the meantime the Lillywhites suffered troubling off-field problems, leading to the end of Geoff Butler's seventeen year stint as Manager. But 2005/06 was a good season. Under the management of former Southampton midfielder, Nick Holmes, Salisbury won the League and along with it, promotion. I didn't know at the time, but I was to meet the Lilywhites again in the not too distant future.

Notwithstanding any of the above, I will remember the season with great sorrow. We lost Doug Gillard on 11th November 2005. The 'workaholic' set off from his Charing, Ashford home early in the morning to attend a meeting at the FA. On his way back to Charing Cross he collapsed. Despite what I believe was about two weeks in hospital Doug never fully regained consciousness. I visited him in hospital. I don't believe he knew I was there but I brought him up to date with the latest news. Upon leaving I kissed his cheek not knowing it was our final farewell. God Bless Doug.

Vice-Chairman Ken Turner, a former Secretary of Gloucester City FC, was appointed Chairman for the remainder of the season and the assignment was confirmed at the 2006 AGM. Soon after the meeting I prepared the fixture list manually and computerised the solution upon my return to the Office. As soon as the list had been published, like every other year, I sneaked off for a fortnight's holiday. But I had a shock upon my return. My laptop, i.e. the League's laptop, was missing. It contained all the League's historic records and, for example, player registrations. Nobody appeared to know what had happened to the device, not even my Assistant who had worked in the Office each day during my absence. Looking back, I am not certain if anyone even realised it had disappeared let alone knew of its whereabouts, other than, perhaps, the person or persons who lifted it. I reported the loss to the police but acknowledged there was little chance of it being recovered. It was a mystery, and remained so.

Part Three – The Football Conference 2007-2015

My 25th season with the Southern League progressed normally until, that is, the Chairman and Vice-Chairman began to act curiously and unprofessionally. I could not reconcile their conduct with previous Officers I had served under, principally Bill Dellow and Doug Gillard. Without any explanation their antics led to a very uncomfortable time for me. I was made to feel very embarrassed at a Board meeting when, without warning, a well rehearsed but juvenile prank was played upon me. The personal content and timing of the prank was inappropriate. Neither was it the time or place for such insulting behaviour. Even with my strong sense of humour I was not amused and the remainder of the Board was taken aback. A little later I was asked by the Vice-Chairman to take ownership of the sponsored Company car or he would come to my house and take it away. I was staggered by this unexpected demand. After due consideration I complied with the order provided the vehicle was serviced, and any defects rectified, before I made the transfer of ownership. After 25 years of total commitment to the cause I did not understand the change of atmosphere and I was not advised of anything I had done to effect such a rude approach. No meeting(s); no warnings; no advice; nothing. Inexplicably, the management towards me from these two gentleman changed. I didn't know why. I just got on with my business.

I cannot remember precisely when, but fairly soon after the above unhappy events, I took a telephone call from Keith Allen, a good friend and ally on the Board. It wasn't unusual to receive a call from Keith but on this occasion the brevity was uncommon. *"Buy Saturday's Daily Mail"*, Keith said, and quickly hung up. Once again I complied with an instruction, albeit a polite instruction on this occasion.

On the back page there was an advertisement inviting applications for the post of General Manager of The Football Conference. Notwithstanding my disillusionment at recent events this was an opportunity I could not allow to pass, under any circumstances. Without hesitation, I carefully and extensively prepared my application and got it in the post, at the appropriate time of course.

An acknowledgement was received in a timely manner. This was soon followed by a letter granting me an interview in the Offices of a famous central London Solicitors. But, argh! I was due to be in Spain on the selected day. Determined this wasn't to be a problem, I took all my preparation work with me, curtailed the holiday and booked an early flight back to Blighty, leaving Jan alone in our Iberian home. Twenty-four hours later I took the train from Birmingham to London, arriving on Drury Lane more than an hour before my appointment time. When the waiting was over I was greeted by Bill King (Chairman), Charlie Clapham (Vice Chairman) and Brian Lee (Vice-President). It helped me to know I had met them all during my career and knew them well. But that didn't make the process any easier; the questioning was intense and thoroughly professional. Seventy-five minutes later I was back on Drury Lane carrying out my own post mortem, wondering if there was anything I could have done differently, i.e. better. The waiting game began.

Two days later my mobile rang, showing an unfamiliar number. After my cautious greeting a voice said, *"Hello Dennis, Lee here. When can you start?"*

The announcement of my new role the Football Conference's Dartford Office.

The answer to the question, upon which the Southern League was to insist, was *"in three months"*. So I gave the required notice to the League Chairman. I didn't expect a verbal bouquet of flowers but after 25 years service I wasn't ready for the icy response I received in one simple inquiry, *"Had I been approached?"*

I was pleased to say *"No. I did this of my own accord"* and proceeded to prepare for my 26th Southern League AGM. Prior to 'D' Day, whilst working my notice period, I used my spare time and a few days leave, to gather information on my new role. I attended three Conference Board meetings and the Competition's Play-Off Final at Wembley Stadium – a game between Morecambe and Exeter City. It was immediately obvious, I was about to make a giant step up! But Morecambe's victory left me saying goodbye to a quickly made friend, the 'Shrimps' Chairman and Conference Director, Rod Taylor; yes another Rod Taylor. Rod was particularly helpful and welcoming during my induction period. He also provided countless bags of sweets at Board meetings.

I left the Southern League on 31st May 2007 after a little over 25 years service without an invitation to the Annual Presentation Dinner. But I was told I could attend the AGM, for which I had made all the formal arrangements and prepared the Dinner programme, *"if I wished."* To embark on a 300 mile round trip to Torquay to attend a thirty minute meeting and leave before celebrating the season I had worked on; saying goodbye to the clubs, many of whom I had worked with for a quarter of a century, was not an attractive proposition. It really was time for me to go. Departure day could not come soon enough.

Untaken holiday enabled me to leave the Southern League in time to assist the Conference with its own end of season formalities. The uplift in status of the two competitions was immediately apparent. But the first three months in my new role was spent working from the Conference's office in Dartford, spending four nights in a hotel and travelling between Worcester and

Dartford on a Monday morning and Friday evening. The greater professional approach and capabilities of the clubs left me with little weekend work, other than to attend a match. Although player registrations were always open so a mobile phone and 'a finger on the button' was always required.

I was soon to learn one of the League's objectives was to move its administration from Dartford to somewhere more accessible and/or practical for Directors and member clubs to visit. One of my first jobs was, therefore, to compile and present a paper to the Board proposing a new centre for its operation. Realising this might be a sensitive subject I began by stating I meant no offence, nor did I wish to cause any inconvenience to existing personnel, by suggesting Birmingham. All current staff, including the Chief Executive John Moules, lived in the Bexleyheath/Dartford area. Having moved from Horsham to Worthing to Worcester in preceding years I was open minded about relocation and Worcester was only 26 miles from 'the second city'. My unbiased opinion for the new venue was supported by the motorway network that surrounded the 'Second City'. Also, Birmingham was served by three railway stations with direct access to most major towns around the country and two nearby airports, if need. And so it came to be. My next tasks were to find a suitable premises and recruit staff to replace those who chose to remain in Kent.

John remained completely helpful to me. He answered all my questions about the company and its procedures at the top end of the FA's National League System. There was one thing, however, he could not do. With his children at a vulnerable time of their school lives he said he would not relocate. Whilst we continued to work well together I could not understand how this arrangement would work in the long term. And whilst I searched for the Company's next home, with Andrew Shaw a Conference Board member associated with Altrincham FC, I did not anticipate what came next.

I was making my way to a Board meeting, only about the fifth one I had attended; in other words, very early in my new role. My phone rang. *"Den, Andy here. Where are you?"* I nearly wet myself. My mind raced. Where was I meant to be? I was in fear. Was I meant to be elsewhere? *"I'm walking through Covent Garden, on my way to the Board meeting at Clintons, Mel Stein's office"*, I replied. *"Stay where you are. I've been sent to intercept you. You must not go in."* More shivers went down my spine. What was going on? Andy met me passing The Theatre Royal and explained the Board was just agreeing terms with John for his departure. I hadn't bargained for that. I was suddenly on my own. But not for long.

Keith Allen had recommended an Assistant working with him at Wycombe Wanderers Football Club who wished to further her career. Kierina Rowland joined me at our new abode in Waterloo Street, Birmingham where we spent one particular Sunday, helped by Jan, receiving and unloading all the League's files and furniture delivered to us from Dartford. That was one long, long working day. We were all set to go, and the team was soon enlarged by the recruitment of a Financial Accountant. Fraser Tooley joined the staff. Keirina and Fraser brought strong skills to the Office team, and we were all quickly tested, even before our first season commenced.

Settling into the new Football Conference Office suite at Waterloo Street, Birmingham

One of my first tasks was to compile the fixture list, manually. The Conference was dissatisfied with the computer solution used in earlier seasons and I was asked, at my interview, if I would replicate my work at the Southern League. I had enough experience not to be intimidated by the task. Besides, with Torquay United being relegated from the Football League, to schedule a Boxing Day/ New Year's Day with Devon rivals Exeter City was too good to ignore. Boston United accompanied Torquay in being relegated, having suffered a ten point deduction, and joined whilst still being in a Creditors Voluntary Arrangement (CVA). Failing to pay its creditors, in particular its football creditors, gave Boston a huge 'sporting advantage'. So with the agreement of The Football League, with whom the Conference had a promotion/relegation agreement, Boston was placed a further Division down the pyramid, into Conference North. The double demotion saved Altrincham from relegation, the third successive time Alty had been saved in such a way. And financial issues that tested our administration did not end there. Crawley Town was deducted six points for breaching salary payment regulations; Halifax Town was deducted ten points for entering Administration, and folded at the end of the season; and Nuneaton Borough was liquidated, also at the end of the season. Notwithstanding my hopes for greater professionalism amongst full-time Clubs, big issues prevailed and tested the League's management. The Board responded by strongly enhancing its financial controls in what was to become one of the industry's first financial fair play regulations.

On an early day off in my Football Conference career I joined several ex-Players, Colleagues and Fans to say goodbye to Horsham's Queen Street Ground.

The Competition's core business, football, ran smoothly despite having some difficult decisions to make. Torquay took to their new position in the football pyramid well and finished the League season in third place, missing out on an immediate return to the League by defeat in the Play-offs. Boston United were still subject to the financial event at the end of the season and, therefore, suffered a further relegation, to the Northern Premier League. On the playing front Oxford United continued to attract the highest average League attendance, approaching the 10,000 mark, but could only muster an eighth place finish. Aldershot returned to the Football League as Champions of the Conference, under the new title of Aldershot Town having gone out of business as Aldershot in 1998; and Exeter City also won back their Football League place following a Play-Off victory over Cambridge United at Wembley. This match at the National Stadium attracted an attendance of 42,511, another big test for the Competition's new administration. Exeter's promotion sadly meant I lost a person with whom another early friendship had been formed. Conference and Grecian's Director, Julian Tagg, returned to the Football League.

Financial issues were not confined to Boston. Crawley Town fell behind with players' wages and was deducted six points for fiscal irregularities; Halifax Town struggled to meet its creditors and was deducted ten points when it entered Administration. The club subsequently folded. And Nuneaton Borough was liquidated after the end of the season. One way or another, my first year at the head of the FA's 'National League Structure' had been a busy one, and traumatic at times. The Competition's financial controls/regulations for the governance of clubs had to be strengthened. And if I thought my first term was tough, year two was even harder.

I was enjoying the greater professionalism of the clubs, the majority of whom had full-time Secretaries. And with the distances teams had to travel on a Saturday very little business was left to the last minutes of a match day morning. This helped me fulfil a requirement of my job description, i.e. to attend a weekend game. My trust in the clubs' administration

was, though, misplaced in some cases. In the early weeks of the 2008/9 season my colleagues in the Office found four clubs had fielded ineligible (unregistered) players, including three clubs in the Premier Division, all of whom had full-time administrations. How could a professional football club field a player they had not registered with the Competition? I still ask myself that question today.

Sadly, some clubs had fielded ineligible players on more than one occasion so my team, principally me, was criticised for not spotting the errors immediately they occurred. I argued, this was impossible as games at this early time of season were being played thick & fast and in some cases clubs had repeated their error before we had received the required match reports. Besides, it would entail checking over two thousand players each week whereas a club had only sixteen to check on a match day. And surely a professional football club, especially one with a full-time administration and full-time players, knew precisely who they had on their payroll, with whom they had a written contract and had registered with the Competition. Seemingly not. It was more expedient to apportion blame elsewhere. Anyway, it was not a Competition's responsibility to check a club played only eligible players, that burden fell entirely upon the club. An unregistered player was not ineligible until he played, so a Competition could only act retrospectively, after a club had committed such an offence. It was club's duty to ensure it fielded only eligible players, i.e. those registered with the Competition. Despite the grief the clubs gave me over this issue I was comforted throughout by a letter from a senior member of the Football Association who confirmed I was not in any way culpable for the maladministration of the clubs and a League was not obligated to check registrations. Furthermore, a player could be ineligible for many reasons so a routine check that a player was registered would not reveal all possible transgressions and was, therefore, inconclusive. As a consequence of the above event Bognor Regis Town, Crawley Town, Mansfield Town and Oxford United all had points deducted from their League Table score. No League likes to see an asterisk indicating a club's loss of points for rule infringements, so to see three such breaches in the 'shop window' Division was damaging to the Competition's image. Crawley and Oxford, in particular, sought to aggressively advance their futile dissent but neither could explain their negligence of playing a player they had not registered with the League. To seek to deflect blame and/or responsibility onto my team and I, hurt, when our only 'crime' was to detect the inefficiencies of others. Why on earth did these clubs, and their appropriate staff, not know what they were doing. Happily, the rest of the season passed trouble free.

Burton Albion won the Championship despite a nail biting 2-1 final day reverse at Torquay United. The 'Gulls went on to defeat Cambridge United 2-0 before 35,089 spectators at Wembley, to regain its status in the Football League. The Conference's tightened monetary controls appeared to be having a positive affect. The Board sought to monitor expenditure on players' wages against income, seeking to ensure salaries did not exceed 60% of income. The Competition developed Rules relating to the payment of creditors, especially football creditors. This caused some angst with HMRC as it was concerned its position as a preferred creditor was being usurped. That was not the Conference's intention so it entered into negotiation with the Revenue to create arrangements that would allow the Competition to monitor payment of PAYE and NI. There were no fiscal failures during, or at the end of, the 2008/09 season. There was, however, a significant decision with the Football League that would subsequently affect the Football Conference.

Since the establishment in 1987 of a promotion/relegation agreement between The Football League and the Conference the competitions had worked closely together, particularly on issues related to Ground Grading of Stadia and the financials at each member club. The competitions had become especially concerned about sustainability and continuity of membership. During the 2008/09 season the Football League had imposed points deductions upon Southampton (10 – imposed in the following season as the club had already been relegated); Stockport County (10); Darlington

(10); Rotherham (17); Bournemouth (17) and, at the beginning of the season, Luton Town (20). The Hatters had also been deducted 10 points by the Football Association for making irregular payment to football agents. The 30 point deduction proved too much for Luton to overcome and relegation to the Conference was confirmed with four matches of the 2008/09 remaining. It proved to be a bitter pill to swallow and one that, looking at banners within the Kenilworth crowd even now, has still not been fully digested. Bitterness ran deep. Luton had become the first team to drop from the Championship to the Conference in successive seasons, ending an 89 year stay in the Football League. But brighter days were to come for the Hatters, which contrasted sharply with the club that accompanied them in relegation from the League, Chester City.

The 2009/10 Champions, and winners of automatic promotion, were Stevenage Borough. The club's effervescent Chairman, and former Conference Director Phil Wallace, had finally fulfilled his ambition. Luton turned their fortunes around and finished Runners-up, but then lost to 5th place York City in a Play-Off semi-final. The Minstermen lost the Wembley Final to Oxford United. Oxford's scheduled league matches against Luton represented the first time two clubs faced each other in all of the top five steps of England's football pyramid. But in an otherwise super season there were two major sources of disruption, which made for a testing time in our Office.

Luton's companions in demotion, Chester City, were in serious financial difficulty and were placed in Administration, thereby incurring a ten point deduction and a further 15 for financial irregularities. Amid a change of ownership in the shape of Chester City (2004) Ltd, a Company set up by former Chairman Stephen Vaughan and his family, the FA withheld the transfer of affiliation. This meant the Club could not fulfil the first game of the season at Grays Athletic. Within the next three months Mr Vaughan, a businessman from Liverpool who once bid to buy Wrexham FC, was disqualified from acting as a Director for a period of 11 years following his involvement in a £500,000 VAT fraud whilst being a Director of Wigan Vikings, a rugby club. He became the first owner of a professional football club to fail the FA's Fit & Proper Person Test. Chester City then stumbled along for the first few months of the season before being served with a winding-up order by HMRC for £29,000 in January 2010. Players were not being paid on time, if at all, and began to express their dissatisfaction by refusing to play and/or travel to away games. The Club was clearly in breach of several Competition Rules and Financial Regulations. I made it my duty to attend a home match, with Jan. Whilst we were treated hospitably in the Boardroom the atmosphere elsewhere was toxic. The 'air' amongst supporters outside the Clubhouse was simmering. Inside the corridors it was evident from the noise of a physical altercation, some unwelcome visitors were being ejected. It was an uncomfortable afternoon.

The writing for Chester City FC was on the wall when the Club failed to honour another fixture at Forest Green Rovers as players failed to board the coach. The Competition's Board suspended the Club for seven days to enable it to 'get its house in order'. No good news was forthcoming and on 26th February 2010 Chester City FC was expelled from the Football Conference by the member Clubs at a Special General Meeting held at Nene Park, Rushden. Just a few months later that year Mr Vaughan, a former Boxer and Boxing Promoter, was arrested and subsequently jailed for punching a Police Officer, breaking his jaw.

Business was made equally as eventful by Salisbury City. In recent years the 'Whites' had enjoyed a successful time under the management of Geoff Butler, in the Southern League. The Club had won a place in the Conference South in the 2004 restructure of the football pyramid and had subsequently gained promotion to the national Division. After finishing 12th in the top Division the previous season (2008/09), finishing only ten points off the play-off places, Salisbury entered Administration in September (2009) with debts amounting to £200,000. Five months later, in February 2010, the Club was taken over by three local businessmen, William Harrison-Allen, Chris

Brammall and Jeff Hooper who took the Club out of Administration. But by June of that year the Club was forced to take a double demotion after missing a deadline to pay creditors. These issues consumed an incredible amount of time and patience within our Office but had to be dealt with whilst continuing to manage the Company's core business – running a football competition containing 68 professional and semi-professional clubs.

Whilst preparing for the Competition's 32nd season Jan & I began planning our wedding. Having fallen 'head over heels' for New York on our first visit to the Big Apple in 1998 a return visit was the unanimous choice. But where in NYC? Well, there was only one place that would do for me – The Empire State Building. And so it came to pass. Thanks to my colleagues in the Office I was able to do something previously unheard of, I took six days off work in the football season! Upon arrival in America we checked into the Waldorf-Astoria and soon made our way to the City Hall to follow up our 'on-line' application to marry in the city. It all went like clockwork and we were married on the 55th floor of what was once the world's tallest building, the ESB on 20th October 2010 (20.10.2010.)

Meanwhile, back in Birmingham, the drive for financial fairness and prudence continued the following season. Kidderminster Harriers, Histon and Rushden & Diamonds, all in the Premier Division, were docked points for submitting misleading financial information. Redditch United, St. Albans City and Welling United, in the regional Divisions, all suffered a similar sanction. On the playing field, Crawley Town, now in a new stadium at Broadfield won the Championship and were promoted to the Football League for the first time in the Club's history. The reincarnation of Wimbledon, AFC Wimbledon, joined the Newtowners when they defeated Luton Town on penalties in the Play-Off Final held at Manchester City's Etihad Stadium, as Wembley had been selected by UEFA to stage the Champions League Final. The Conference, and my Office in particular, received a lot of criticism from supporters of the Finalists for choosing Manchester for a Final containing two southern based clubs. But it was not possible to wait until the Finalists were known before deciding on a venue. It needed to be established a year in advance. And we were grateful to Conference Director, Andy Shaw, for his connection to Manchester City FC and the 'Citizens' for accommodating us. It is a wonderful stadium and the most important aspect, the pitch, was perfect! I know. We were allowed a brief kick-about!! Never had I 'played' on such true surface.

Call this work?

A day out at the Offices of Littlewoods Pools' at Walton Hall Avenue, Liverpool and another chance to meet 'Sir' Roger Hunt and Gordon 'One Save' Banks.

In 2011/12 Fleetwood Town FC continued its meteoric rise up the football pyramid. Under the leadership of its Chairman, Andy Pilley *, the Club had already achieved 4 promotions in 8 years. Its fifth elevation

* It came as a huge surprise to me when, in July 2023, I read Andy Pilley had been sentenced to 13 years in prison for fraud after a trial lasting nine months. And even more surprised to learn he had, in 1998, served 4 months for conspiracy to steal whilst working for the Post Office.

came with the Conference Championship having amassed 103 points while scoring 102 goals in its 46 league matches. 31 of the goals had been notched by Jamie Vardy who subsequently moved to Leicester City where he won the Premier League and 26 England caps. Wrexham finished second in the table but were defeated by Luton in the semi-final of the Play-off matches. The Hatters were in the Final for the second consecutive season but also tasted defeat for the second time. On this occasion York, in their second Final in three years, ran out 2-1 winners in front of 39,265 fans. It was a superb match to end a fine season although the campaign had not passed completely trouble free.

The Board made efforts to strictly monitor for sound fiscal practice. Too many Clubs, it seemed, were prepared to sail too close to the wind when it came to measuring expenditure against income. Evidently, there was too much debt owed to HMRC and, from the size of outstanding amounts in some cases, the Revenue was not being particularly vigilant until it became time to issue winding-up petitions. Thereafter, enforcement became heavy. The Competition, therefore, negotiated an arrangement for HMRC to share information on settlement each month. With the threat of a player registration embargo for non-payment of, say, tax, NI and VAT, collection became more regular and timely. But the odd contentious case still arose.

After losing the use of its Rockingham Road Ground in 2011 Kettering Town, under the ownership of Imran Ladak, was deducted 3 points for failing to pay football creditors. The Club finished bottom of the League, entered Administration and was demoted by the standard sanction of two Divisions.

Darlington was also in troubled waters. Relegated from the Football League just over a year ago and having relinquished its home of 120 years at Feethams, the Quakers were playing home matches at the lavish 25,000 capacity Darlington Arena. The Club brought with it, to the Conference, substantial debt and began failing to meet the players' monthly wage bill. Complaints from the players regularly came in to the Office and I remember some gave appropriate notice to terminate their contracts. The

Club was placed under a player registration embargo which limited the Club to signing non-contract players and/or youth or Academy players from other clubs without incurring further cost. Darlington was clearly troubled by this and pestered the Office with claims it could not compete in the Conference without signing new/better players. But I was obliged to apply the rules and advised the Club, how could I let it take new players onto its payroll when it was not paying the players it already had. I had to weather the rancour for the sake of the Competition's integrity. And on one particular Friday whilst still articulating its disapproval of my decision the club complied with my order, albeit reluctantly fearing a drubbing, and borrowed a 17 year old goalkeeper from Sunderland's Academy on a short term youth loan. Unafraid of putting my head in the lion's den I went to Darlington's home match the following day. Obviously I faced a barrage of questions and disapproval throughout the afternoon, albeit politely. How could they compete with a youth in goal, they protested? I accepted such appeals go with the territory. I cannot remember the result, nor Darlington's opponents, but I vividly recall saying to Janet upon my return, I have seen a future England goalkeeper today. As it was late by the time I got back to Worcester and due to the hour Jan's response was fairly unenthusiastic but sufficiently interested to ask, *"What's his name?" "Jordan Pickford"*, I replied. And we retired without giving the game any further thought. Sadly, at the end of the season, Darlington FC was also put to bed. The Club folded.

I thank the lucky stars that brought Jan & I together. Her upbringing meant our interest in football made us very compatible. So, after some personnel changes in my Office, when Kierina moved on to pastures new and Hannah Brown & Tahli Jenkinson came and departed, to be replaced by Louise Edwards and Michaela Lock, Jan also joined the team for a three day each week stint. As a senior Civil Servant at Worcester Combined Court, already known to Louise, Jan's experience and maturity was of great benefit to the organisation. And after about 17 years together, at that time, she knew my work and my thoughts inside-out.

While some Clubs continued to abuse creditors, and consequently fall foul of the financial regulations, others were resurrecting their fortunes. Premier Division clubs in the 2012/13 season were all onside regarding such sanctions. But Hinckley United, in the Conference North Division lost three points for failing to pay football creditors. A further 3 point deduction followed for failing to fulfil a fixture. In the South section Farnborough lost 4 points for fielding an ineligible player before losing another 10 points for entering Administration. But they were not alone. Truro succumbed to the same fate. The Club's Chairman, property developer Kevin Heaney, stood down at the beginning of the season after being declared bankrupt. He had previously funded the Club during 5 promotions in 6 seasons. Last season had been extremely tough and I remember travelling to Cornwall five times in the hope of helping the Club survive. It was all to no avail. The Club went into Administration; it was deducted 10 points and finished bottom of the Division, 15 points adrift.

As for the Premier Division Championship, the race for the automatic promotion place to the Football League was one of the closest I had overseen. Wrexham, Grimsby Town and Newport County were all in contention until their challenge fell away during the final weeks of the season leaving Mansfield Town and Kidderminster Harriers clear at the top. After 45 rounds of matches the destination of the trophy would not be determined until the final games, on the last Saturday of the season. So, where should I be with the trophy and medals? Subject to their results either could win. And there was 87 miles between the respective Grounds. I decided to position myself somewhere in between.

I parked at Donington Service Station, where the A42 meets the M1 and followed the scores via radio and telephone contact. Neither match was proving to be conclusive; both were level in their respective games. So before it was too late for me to reach either Stadium, I had to make a decision. But both games were level. Mindful that Mansfield began the day at the top of the Division and had to lose for Kidderminster to have a chance of overhauling them, I took a chance and set off for Mansfield. It was the correct choice. I was hastily escorted into the Ground and warmly welcomed. The trophy and medals were in the right place at the right time, and were presented. All was well that ended well; until, that is, a few days later.

It was about Thursday of the following week when the postman delivered a parking fine. I had overstayed my welcome at Donington Services. Naturally, I lodged my mitigating circumstances and that I had used the services for several cups of tea, biscuits and a sandwich during my anxious wait, adding that I had several thousand pounds worth of silverware with me and could not leave my vehicle. I was not idly parking. I also had the support of BBC Radio 5 live which had reported what I was hoping to achieve throughout its Saturday afternoon sports programme! I was pleased to learn a further few days later, the fine had been rescinded.

With another Congress weekend at Celtic Manor completed, and the new fixture list compiled, August 2013 and the start of another season soon arrived. A personal letter, on behalf of the Football Association, arrived too. As part of the FA's 150th birthday celebrations I had been selected to be one of 150 people to receive an award for services to football. The wording of the award appeared to be honouring volunteers who had given their time to our great game. My first reaction was, therefore, to advise the governing body I was not eligible. I was a full-time employee, not a volunteer. I was informed I had been nominated out of over 40,000 people who contributed to running the game each week and my nomination had been approved. I qualified; I had been selected; and I should accept. So I did.

The letter informed a presentation would be held at a central London location on a date to be advised. In the meantime recipients were asked not to disclose the content of the letter with anyone. Jan & I were intrigued. And I would not be telling the truth, knowing who the President of the FA was, if I said we did not speculate. Of course we did; and our hopes were realised. We were subsequently invited to Buckingham Palace on 13th October 2013 for me to receive a medal from HRH Prince William, followed by a luncheon. The council house kid was going to the Palace! What a wonderful day it was. I am sure Mum & Dad would have been bursting with pride. I am certain they were watching.

Buckingham Palace – The 150 recipients of The FA's award for services to football.

Top photo – I am somewhere in the back row, towards the centre.

Bottom photos – I get to meet the future King and show off my award in the Queen's back garden.

The above event came early in another eventful season. It began when Blue Square Bet, the Conference's title sponsor for six years, was taken over. The new owners of the Company chose not to renew its partnership with the Competition. Thanks to the tireless Charlie Clapham, the Competition's Vice-Chairman, a new sponsor was quickly found. An on-line payment/money movement Company called Skrill took over. Sadly, the arrangement was not blessed with longevity. It lasted only one year but Charlie's efforts were no doubt appreciated by the member Clubs.

As the season progressed a clutch of Clubs fell foul of the player registration rules. It was frustrating and disappointing that not all senior professional Clubs were still not being sufficiently diligent. Alfreton Town, Oxford City and Harrogate Town were deducted points and incurred the dreaded asterisk on the League Table. Even more 'Office' time, however, was consumed by the financial troubles of Aldershot Town, Hereford United and Salisbury City. The 'Shots were deducted ten points for entering administration and Hereford, having been plagued with growing financial issues throughout the season, were expelled on 10 June 2014. The demise of the Bulls was a huge irony, given they had saved their Premier Division status with a 1-0 win at Aldershot on the final day of the season. Salisbury, promoted via the play-offs at the end of last season, finished in 10th spot despite spending much of the campaign under a player registration embargo. Now under the stewardship of an unknown Dubai based Moroccan businessman (or so we were led to believe), Mr. Outail Touzar, the Club remained in trouble. Joined by local businessman, Mark Winter, the pair took over the Club in May, for allegedly £1 and the inheritance of an estimated £150,000 of outstanding debt. Much debt, however, remained unsettled and the Club was again relegated, this time to the South Division on the understanding all creditors would be satisfied, i.e. paid, by the 4th July. The deadline was not met and the Club was expelled. The Club subsequently went into liquidation whilst challenging the legitimacy of Mr Touzar's take over.

Apart from the player registration issues mentioned above the Competition's core business passed without any more problems. Luton Town, despite being close to honours during its sojourn in non-league, finally 'produced the goods'. They won the Premier Division by a country mile, 19 points above Cambridge United who won promotion back to the Football League through the play-offs. Little did we know Luton's elevation to League 2 was the beginning of its nine year climb to the Premier League. A wonderful achievement and just reward for Luton's CEO, Gary Sweet, who spent the duration of the Club's tenure on the Conference Board.

Another new season brought with it a new title and a new main sponsor. The Football Conference was re-branded as The National League and for sponsorship reasons became known as The Vanarama National League. Hereford's expulsion saved the reborn Chester from relegation but Salisbury City's exit, following relegation to the South Division occurred too late to save a Club and the section played with a team short. Almost inevitably, but equally disappointingly for professionally run members, three clubs in the Premier division were found to have fielded ineligible players and each had three points deducted. Forest Green Rovers, Nuneaton Borough and Telford United all suffered that ignominy. Barnet, relegated from the Football League only two seasons ago won their place back by the margin of a single point over Bristol Rovers. But Rovers, relegated only the previous May, were compensated with a Wembley Play-Off victory over Grimsby Town in front of a Conference record attendance of 47,029, which still stands.

The Office team leaves for Wembley Stadium for the 2014-15 Play-Off Final.
Left to right:- Louise, Michaela, Janet

Above:- The Strudwicks survey the National Stadium. Below:- Closer to kick-off, a former Carshalton Athletic full-back renews acquaintance with former Horsham full-back whilst waiting to be presented to the teams.

CHAPTER FIVE

The Final Whistle – October 2015 to date

At the time of concluding the 2014/15 season I was in my 69th year and more than three years beyond State retirement age. I had begun playing organised football from the age of 9, subsequently graduating to a senior level. I had played the game for approximately 21 years, largely for my hometown club. During a 52 year working career I had completed the equivalent of just over 38 seasons in football administration, almost entirely in full-time employment. In summary, the majority of my working life had been spent in my hobby. I had indeed been very, very fortunate.

Preparing for whatever lay ahead I sought the appropriate financial advice to see if I could viably face the future without a full-time income. The answer was in the affirmative, should I wish to step off the treadmill. This prompted serious heart-wrenching discussions at home. If I was to retire, we agreed Jan would also have to leave her part-time employment at the Football Conference. It was going to be hard enough for me to 'let go' without Jan continuing her role at the Competition Office. Fortunately, Jan understood and agreed. I was grateful for her support in making a joint decision. We remained focussed on completing the regular season, in which Barnet won the Championship for the third time, and we then concentrated on the series of Play-Off matches in the three Divisions. The National League Final at Wembley was contested by Bristol Rovers and Grimsby Town. It proved to be one of the most exciting games we had staged. The match was level at 90 minutes and still tied after extra-time. The Rovers won on penalties. Along with my colleagues the Office team then turned our attention to the AGM and wound up the affairs of my eighth season solely in charge whilst at the same time setting the stage for the next campaign. Only upon reaching a satisfactory and tidy conclusion would I call time on my career. So two days after a magnificent celebration of the season, held at Celtic Manor in Newport, South Wales I posted a letter to the Chairman giving six weeks notice of my departure. It is fair to say, the Board was surprised.

Once the Chairman shared the news with the Board my phone started ringing and the meetings began, some scheduled; some unofficial. Everyone wanted to know why I wished to leave a job that meant so much to me. I didn't find the arguments for me to change my mind sufficiently persuasive for me to stay in office, but I did agree to remain in post a little longer, whilst a replacement was sought. In the meantime, determined not to leave any aspect incomplete and/or unfinished, I carried on as normal. I compiled the fixture list for the forthcoming campaign and prepared for, and attended, the pre-season Clubs' meeting at Telford. The Chairman advised the Clubs of my decision and I was asked to address the meeting after which I received a standing ovation accompanied by what appeared to me, a thunderous round of applause. It left me with a memory I will never forget.

Looking back, I would be telling 'porkie-pies' if I said I have not missed my total involvement in the game. But it was the intensity, the daily commute and the long hours that contributed to my decision. I missed Brian Lee, too. Brian had stood down at the AGM a year ago. My voice and access to 'the Chair' following the appointment of Brian's successor, Brian Barwick, was not as direct. Mr. Barwick, it seemed, had many other responsibilities and much of my contact had to be carried out through a Secretary. Whilst my position within the structure was unaffected the introduction of a 'third party', between me and my direct line Manager, was unhelpful. It added another layer in the line of communication to my Boss. There were times when quick decisions were needed and/or advice given. This was not always possible under the new management. I didn't enjoy the times when I could not pass on the Competition's direction promptly. It was time for me to go.

My three jobs in football were vocations more than occupations. I had worked my socks off for 39 years. It had been far from easy but there had been hundreds of good times and many memorable moments. During my playing career I had met and befriended many players and other people. In my administrative career I had met and worked with 'household' names from within the game, many that I have already mentioned. One 'magic moment' not so far mentioned is the day I discovered England International and Portsmouth stalwart, Jack Froggatt, ran 'The Green Man' Public House in a village near my home. I visited him and sought his autograph on three match day programmes from Pompey Championship years, 1949/50 & 1950/51. I had already acquired the signatures of four of his team mates, including Jimmy Dickinson and Duggie Reid, so when Mr. Froggatt saw what was in front of him, he was visibly moved. *"I will have to sit down"* he said, wiping his eyes. After several minutes his name joined the signatures of his colleagues. We stayed in touch; his son or daughter I cannot remember which, owned a restaurant near Worthing, which I frequented. Occasionally, he would call in for a nightcap and would say "hello" if I was there. Jack Froggatt would come to my table!! If only my Dad could see that! More moments I could not have bought.

Notwithstanding all of the above, Bill Dellow's admiral advice, to *"pack up the year before they start taking the piss"* was always in the back pocket of my mind. I believe I comfortably met that threshold. I had a few good years left in me but my overriding thought was, I was prepared to go. And, above all, I wanted to go. Like everything else in life day to day circumstances, personnel and working conditions change. I found myself in the fortunate position I was no longer obligated to work with all these changes. I was verbally encouraged to stay and as an alternative I was invited to continue the management of the Competition's football business, only, working for a reduced number of days. But I knew that would not work for me. I could not work for, say, three days each week and just put the job down for the remaining time. I had always been involved 'up to my neck' and that was the only way I could continue. But, I had selfishly indulged myself in my chosen career; it was now time to pull my considerable weight at home, with Janet. I had played and administered football for sixty years, or thereabouts. My career had eliminated, almost to zero, any time off in the winter months. I had never, for example, been able to go away at Christmas time; I was always on duty at such a critical and busy time. I was determined to change that scenario. And I have, for the past nine years or so. We, Jan & I, have celebrated the festive season in Prague, Washington DC, New York, Boston and our homes in Worcester, and the warmer climes of Aigues, Spain. To celebrate the beginning of our 'new lives', without full-time work, we rode the Rocky Mountaineer train from Banff and Jasper to Vancouver from where we cruised to Alaska. Our stay in the 49th State enabled me to fulfil a 'bucket list' wish, i.e. to see whales in the sea. When back on dry land we came within feet of enormous brown bears. Alaska is one of the most beautiful and hospitable places I have visited.

I didn't suffer from any withdrawal symptoms when leaving football behind, but I purposefully stayed away from games to help me 'let go'. Having an indefinite time to ourselves has enabled us to visit our home in Spain more often, and for longer periods. We have forged many friendships during our 21 year occupancy in Aigues, Alicante. In this respect we have been able to give something back to our Spanish pals, Oscar & Ruth Gonzales and their children, without whom our home would not be so well taken care of. Muchas gracias, amigos.

Also, being able to watch football in Spain without responsibility and/or duty, helped me to re-integrate into the game at home. Visits to Real Madrid, Atletico Madrid, Valencia, Barcelona, Elche, Hercules (Alicante) and other teams more local to Casa Strudwick have been therapeutic. I can now comfortably visit clubs local to my Worcester home, as well as making the occasional visit to Horsham FC and Jan's team, Halesowen Town FC. This enables me to stay close to, and in touch with the work within the game I continue to serve.

CHAPTER SIX

'Time Added On' – October 2015 not out

I called time on 31st October 2015. After a final lunch with my colleagues, gratefully gate crashed by Brian Lee, I made the train journey home from Birmingham New Street Station to Worcester Shrub Hill for the last time. I had no regrets. And, if at any time I felt uncertain about what I had done, I reminded myself how I felt when I posted ***that*** letter back in June. I felt a weight had been lifted from my shoulders. I was relieved. Besides, I still had my role on the FA's Judicial Panel to look forward to, should I feel 'unemployed' at any time. I had a new hobby, too. During the four month wind down spell Jan, with her brother Steve, had signed me up for an allotment. *"I had to have somewhere to go"*, Jan insisted. *"But I have rarely turned an angry sod in the garden, let alone an allotment"* I retorted. My protest was in vain. It was all too late. The deal had been done. Whilst I am not 'in love' with my new past-time I have become spellbound by what mother earth, a tiny seed, water and a bit of tender loving care can achieve. Nothing beats home grown fruit & vegetables, particularly for two vegetarians. Notwithstanding the allotment, it wasn't long before I had somewhere else to go.

Within a few weeks with my feet metaphorically up, the FA asked me if I would like join its Registrations Department for a month's temporary secondment to help during the January 2016 transfer window. I was pleased to accept. It was a new experience and an opportunity to work next to the people with whom I had worked with remotely, for many years. The task entailed a journey to Wembley Stadium very early on a Monday morning to field questions from clubs about Contracts, Registrations and to answer Player status inquiries. After four nights in a nearby hotel, and four over indulgent breakfasts, I travelled home on Friday.

I must admit, although I had to get used to the FA's software, I wasn't overworked. I had time on my hands. So I began to work on something that I never quite understood during my career, the structure/order of the Competition Rules for the level of football to which I was accustomed, i.e. the Standardised Rules for the National League System. I couldn't, and didn't, change any Rules I just re-assembled them in a chronological order ranging from organisational requirements and obligations; pre-season arrangements to pre-match; match day duties; and post match responsibilities. Not knowing what might happen to my 'paper' I left my work with two senior colleagues, Neil Prescott and David Newton. Two years later I found the principle of my re-structure had been adopted.

Throughout this process I continued the work I began in 2014 as a member of the FA's Judicial Panel, sitting on Disciplinary Commissions as an Independent Football Panel Member. One of the first assignments I received, after I retired was held at Carlisle. For reasons I am unable to mention, the meeting was adjourned and I had to travel again the following week. On hearing this my son Ben said, rather protectively, *"Don't they know you have retired."* I have since been appointed to the General Appeals Panel, which involves Clubs and/or participants appealing against decisions of Commissions and Competitions. As these frequently involve a challenge to the interpretation/application of Competition Rules, they replicate the work I have done for the past 38 years. I have been involved with many levels of the game, professional and non-League. I was subsequently appointed to the Regional Disciplinary Panel which deals with the cases of several County FA's. More recently I have been assigned to the National Serious Case Panel. My participation has taken me to many places, as well as Carlisle, big and small, including many visits to the magnificent Wembley Stadium. But since Covid all the Hearings have been held 'remotely' by Microsoft Teams.

There is an old adage in soccer, 'you are quickly forgotten in football', as the game moves on rapidly. I am, therefore, grateful, to the FA for remembering me and for allowing me to still be involved. My continued involvement gives me a 'raison d'etre'. I thank The FA for that.

It is, you know, the greatest game on earth. And it's more than just a kick in the grass.

A thought for those friends; team mates; opponents & colleagues I have lost along the way. The final whistle may have blown but, for me, they are all still on my field of play. God bless them.

Ian Agate – Larger than life goalkeeper who played for several Sussex County League clubs

Mike Appleby – Forever helpful Leagues Manager at The Football Association

Kevin Barry – Formidable opponent. Tall Centre forward for Hastings United FC

Peter Bentley – A giant of administration in Sussex soccer. Secretary of the Sussex County League

Peter & Janet Brackley – Peter, a radio & TV broadcaster. Janet, my Secretary in Brighton

Paul Britton – Highly respected & popular Secretary of Bath City FC

Micky Browning – Possibly the most respected Horsham FC player. A tremendous centre-forward

Kenny Carter – Highly successful Manager with Lewes FC

Steve Cosham – Amazing pace & tenacity. Dynamic striker. Scored goals for fun

Peter Cull – Southwick's most uncompromising and dependable defender of the '60s & '70s

Steve Danaher (The Hat) – Newick Rangers' biggest supporter

Bill Dellow – Ex-Referee & top Administrator who bravely passed me The Southern League reins

Barry Dendy – Footballing pal during the early days. A goalkeeper aka Bendy Dendy

Ron Eastwood – Manager, Newick Rangers FC. The most successful Boss in the Sunday League

Tony Elkins-Green – Talented Manager of Crawley Town FC and Horsham FC

Keith Etheridge – An excellent goalkeeper. Almost as good when playing centre forward

Peter Faulkner – Chairman of Waterlooville FC; Vice Chairman of Southern League; and friend

Ian Fenton – Centre-half for Pagham, Littlehampton & Burgess Hill

Dave Fitzgerald – A loyal team mate at Horsham FC. Played most of his games in the Reserves

Tom Foster – A pioneer of Sunday football in Sussex

Terry Gill – Centre-forward for Bexleyheath & Welling FC before Worthing and Littlehampton

Doug & Pat Gillard – Doug, Chairman of the Southern League. Pat, Doug's First Lady

Trevor Gregson – Reliable defender and team mate at Horsham FC for a short while

Alan Gunn – Former Whitehawk player, Secretary of Sunday League who became a top Referee

Dave Haining – A tough defender for Crawley Town FC who became Secretary and a huge friend

Morty Hollis – Mr Worthing FC. Morty devoted his life to the Woodside Road club

Dick Hounsome – No nonsense defender & team mate. Also played for Three Bridges FC

Frankie Howard – Popular former Brighton FC player who became the Goldstone Groundsman

Gordie Howieson – Much loved impish winger. A thorough nuisance to play against

Anthony Hughes – A martyr for Merthyr Tydfil. Gave 30 years service to the club.

Mike Hughes – Popular Secretary of Stafford Rangers FC and Southern League Board member

Wilf & Sonia Hugill – Wilf, an outstanding player & gentleman. Sonia, a well respected teacher

Dr. Rod Ingham – Genius Dentist who repaired my broken teeth and looked after me for 42 years

Bill King – Ex-Chairman of the Football Conference who gave me immense support

Frank King – There is nothing this man did not do for Horsham FC. But terrible driver!

Jimmy Knox – Tricky winger who played for several Crawley based clubs. Lost far too soon

Alan Lancaster – School pal and Horsham FC team mate. Alan didn't appreciate how good he was

Tony Lee – Former Horsham full-back who then served years as Club Secretary

Brian & Shirley-Ann Lee – Giants in the game at 'our' level. Life long Wycombe fans

Barry Lloyd – Chelsea, Fulham, Hereford & Brentford player who managed Brighton & Worthing

Stan Markham – Former goalkeeper, Manager & Secretary for Crawley Town; outstanding servant

Ken Marsden – Long time servant & Chairman of the Northern Premier League

Dai Mason – Horsham FC team mate and the finest goalkeeper I played in front of

Ernie Miles – A team mate in my early days at Worthing FC

Terry Molloy – A better player than he imagined. Spent 30 years as Chairman of Banstead Athletic

John Motson – Iconic broadcaster. Met several times at matches; always phoned for a Handbook

Ron Pavey – My mentor at Sunday League. Great football brain. Became Secretary at The Albion

Mickey Peters – A cultured local player. Supported Sunday football with Datsun FC

Steve Piper – Local lad who became stalwart defender for the Albion and then Portsmouth

Alan Prebble – Skilful Inside-forward for Littlehampton. Always a handful.

Rodney & Duncan Ralfe – Father & Son football duo. Rodney was a team mate at Horsham FC

Peter Ranson – Class player. Came to Horsham FC after being released by Crystal Palace FC

Ron & Betty Reeve – Popular man & wife team who administered the Sussex County FA

Tony Reid – A great lad & good 'keeper who played for several Crawley based clubs and Horsham

Stephen Rooke – Journalist; Secretary for several clubs and administrator at the FA

Harry Rudge – Mr Halesowen. Resurrected club after WW11 and fulfilled every role at The Grove

Roy Scutt – Horsham stalwart as a wing-half who then spent years on the Club's Committee

John Shepherd – Former polio victim who enjoyed professional career that ended at Southwick

Ray Smith – Fine all-round player for Horsham & Lewes FC's. Teacher at Collyers school

Paul Steer – Reliable team mate when in Horsham FC Reserves. Brother to Barry

Mel Stein – A top London Lawyer and Author. Legal Advisor to the Football Conference

Robin Stepney – Player at Aldershot; Coach at Tottenham & in Bahrain & Sweden. Family friend

Trevor Still – Tough tackling midfielder for several Sussex clubs, incl. Worthing and Lewes

Tony Stones – School pal and football team mate throughout the early years

Ken & Dorothy Swallow – Former team mate at Horsham. Died together in accident at home

Graham Sweet (aka Boo-Boo) – Powerful, skilful player and one of the funniest men I have met

Andy Tasker (aka Whisker) – Superb full-back for Ringer, Lewes and Horsham

George Templeman – President of the Southern League and Dorchester Town stalwart

Phil Tidy – Tricky winger for Worthing who could terrorise defences with his skill and pace

Pat Tobin – Meticulous planner and knowledgeable Coach. Revitalised Horsham FC

Kevin Townshend – Strong centre-forward for Whitehawk. Asked no favours and didn't give any

Jason Turner – Hugely popular Secretary for Bath City, Cardiff, Plymouth & Notts County

Alan Turvey – Football League Referee & Officer for the Isthmian League for many years

Sid Viccars – Ex-Referee & Sussex County FA Councillor who gave me his time and advice

Keith Welham – The thinnest legs I've seen on a football pitch disguised the hardest shot I have seen

Peter Wells – Loyal player for Arundel FC and administrator for Sussex County League

Ray Wheatman – A wasp of a striker who could not be swatted away. A chaser of lost causes

Gary Willard – From Sx Sunday League to Premier League to FIFA. A good lad; excellent Referee

Terry Wiltshire (Tex) – A polished gem with a cutting edge. Most charismatic player I played with.

ACKNOWLEDGEMENTS

Ursie Emma (1909-1985) & Horace Edgar Dean Strudwick (1910-1981) aka Mum & Dad.

My siblings & partners (left to right), Margaret, Patricia, Gordon, Brian (Pavey), Maureen, Brian, and Derek. (Apologies for Betty's absence – perhaps she was the photographer) Nieces & nephews (at the time) at the front:- Ian, Susan, Dean, Sally, Sandra, and Jackie.

All my Team Mates – Play on

Keith Allen –
for encouraging me to write this book

John Kendall –
without whom I could not have written this, or any other book

Mark Wells –
Keeper of Horsham FC archives, without whom I would
have only half a book

The Football Association & Staff –
without whose help I may not have had a career, nor book

Adam Metcalfe-Pearce –
computer wizard without whom this book would be on parchment

Ilse & Colin Tivenan –
for pointing me towards Aspect Design whose skill and
professionalism produced my book

Janet Strudwick –
Thanks for your loving support and for looking after me the last 29 years

Benjamin Strudwick –
My number One Son. My love for you is exceeded only by your loyalty

And finally –
FOOTBALL –
it's more than just a kick in the grass.
Thank you.

The Football Conference Annual Congress Weekend
Celtic Manor, Newport, South Wales
June 2012